ART EDUCATION BEYOND THE CLASSROOM

ART EDUCATION BEYOND THE CLASSROOM

PONDERING THE OUTSIDER AND OTHER SITES OF LEARNING

Edited by

Alice Wexler

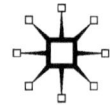

ART EDUCATION BEYOND THE CLASSROOM
Copyright © Alice Wexler, 2012.
Softcover reprint of the hardcover 1st edition 2012 978-0-230-11430-2

All rights reserved.

First published in 2012 by
PALGRAVE MACMILLAN®
in the United States—a division of St. Martin's Press LLC,
175 Fifth Avenue, New York, NY 10010.

Where this book is distributed in the UK, Europe and the rest of the World, this is by Palgrave Macmillan, a division of Macmillan Publishers Limited, registered in England, company number 785998, of Houndmills, Basingstoke, Hampshire RG21 6XS.

Palgrave Macmillan is the global academic imprint of the above companies and has companies and representatives throughout the world.

Palgrave® and Macmillan® are registered trademarks in the United States, the United Kingdom, Europe and other countries.

ISBN 978-1-349-29587-6   ISBN 978-1-137-07238-2 (eBook)
DOI 10.1057/9781137072382
Library of Congress Cataloging-in-Publication Data

Art education beyond the classroom : pondering the outsider and other sites
   of learning / edited by Alice Wexler.
        pages   cm

   1. People with disabilities—Education.   2. Art—Study and teaching.
   3. Educational sociology.   I. Wexler, Alice, 1942– editor of compilation.
   LC4025.W494 2012
   371.9′044—dc23   2011052098

A catalogue record of the book is available from the British Library.

Design by Integra Software Services

First edition: August 2012

For the extraordinary artists who have graciously given their artwork and their time to make this book possible

Contents

List of Figures		ix
Acknowledgments		xi
Introduction		xiii
1	The Messages of Linda Persson *Roger Cardinal*	1
2	Working with the Young Outsider Artist: Appropriation, Elaboration, and Building Self-Narrative *David Henley*	7
3	How Do You Get to Prospect Avenue? *Tim Rollins*	31
4	Young and Disabled in Harlem: Making Art Like It Matters *Alice Wexler*	47
5	The Art of Living and Dying: Linda Montano *Linda Weintraub and Alice Wexler*	71
6	Truth, Goodness, and Beautiful Art: Set Free in the Penitentiary *Phyllis Kornfeld*	93
7	Following the Siren's Song: Scott Harrison and the *Carousel of Happiness* *Doug Blandy and Michael Franklin*	117
8	Digital Ethnography: Artists Speak from Virtual Ability Island in Second Life *Mary Stokrocki, Alice Wexler, and L. S. Krecker*	135

9 Outside the Outside: In the Realms of the *Real*
  (Hogancamp, Johnston, and Darger) 159
  Jan Jagodzinski

Author Biographies 187

Index 191

List of Figures

Cover: Gregory Smith, 1990. Title: *Faces in the Red*. Acrylic on canvas. 48 X 60 inches, photograph by Alice Wexler

1.1	Linda Persson, c2001–05. *Black House,* 22 × 20 cm, ink, photograph by Martin Nauclér	3
1.2	Linda Persson, c2001–05. *Horse and Rider,* 21 × 29 cm, pencil, photograph by Martin Nauclér	3
1.3	Linda Persson, c2001–05. *Bird with Large Claws,* 32 × 25 cm, ink and acrylic, photograph by Martin Nauclér	4
1.4	Linda Persson, c2001–05. *Creature with Bristles,* 22 × 21 cm, ink, photograph by Martin Nauclér	5
2.1	R. J. *Untitled*. No Date. Graphite, 12 × 17 inches, photograph by Dawn Henley	19
2.2	R. J. *Untitled*. No Date. Graphite, 12 × 17 inches, photograph by Dawn Henley	21
2.3	R. J. *Untitled*. No Date. Graphite, 12 × 17 inches, photograph by Dawn Henley	24
2.4	R. J. *Untitled*. No Date. Graphite, 12 × 17 inches, photograph by Dawn Henley	27
3.1	Untitled photograph of Tim Rollins and KOS 1988, photograph by Tim Rollins	38
3.2	*AMERIKA*. 1988. Watercolor on book page, photograph by Tim Rollins	43
4.1	*Five Young Painters*. From left: Gregory Smith, Louis Donaldson, Abraham Daniel, Jason Butler, seated—Chappell Williams. 1990, photograph courtesy Ricco/Maresca	51

List of Figures

4.2	Louis Donaldson. *Brook's World.* 1990. Acrylic on canvas. 58 × 80 inches, photograph by Alice Wexler	63
5.1	*Linda Mother Waits.* 2011, photograph by Tony Whitfield	89
5.2	*Linda Mother Giving Blessing.* 2011, photograph by Tony Whitfield	89
6.1	Braulio Valentin Diez. 1983. *Untitled* (church of the roses). Mixed media on paper, photograph by Phyllis Kornfeld	95
6.2	Arthur Keigney. 1991. *The Booking Room.* Acrylic on canvas, photograph by Phyllis Kornfeld	97
6.3	Ronnie White. 2001. *Spiritual Confrontation.* Ballpoint pen on matboard, photograph by Phyllis Kornfeld	104
7.1	Postcard: Saltair Pavilion from Top of Roller Coaster	119
7.2	*Harrison and Carved Gorilla.* 2011, photograph by Michael Franklin	124
7.3	*Harrison and Carousel Animal in Progress.* 2011, photograph by Michael Franklin	125
8.1	*Welcome to Linden Lab*, Nana and Ronin, photo capture by Alice Wexler	142
8.2	Carla Broek, 2009. *Lights On_.* Machinima, photo capture by Carla Broek	144
8.3	*Bubbles*, Levi, and Nana, photo capture by Alice Wexler	146
9.1	Mark Hogancamp. *Marwencol* (2010). Documentary. Directed by Jeff Malmberg (film grab, Jagodzinski)	164
9.2	Daniel Johnston. *The Devil and Daniel Johnston* (2005). Documentary. Directed by Jeff Feuerzeig (Film grab, Jagodzinski)	174
9.3	Henry Darger. *In the Realms of the Unreal* (2004). Documentary. Directed by Jessica Yu (Film grab, Jagodzinski)	177

Acknowledgments

I am indebted to the excellent artists, art educators, art therapists, and art critics who were part of the assembling of this book. First, I would like to thank the authors who contributed original essays to this volume: Doug Blandy and Michael Franklin, David Henley, Jan Jagodzinski, Phyllis Kornfeld, Tim Rollins, Mary Stokrocki and L. S. Krecker, and Linda Weintraub. In addition, I thank Roger Cardinal, who generously granted permission to reprint his text originally printed in the catalogue *Linda Persson. Korta Möten/Brief Encounters*. Finally, I thank the many artists who have given the authors permission to print their works and tell their stories.

Introduction

This compendium has been gestating in my mind since 2004, and its many iterations have reflected the changing Outsider label. Well before 2004 the concept of the "Outsider" had been commercialized, institutionalized, and compromised to such a degree that in order not to perpetuate the myth, its definition and meaning are best left to the purview and discretion of the authors and readers of this text. Nevertheless, I believe that the authors herein use the term with metaphorical integrity. "Outsider" is the term that the authors, as art educators, art therapists, and art critics, use as a reminder of the limits of the dominant culture to which we are tethered. Mainstream culture also efficiently obscures us to the experiences of those who are attached to the world by a mere thread. Outsiders teach us about the arbitrary—sometimes sterile or even laughable—conventions we use to adhere to the world. Possibly no group of people does this more efficiently than autists, a population that is the subject of several chapters in this text.

Autism, like all disabilities, exists only in the context of the "normal," or an ideal construct of being and behavior. For instance, Sue Rubin describes her philosophical viewpoint about the social convention of concealing emotion.

> In a society that has not yet accepted us as being normal, what a great advantage it would be to always appear like everything is rosy. That, all-is-well look is something I see most often: people, normal people, falling to social context, walking around with a permanent smile shielding what they really feel. Yet *we* are termed abnormal or peculiar.
>
> (In Biklen, 2005, p. 83)

As an autist who typically learned to talk late in life, Lucy Blackman observes that non-autists who learn to talk in a timely way do not have the same sensitivity to non-talking, nonhuman species.

> What is speech? I laugh to myself when the scientific community privileges our interaction over [that of] the animals.... How can we say a sardine doesn't know the meaning of life? They don't necessarily become part of a silver flowing school by chance. To suggest that a cat doesn't know what death is would seem to be downright totally unobservant. But we big brained apes, because so much else is going on in our heads, have to work so hard at this, using different social construction to do so.
>
> (as cited in Biklen, 2005, p. 153)

Autists pose an existential question about alterity with their exceptional gifts, such as inter-species communion, their unworldly sensitivities to their environment, and a sensual knowledge about the natural world that is an artifact of a visual, rather than verbal, language. Is our conceptual construction of the world superior to their concrete and sensual one?

*

I have been an art educator working in the field of disability for about 15 years. During most of that time I believed that I had fallen into the field accidentally or, perhaps, serendipitously. It was in fact neither. I have never felt entirely in the center of the world, inside of things, and many of my dreams are literally about being on the outside of a window looking in. But my actual connection to disability is with a history of mental illness in the maternal side of my family. At least one child in each of my mother's siblings' families has been severely mentally ill. My sister became schizophrenic in her early teens, and she died a self-induced bulimic death. My mother too, although undiagnosed, certainly had a mental disorder. The proximity of the two women to me, needless to say, influenced my life in such depth that I will always be exploring its ramifications.

A recent article in the *New York Times* (2011) about Marsha Linehan's exposé of her hidden borderline disorder, and a discussion of her therapy of *radical acceptance* that followed, invigorated a more objective interest in my family's ailment. Her basis for treatment is appropriate for the paradoxical and existential experience of mental disorder: "[a]cceptance of life as it is, not as it is supposed to be; and the need to change, despite that reality and because of it" (p. 3). The juxtaposition of the seemingly contradictory terms, "acceptance" and "change," and "despite" and "because," is necessary when working through the incongruous emotions and distorted thoughts of the young and old with mental, neurological, and physical disabilities. While the concept of radical acceptance can raise reasonable questions of indulging people with mental illness to the point of divesting them of responsibility, I would argue that it is also our responsibility to take these risks. It is our overindulgence in caution rather than our reasonableness that keeps us at a safe distance.

I believe that I devoted my life to disability as a kind of metaphor, or replacement for my imposed denial of and distance from schizophrenia. In my course *Disability Studies in Art Education,* I have consciously or unconsciously stayed clear of it. But with this concept of radical acceptance, my thoughts have turned toward schizophrenia, not as the ultimate other in my midst, but as one of the many permutations of humanity.

Included in the *New York Times* article about Dr. Linehan was a note from Elyn Saks. She said, "There's a tremendous need to implode the myths of mental illness, to put a face on it, to show people that a diagnosis does not have to lead to a painful and oblique life" (p. 1). Saks (2007) is the author of *The Center Does Not Hold: My Journey through Madness,* the only autobiographical narrative about schizophrenia that I am aware of, and therefore an awakening comparable to Temple Grandin's (1986) groundbreaking book about autism, *Emergence: Labeled Autistic.*

Saks was fortunate to have had her first full blown episode of schizophrenia in 1977 as a graduate student at Oxford University in the United Kingdom. Unlike the United States, the United Kingdom had banned any form of restraint or use of force for many years. After four months of hospitalization, she was referred to the well-known Dr. Anthony Storr, and for the first time she was heard rather than judged. In an environment with such empathy, she released her "darkest" thoughts, and thus began therapy.

> I told Dr. Storr everything, and edited nothing in the telling. His eyes didn't widen in surprise or horror; he didn't tsk-tsk, he didn't shake his head in dismay. He simply leaned forward, kept eye contact with me, and listened intently, without flinching, to every word.
>
> (p. 86)

Storr's remedy was to resume the work she loved and made her happy (studying philosophy at Oxford, but with the addition of daily intensive talk therapy). On the contrary, the medical field in the United States theorizes that psychoanalysis is fruitless for the severely schizophrenic. Saks's doctor was to be a Kleinian psychoanalyst, of which talk therapy was the

> [D]ensest, most intellectually rigorous, challenging and unsettling sort....Kleinian interpretation calls for using the same kind of language that the patient's fantasies are couched in. To do this, Kleinian analysts

employ the same words and images that the analysand uses—and as a consequence, Kleinian analysts can sometimes sound just as crazy as their patients do. These simple but startling exchanges between doctor and patient operate something like arrows shot directly at whatever it is that's upsetting the person being analyzed. If the arrow hits, it punctures the target; what results is something like a valve opening and long-pent-up steam being released.

(pp. 89–91)

The narratives of people with disabilities are indeed becoming welcome in the field and are one of the flash points of disability studies, as Saks's book highlights. Their stories recounted in the visual arts, theater, music, poetry, and prose are disrupting mainstream assumptions. They describe how a diverse spectrum of bodies and minds exist in the world. They are replacing old metaphors with new ones learned from their bodily experiences. Given new interest in post-postmodernist inquiry of embodied knowing, these viewpoints, which are strictly about, of, and from the body, are of growing interest. Disability and difference of all kinds influence and change the way one communicates and processes information. "Only this body, this voice, can communicate in this time and place" (Swan, 2002, p. 294). Ultimately, what we find out is how people labeled with a disability perceive the "experts'" representations of their bodies and performance, and that they often conflict with their own experience.

The authors of this text describe the subjects of their chapters with not only empathy, but also a mutuality that explores, and eventually disrupts, the barriers between the "sane" and the "not sane," the "abled body" and the "disabled body." What the authors hope to arrive at is not a division, but rather a continuum suitable for the human condition, and how that continuum plays out in our respective fields of study.

In the first chapter, "The Messages of Linda Persson," art historian Roger Cardinal confesses his all too common presumptions about autistic art—the inapproachable distance, the idiosyncratic vernacular, the indifference to communication—with which he approached the work of Persson. After his first introduction, however, Cardinal found her communicating directly to him, with deliberate and meaningful images that are interpretable. At the end of his poetic story, Cardinal raises the question of the autistic "self," particularly as it is presented in the work of autistic artists such as Stephen Wiltshire, Jessy Park, and Nadia C. Cardinal suggests that his communion with Persson's work is testimony of a creative self within, "untouched by a supposed abnormality of brain activity."

In "Working with the Young Outsider Artist: Appropriation, Elaboration, and Building Self-Narrative" David Henley departs from a career-long emphasis on clinically based art therapy research. Rather than searching for a "cure," or the normalization of the client's identity, and therefore artwork, Henley shifts from diagnostic labeling to empathy, wonder, and biography. A young autistic artist is also the subject of this chapter, who Henley engages with as the complicated product of environmental and social phenomena. At the time of the writing, R. J. was a 12-year-old African American male living in a "cottage" in the south side of Chicago, next to a freeway and neighboring a construction plant. R. J.'s artworks were understandably perseverations of the construction vehicles and heavy equipment that populated his neighborhood. However, this narrative, says Henley, "is not intended to be yet another tiresome, heartwarming story. It serves as a point of departure to examine and debate ideas and interventions."

In Chapter 3, artist and educator Tim Rollins describes the genesis of K. O. S. in "How Do You Get to Prospect Avenue?" Under Rollins, a group of teens in the South Bronx, destined to drugs, poverty, and prison, became internationally renowned artists. "Self-satisfaction and congratulation are not enough," writes Rollins. His social commitment as an artist, educator, and citizen led him to seek a place outside the classroom where he found it more hospitable to influence public education in dire economic and moral distress. The constant interruptions endemic in public schools—bells, intercom messages, late arrivals, and early dismissals—sent a message. But beyond these inconveniences was the more dangerous culture of denial.

> Condescending, well meaning, good intentions were all around: lots of high fives, backslaps, and "good jobs!" as praise for even the slightest accomplishments. Kids who showed up on time and never cursed out the teacher were assigned to classes for the gifted and talented students who did the opposite were placed in special education.

Rollins bears witness—as many young and motivated teachers do who want to make change—to the lack of high expectations, rigor and, most regrettably, to the open contempt from teachers, administrators, and staff who are determined to maintain the status quo. "After my first year of acclimation, something had to give."

In Chapter 4, art educator Alice Wexler narrates brief case studies of children who have gone under the public radar because of the severity of their physical disabilities. In "Young and Disabled in Harlem: Making Art Like It Matters," the author writes about an art studio in the Harlem

Hospital Center in the 1990s where five young boys and founder Bill Richards defied the odds. Richards's hands-off approach quickly generated eloquent artworks from the five children, which received attention from New York City curators, art critics, and journalists. Because Richards's approach falls outside the purview of art education and art therapy, the children's artwork is more closely aligned with the idiosyncratic work of Art Brut or Outsider Art. Wexler follows four boys: two entered the hospital with injuries in 1989, one youngster with cerebral palsy, and one with spina bifida. She records their developing artistry and healing throughout the decade.

In Chapter 5, "The Art of Living and Dying: Linda Montano," art critic Linda Weintraub and art educator Alice Wexler reflect on Montano's performance art. Through interviews, the authors illuminate how Montano's lifelong work of endurance, risk taking, control, and spirituality emerged from her preponderance on the life process. They discuss how her roles as Mother Teresa, the chicken woman, resident counselor of the New Museum, and finally full-time caregiver to her Dad conform to a legacy of therapeutic art she inherited from her parents and grandparents. Dad Art is the culmination of what Montano calls "Art/Life counseling," a practice she used for over 30 years. Weintraub writes, "The words 'art' and 'life' do not refer to the 'life' of the people or the 'life' of the era. They are specifically the life of the artist as she forms her identity, matures, and awakens."

In the next chapter, "Truth, Goodness, and Beautiful Art: Set Free in the Penitentiary," Phyllis Kornfeld narrates how after a series of teaching positions she arrived at her calling: making art in prisons. She says, "I remember feeling constrained, overworked, under-joyed, and restless. It wasn't for me." In 1983 she was hired to teach painting and drawing to men and women incarcerated in state prisons, and taught her first class in a medium security men's facility in Lexington, Oklahoma. As a result, she experienced a sense of belonging to the art teaching profession that has not abated. For the past decades she has campaigned against the predictable stereotypy of pain and victimhood: the kissing swans and bleeding hearts that are so popular in "prison art." They are replaced with earnest and personalized images.

"Following the Siren's Song: Scott Harrison and the Carousel of Happiness," by art educator Doug Blandy and art therapist Michael Franklin, is a story of Scott Harrison, a Viet Nam veteran and cofounder of Urgent Action Network Office of Amnesty International USA. Harrison is also a wood-carver and mechanic, and over the past 25 years has carved 58 animals for a carousel initially built in 1910 and dismantled in 1987. The carousel now operates as the nonprofit *Carousel of Happiness* in

Nederland, Colorado, with a mission dedicated to "inclusiveness and giving." Blandy and Franklin discuss Harrison's *Carousel of Happiness* within the larger context of art created by veterans from both an art therapeutic and an art education perspective.

In Chapter 8, "Digital Ethnography: Artists Speak from Virtual Ability Island in Second Life," Mary Stokrocki, Alice Wexler, and L. S. Krecker investigate the coalescence of disability and technology within an island on Second Life called Virtual Ability, and how identity is reconstructed in the commingling of real and virtual worlds. Digital ethnography in Second Life is different from other forms of qualitative research in the role switching that occurs between observers and subjects during the interchange of technical information and the forming of friendships that are built into the Second Life community. The avatar identity levels the playing field, which is one of the benefits of being an individual with a disability in Second Life. In Virtual Ability Island, however, as opposed to most other sites in Second Life, disability is recognized and supported. At the same time, having an avatar permits accessibility and participation not available in real life. The authors interview five artists who live and work on this island.

In the final chapter, "Outside the Outside: In the Realms of the Real (Hogencamp, Johnston, and Darger)," Jan Jagodzinski invites the reader to question the political implications and the legitimacy of the phenomenon "Outsider Art," which suggests exclusion but quickly captures the interest of the gallery and museum as transgressive and innovative. Jagodzinski wonders whether inclusion by these institutions is benignly democratic and embracing, or "vampiric" in their capitalistic search for the newest spectacle. " ... in the name of equality and justice, the distribution of power remains unchanged." Institutions and galleries then make safe and tame the ultimate otherness of madness, "and readied for tasting as exotic, mad, violent... " Jagodzinski presents three schizophrenic artists who have entered the gallery walls while paradoxically remaining outside society's empathy.

References

Bilken, D. (2005). *Autism and the myth of the person alone: Qualitative studies in psychology.* New York: New York University Press.

Blackman, L. (2005). Reflections on language. In D. Bilken (Ed.). *Autism and the myth of the person alone: Qualitative studies in psychology* (pp. 146–167). New York: New York University Press.

Carey, B. (2011, June 23). Lives restored: Expert on mental illness reveals her own fight. Retrieved from the *New York Times:* http://www.nytimes.com.

Rubin, S. (2005). A conversation with Leo Kanner. In D. Bilken (Ed.). *Autism and the myth of the person alone: Qualitative studies in psychology* (pp. 82–109). New York: New York University Press.

Saks, E. R. (2007). *The center cannot hold: My journey through madness.* New York: Hyperion.

Swan, J. (2002). Disabilities, bodies, voices. In S. L. Snyder, B. Brueggemann, and R. Garland-Thomson (Eds.). *Disability studies: Enabling the humanities* (pp. 283–295). New York: The Modern Language Association of America.

CHAPTER 1

THE MESSAGES OF LINDA PERSSON

ROGER CARDINAL

WORKS OF CREATIVE EXPRESSION SPEAK TO US in an idiom that is nowhere quite the same. Culturally alert artists will tend to situate their individual statements within the wider context of art history, and of history at large, by alluding to famous works from the past, or referring to public events that we are likely to recall. Autistic creators, on the other hand, may be expected to ignore the cultural heritage and the great fund of shared information of their community. Given that they are psychologically distanced from the majority of other people, and enjoy only a limited dialogue with their immediate carers, they must develop an idiom—or more precisely an idiolect—that derives from their unusual way of seeing things, a vision conditioned by autistic perception and understanding. Such a private world is bound to diverge fundamentally from our habits of social and aesthetic recognition.

These were the assumptions that I had in mind when I first approached Linda Persson's images, having been told that she was autistic and a keen painter. Surely this person's sensibility must be at odds with my own? And surely her ideas about the world must be sufficiently remote as to make it very hard for me to grasp what she is saying?

Fortunately, there was little difficulty in bridging the gap. Linda's artwork struck me at once as possessing a quality of urgency. This has something to do with the way her brushstrokes and the motions of her pencil or felt-tipped pen assert themselves as they cross the surface of the paper. I become aware of an intentionality, for I cannot imagine these marks to be idle, the arbitrary result of mindless scribbling. And, of course, while it is true that a good deal of the material escapes immediate construal, a high percentage of lines and contours do introduce legible configurations. Thus, I make out a horse, then a man on a horse. I am starting to find shapes that appear deliberate and meaningful, and this prompts the thought that Linda is indeed sending out messages that I am in a position to receive and interpret. It is perfectly possible that she had no other person in mind while she was making her marks, and yet the supposition that she is engaged in acts of communication becomes all the more compelling as I identify more and more of her visual references. Indeed, it takes very little time for me to realize that she is actually speaking quite clearly, and indeed speaking *to me*. Despite the inhibitions and confinements that may be thought to have affected her, she is indeed capable of emitting signals that I can receive and interpret. Hence, in a fundamental sense, and even though we have never met, she is getting in touch with me, telling me her stories, offering me her thoughts and reflections. The conditions of dialogue are there, except insofar as the artist's death means, sadly, that I cannot reply to her messages.

WHAT SORT OF MESSAGES HAS LINDA PERSSON LEFT?

Dark lines are in motion, traveling up and across the paper surface. I can imagine the artist pressing her face close to her work, so that the movements of hand, pen or brush lead her gaze in shifting directions. A dense mass of black ink designates a building, and that bright gap in the blackness reveals a window (see figure 1.1). Light is penetrating the realm of opacity. Elsewhere, errant black lines convey a kind of rumor of space, something virtual rather than actual; yet there is room for the viewer to imagine entering the image, to look behind and beyond certain objects and to catch sight of what is not ordinarily visible. Linda helps the discovery along by simply *drawing over* what is already depicted, treating existing forms as if they were transparent and bringing fresh forms into explicit focus. A horse and rider gallop noisily into one evocative sketch: the creature's head is massive and authoritative, but the rider is less distinct, and his steed's back legs shrivel into a messy gathering of tentative lines. (The motif of the scrawled horseman is reminiscent of the early drawings of the well-known English autist Nadia C.) It's as if Linda's horse embodied a wonderful idea that she couldn't sustain—it looms up boldly and confidently, then dissolves into indecision and vagueness (see figure 1.2).

Elsewhere, animals abound: fish, birds, a bull, even a leaping giraffe. There is one drawing in which a kangaroo seems to encounter a cow; the firm outlines are reminiscent of prehistoric drawings, from the French cave of Niaux perhaps, where black pigment was dominant. Several of

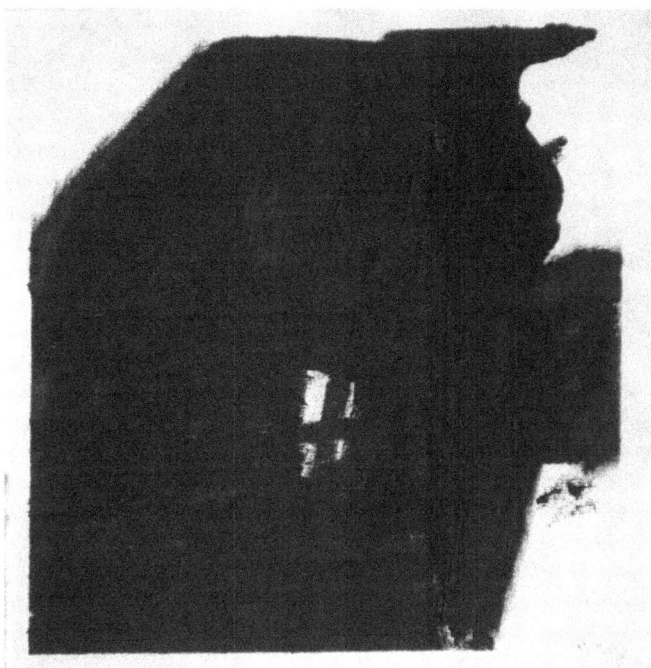

Figure 1.1 Linda Persson, c2001–05. *Black House,* 22 × 20 cm, ink, photograph by Martin Nauclér

Figure 1.2 Linda Persson, c2001–05. *Horse and Rider,* 21 × 29 cm, pencil, photograph by Martin Nauclér

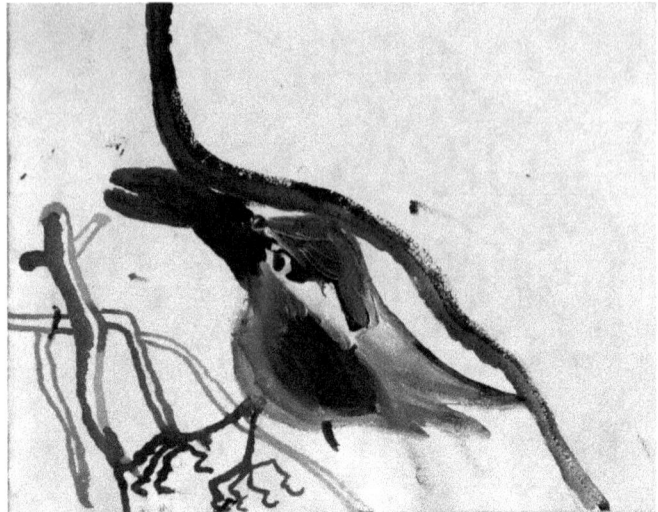

Figure 1.3   Linda Persson, c2001–05. *Bird with Large Claws,* 32 × 25 cm, ink and acrylic, photograph by Martin Nauclér

Linda's sketches delight in the meanderings of leaves and flowers. Sometimes birds chase one another into the foliage, and there is even a bee or a wasp sheltering beneath a leaf. All these little figures are the product of swift strokes; indeed, those done in paint are typically slurred or smeared, in a form of shorthand, as if the artist were not too concerned about accuracy (see figure 1.3). Or perhaps she has no need of precision, given that the autistic creator is operating within her own singular field of vision, and knows exactly what she has in mind in every dab and smudge. Again, perhaps it is the case that she attends carefully to a given shape when it demands to be fully rounded off, while she is content to let others remain sketchy and incomplete. However, these less defined configurations might be equally as appropriate, being faithful transcriptions of states of a pleasant vagueness. There is, after all, an art of creative suggestion here and it thrives on avoiding the explicit.

One important cycle of paintings relies on the forceful use of red pigment, and delivers a suite of challenging images of hands with long fingers. I find these superbly expressionistic, and feel that they transmit an interest in hands and fingers not simply "as such," but as important instruments that channel emotion through the marks they make. We may be reminded that finger painting is often a more spontaneous alternative to brushwork. Linda's portrayals of hands, typically in red, tend to include a secondary hand, usually of a different color. A symbolic narrative could arise here, with the meeting of separate hands depicting an encounter, a conversation with another person. Alternatively, we might suppose these to be single hands, each appearing alongside its shadow; whereupon they articulate a statement of self-sufficiency, and a sort of wonder at the miracle of duplication on a sunny day.

Many of the larger paintings shift into dimensions of illegibility while still trailing a few identifiable hints. Some appear to be interiors crammed with agitated, caricatural figures, and remind me of the canvases of the surrealist Roberto Matta, who worked in similarly subdued tones of white, black, and pale pink. Linda stabs at the surface and drives her brush at high speed, anxious to define and capture something fleeting, something that is being generated not by the projection of a mental image but through the eloquent ramblings of the brush. Her pictures sponsor connections between separate configurations and produce "mixed salads" of higgledy-piggledy forms, a crowded combinatory system of overlaps and interlinks that exerts its own special magic (see figure 1.4).

Figure 1.4   Linda Persson, c2001–05. *Creature with Bristles,* 22 × 21 cm, ink, photograph by Martin Nauclér

All in all, Linda's sketches and paintings are the fruit of a mobile mind and an active hand, certain proofs of intentionality and of an expressive gift. True, they differ in several ways from the art of trained and self-assured professionals; yet it is not helpful to impute that difference to a medical condition, as if autism were an implacable mechanism of misconception and mistranslation. To the contrary, Linda Persson's excursions into unexpected spaces, her unlikely colors and illogical combinations, may be the very basis for recognition, the signs of an individual who, in exploiting a range of what we see as unconventional utterances, is in fact attempting to give voice to her own natural self. I believe that this self—the creative self—is fundamentally untouched by a supposed abnormality of brain activity. Rather, it is a self that cultivates its own unique style and thereby brings the reality of an individual sensibility to our notice. Irrespective of supposed deficits, this creative person has become a true presence: her voice is that of a coherent, assured, and knowable person.

*

Text first published in the catalogue *Linda Persson. Korta Möten/Brief Encounters,* a memorial exhibition of Linda Persson's pictures arranged by the Ateljé Inuti and held at the Konstnårshuset in Stockholm, August 2010.

CHAPTER 2

Working with the Young Outsider Artist: Appropriation, Elaboration, and Building Self-Narrative

David Henley

Introduction

An exploration into the art process and art productions of children who are not considered "typical" have traditionally been accommodated using adaptive learning and behavioral programs to compensate for their disability (Henley, 1992, Wexler, 2009). An exception may be the rarest of sub-populations, who, despite their conditions, operate with some success on the "edges" of social and mental norms. Often affiliated with those on the autistic spectrum, some children possess "islands of ability," implies a savant-like capacity to display discrete areas of giftedness. The case of Nadia, is the most noteworthy as she was severely disabled yet somehow able to draw, beginning at age five, with astounding skill and with a verve compared to Daumier, Delacroix, and other masters of art history (Selfe, 1977, Winner, 1982). Inexplicably Nadia's drawing abilities vanished after age eight, once she received speech therapy and suffered the traumatic loss of her mother. She is among the most notable examples of the autistic child Outsider, whose idiosyncratic gift evaporated once her internal world was disturbed by therapeutic intervention. The author observed her as a twenty year old in Britain and found a regression so sweeping that she could then barely draw at the level of a seven year old (Henley1989a). The creative and fragility endemic to this population is a cricitcal issue that runs throughout the narrative.

In this paper I shall depart from a career-long emphasis of clinically based art therapy where the mission was "curative" (Henley, 1989b, 2001). Instead it is purely the art and art process that will be considered, exploring the work of a child whom I shall designate as a young "Outsider Artist". Accommodating the mental state of the artist requires a mindset that accepts much that is contrary to the tenets of art therapy and art/special education. For instance, psychopathology is considered a central component in diagnosis and treatment in art therapy. In the Outsider Art paradigm "mental differences" have long been accepted as an essential ingredient for "originality," even genius. While most Outsider Artists have some form of disability and thus require therapeutic handling in the educational setting, diagnostic labels have no place in *defining* their identities as artists. While much of art/special education deals with "normalizing" the student, in the Outsider paradigm, social eccentricity, indifference to instruction, creating art that stretches the norm can be highly valued. Aesthetic mores in both therapeutic and educational settings are often guided by formal attributes and political correctness. The Outsider aesthetic is raw, untutored, oblivious or rebellious to the ever-shifting norms of the social contract. Dealing with the child "on the margins," then, requires a paradigm shift that questions and redefines the culturally determined norm. To inquire into the artistic nature of the child Outsider, requires a stance of openness, as dealing with those who operate in an alternative cognitive/psychic realm may be alien and unsettling. Celebrating difference also requires a balance that honors marginality without romanticizing mental anguish or social ostracism. Thus this paper endeavors to describe and analyze the unusual gifts of a special child and how he developed with the tutelage of an equally unique art specialist.

The young Outsider refers to a child who creates almost exclusively for self-gratification and displays an obsession with his artwork that is often all-consuming. Most of these children are self-taught with a deeply personal style, yet as is the case with all true artists, they appropriate images from their culture. However, subject matter may be of narrow focus and markedly eccentric (Henley, 1989b, Sacks, 1995). Indifferent to art instruction, these children prefer to work on their own, often in isolation or even secrecy. Roger Cardinal, the preeminent authority on the adult form of Outsider Art, describes an artist "who carves out his own meanings and is propelled by its own idiosyncrasy" (Cardinal, 2004, p. 52.).

Working with the child who is often oblivious or resistant to formal art instruction, once again, presents a unique challenge to educators and other art specialists. Implied within the Outsider paradigm is the need for a pedagogic shift that leans away from structured projects of the specialist's choosing, which may be impossible to implement. Instead, subtle interventions that are unobtrusive or noninvasive, such as open studio sessions, may be more effective, where guidance is available but not mandatory. The art room can then become what psychoanalysts term a "facilitating environment" (Winnicott, 1965), where the child may benefit from being exposed to the social mores of an art community, but is not pressured to actually *join in*. As illustrated in the opening vignette, the delicate nature and art process of the child Outsider may be unduly interrupted or cease altogether if disturbed or intruded upon (Henley, 2007). Thus the art specialist is faced with a contradictory task-To engage these children in programs that foster their development but can also overcome the educator's natural propensity to *over-teach*. An approach is employed that fosters creative and mental growth while also respecting the special child's profound need for personal distance and autonomy (Lowenfeld, 1957).

SHIFTING PARADIGMS

Outsider pedagogy also requires moving between established paradigms, which, more often than not, are professionally territorial, each possessive of their favored theoretical influences and teachings. Moving between fields such as art/special education, psychology, creativity theory, and even neuroscience, one often encounters professional bias. The tenets of postmodernism, however, have freed up a researcher's movement to cross disciplines and paradigms to those that best fit the individual needs of the child (Henley, 2012).

In this case I have chosen from several disparate fields and theoretical constructs which might best inform the art specialist's interventions. These paradigms include that of "transitional space," which is a psychoanalytical concept rooted in attachment theory, exploring the child's interactions between inner and outer reality: Ethology, which includes precepts from the study of animal behavior and, by analogy, attempts to derive insight into the genesis of creativity in human behavior. Child-centered art education, most notably led by Viktor Lowenfeld, coupled with the "art as therapy" approach pioneered by Edith Kramer: The aesthetics of Art Brut, or Outsider Art, which again, examines the art of untrained, naïf, or otherwise display marked eccentricities. Finally, the neuroscience of "self" building, as described by Anthony Damasio (2010), focuses upon "brain-mapping" those neuron-circuits that are the basis of consciousness. Any or all of these constructs may contribute to our understanding, though the author could have chosen others—from cognitive theory, behaviorism, humanism, to Zen Buddhism—providing they are theoretically sound and practical.

Postmodernism, although over-referenced and passé amongst the academic elite, still has its lessons to teach. Its tenets remind us that we can never tease apart each environmental, relational, or neurological underpinning that brings the art of such children into being. Multiple causation factors are inextricably woven and thus defy easy categorization. Analysis requires a tolerance for ambiguity (Flax, 1990). Yet we must persist in this endeavor by telling their stories, to try and observe, reflect, and empathize with their unique perceptions and emotions. Ultimately, we stand ready to support their artistic efforts in whatever remarkable form they take.

THE ART SPECIALIST REDEFINED

In this chapter, the art education/therapeutic work is not drawn from the author's clinically driven studies. Instead, the work was conducted by my wife and colleague with whom I have worked closely for over 30 years. Dawn H. is a longtime therapeutic art teacher whose gentle and welcoming nature created an ideal environment for the child Outsider to flourish. Her unique gift was to connect with the most taxing special education children. Ms. Dawn (as she was known) was a teacher whose approach was wholly intuitive. Unable or unwilling to teach from prepared lesson plans or record behaviors using checklists, she was often at odds with her paper-driven administrators. They were less interested in epiphanies and breakthroughs than formulating state mandated IEP goals that calculated "measurable progress." Her stance was unwittingly postmodern, that as a subjective entity, the child can never be objectively knowable, only described. Even after years of interaction the young man of our study retained much of his mystery. Yet she had become so attuned to the child's needs that a productive relationship became established, permitting her a fleeting glance at his inner and outer world.

Such an accomplishment is no easy task. For instance, I worked with another child who, during seven years of art therapy, never confided that an invisible, fearful being had accompanied us in session. This menacing "presence," as we finally named him, had threatened the child for years, only to remain a closely guarded secret until the final year of our work! Only then did he take me into his confidence and even then he feared "its" retaliation. Thus in working with the young Outsider one must factor in the possibility that a delusional world exists, one that is equally real to that of outer reality. Translated into the learning environment, the child Outsider's development may be markedly non-linear compared with the progression-orientation which most educational programs are predicated upon. Thus Ms. Dawn's studio might best be described as a Zen-like atmosphere where everyone's efforts are honored with an acceptance of what comes.

Departing from structured and academic art exercises, Ms. Dawn's studio environment was akin to that of an atelier. Here, children could gather to interact with the studio's resources (art books, interesting objects), work at media stations, and participate in demonstrations of technique, all of which created a climate of inclusion and experimentation. She was able to survive the special education setting because she possessed the unique temperament to tame the wildest of children and was beloved by her students. This rare capacity, to engage "impossible" children for sustained periods of time, perhaps, *cannot be learned*. Thus Ms. Dawn, with her indifference to the latest trends in art/special education, working straight from the heart and intuition, might be designated as the "Outsider Teacher."

To becalm the most disturbed child is unusually valued within special education. The overarching goal of most programs is upon classroom *control* rather than academic achievement. Classroom management in this guise was characterized by downplaying the authoritative, task-master position and instead fostered an atmosphere of mutual respect for children and their art production. The art room became a sanctuary and laboratory where those who had otherwise failed in other areas of the curriculum could taste success. Regardless of level of functioning, Ms. Dawn sought to tap into each child's interests, however at-odds with the norm. Her focus was to always try and kindle *personal investment* in the art activity, for without self-investment, motivation lags and productivity suffers. However, self-investment may also precipitate expressions that are variously profane, bizarre, or otherwise inappropriate to the educational setting (Henley, 1992). As the children were cautiously freed to take the lead in their artistic explorations, images sometimes arose in the rawest state. Ms. Dawn's response was to accept these within reason, then subtly intervene, affirming the children's interests yet also working toward making them palatable within the educational setting where they were created. Such affirmation becomes complicated without censoring, diluting, or otherwise doctoring the work. At risk was the loss of the artist's integrity, intent, and vitality. More often than not, however, the artwork she elicited among her students was hardly transformational. She was most often presented with expressions of mired developmental arrest, aggression, delusion, stereotypy, or blandly schematic (stick figures as one example). The reader must bear in mind that the child described in this chapter is among the rarest of sub-populations, with only some 5 percent of gifted special needs children being applicable to the Outsider paradigm (Henley, 1989b).

Therefore, what follows is the journey of a remarkable young artist supported by his empathic art teacher. Focusing upon one particular case is not intended to be yet another tiresome, heart-warming story. It serves as a point of departure to examine and debate ideas and interventions. The case study most dramatically brings to life those moments that illuminate those paradigms that may be useful for working children on the extreme margins.

PEDAGOGY

As referenced earlier, the pedagogy described is most aligned with the now antiquated, yet enduring, Lowenfeldian child-centered approach (1957) and Kramer's studio-based model (1971). Each of these seminal theorists sought to assist young artists in becoming aware of their surrounding environment, regardless of how hostile, impoverished, or enriched, so as to gently nudge their students to draw upon their inner sensations and personal experiences and then elaborate upon them through pictorial details. By elaborating both inner and outer facets of the child's world, a personal narrative could then be constructed, a process that is often the most difficult for children with special needs.

The art specialist in this guise facilitates these developments and then functions like a curatorial sieve—reflecting back to the children their selections of form and content, helping them surmount blockages, distilling sensations, and when possible, facilitating a meaningfully critique of their work (Henley, 2004). For a child to articulate inner thoughts and feelings in context with that of the outer world requires what Kramer (1971) and Naumburg (1943, 1973) referred to as a "supreme act of integration," or sublimation (a term not to be confused with its original Freudian meaning). In rare instances, children might artistically transform their inner sensations, fantasies, illusions into images that serve self-expression *and* communication. An ideal seldom realized even in the highest of art forms, sublimation remains the benchmark for expressions that constitute "art" in the truest sense of the word (Kramer, 1971).

Central to supporting the students' bid for self-expression comes the inevitable task of setting of behavioral limits. In cases of behavioral disturbance, the necessity for punitive measures is resorted to only when the safety of the children is at risk. However, in working within the paradigm of the Outsider, where it is the work—not disruption—that is usually the presenting problem, coercion or bribing for compliant behavior were not as necessary. The emphasis then came to be one of *redirection* through their immersion in the artistic process. When a sense of mutual trust was achieved, and a productive studio regimen and rhythm was established, the need to act out became superfluous (Henley, 1992). With their eyes and hands fully absorbed in the media, disruption or other forms of chaos could often be held in check.

THE CASE

R. J.,[1] as we shall designate him, was an African American child born to extreme poverty on Chicago's south side, twelve years old during the period described in this chapter. Neglected as a child at age six, he was removed from the home and placed with his grandmother, who raised him alone in a shotgun style cottage. His home was amongst the poorest of neighborhoods—set within a small enclave that somehow escaped being condemned or relocated. His home was wedged between a freeway off-ramp and a chain-linked yard where heavy equipment and a temporary concrete plant had been constructed. The place was a kind of no-man's-land—a pocket of isolated homes that received the barest services of the city. R. J. was fortunate to be rescued by social services which placed him with his loving grandmother and a private day school in the suburbs where he could escape the anarchy of the surrounding streets and its inherent dangers. Thus he was taken daily to his day school for special needs children—which was at once therapeutic and academically developmental based.

R. J. was a selectively mute child, probably due to developmental disability exacerbated by neglect. Physiologically, he had the capacity to speak, but reserved his speech for only those whom he entrusted. Though quiet and reserved, he was pleasant around others. He posed no behavioral problems as long as he was not harassed. When disturbed by peers or pressured by teachers to perform, he tensed up his body, formed a pair of clenched fists, grimaced, and let out stifled yells. When becalmed, he tended to withdraw completely from his environment. Left to his own devices, he would then remain totally self-absorbed with his art. R. J. made a positive transition from his urban setting to the relatively plush suburban parochial school. Yet as an artist, he never left behind the grit and cacophony of his world of dusty transit yards and rumbling overpasses. His art remained true to his life—as is the case with the most renowned artists in history.

R. J. came to the studio with strong draftsmanship and thematic preferences. His oeuvre consisted of motor vehicles of every conceivable form and function. They were markedly "object based," meaning they conspicuously omitted references to people as a part of the subject matter or composition. Fascination with motor vehicles such as trains, subways and other mechanical objects are a predilection not unusual with children who occupy the autistic spectrum. I have described in Henley (1989b, 1992) the art of children who obsessed over mechanicals, from simple light bulbs to fantastically intricate robotic creatures. In the case of R. J. the obsession with vehicles perhaps reflected the reality of a life lived under the overpass. The daily bustle of his mechanized "companions" became part of the norm. Here, the predictable comings and goings of heavy construction vehicles indicated that all was well with the world.

Although he was open to his teacher's enrichment activities—attending field trips, gardening outside, and other stimulating happenings of the art room—they had little impact upon his work. R. J. was often completely self-absorbed by his work and, again, almost completely nonverbal with others. His artistic output compensated, as his continuous stream of images, drawn throughout the school day and undoubtedly at home, were so prolific that they served as a primary means of communication—the work serving as his "voice."

Despite his intense self-introspection, R. J.'s art was very much of and about this outer world. It is a misconception that Outsiders work from within an autistic vacuum—quite the contrary: They are constantly appropriating aspects of the world around them, albeit in exceedingly idiosyncratic ways. R. J. appropriated from the rich and varied industrial and freeway landscapes that surrounded him at home and that he passed by during his endless commutes through the city. His obsession with construction vehicles, with their masculine and powerful personas could be construed as being wholly appropriate subjects for a boy in the latency stage and thus constituted a healthy interest. It was only R. J.'s obsessionality and limited variation that set him apart from his typical counterparts. His protective defenses of remaining guarded and socially unnoticed were probably a matter of survival, especially at home in his community. Yet they had also adversely arrested his academic and social development. The task, then, was to engage these disparate fragments, a complicated social history, idiosyncratic artistic giftedness, arrested emotional and intellectual skill-sets—and out of this complex dynamic, develop something meaningful. To support this initiative, Dawn H. unwittingly and inadvertently engaged several paradigms that served the child's best interests—several of which I shall now describe.

TRANSITIONAL SPACE

It was the British child psychoanalyst D. W. Winnicott (1957, 1965) who described the concept of "transitional phenomena." This psychological/developmental paradigm has its roots in the earliest mother-child dynamics, wherein the infant transitions from a state of complete symbiotic attachment—of being blissfully merged with the mother—to eventually evolving into something "outside" and separate. To quell this separation, the infant finds an object that provides self-soothing comfort in any number of forms, the most common of these being "transitional objects" such as the proverbial Teddy Bear. With the internalization of the sustenance and love of the mother and others (called introjects), this secure attachment to the mother can be then transferred and assimilated in later stages of life, beyond the infantile objects of comfort to more diverse, autonomous pursuits (Bowlby, 1969, Hartman & Zimberoff, 2005).

R. J.'s limited communicativeness is perhaps due to early deprivations that hindered his capacity to bond with a caregiver and thus feel secure enough to communicate with others. In later stages of life, such as school years, both positive and negative introjects contribute to forming the constellation of later relationships. As early and ongoing trauma can interrupt the forming of later bonds, it was a testament to R. J.'s resilience that he was able to connect with certain staff and faculty at the school, however limited. His school experience served perhaps as an antidote to both his early attachment problems as well as those still suffered in his home community. Winnicott's concept of "transitional space," then, describes an intermediary psychic realm that functions as the meeting ground between one's inner world and the exterior world of school and home relationships. We witness this again with regard to the Teddy as it evolves from an imaginary, inseparable friend to a stuffed toy that offers companionship, rather than symbolically replacing the pre-occupied mother. When a productive balance between illusion and reality can be blended at will, an individual may then "play" within this transitional region. Accessing transitional space is a crucial developmental milestone which sets the stage for enriched creative potential for years to come.

ETHOLOGY AND NATURALISTIC RESEARCH

Ethology is the study of animal behavior that by analogy can be applied to the earliest stirrings of human creativity behavior (Eibl-Eibesfeldt, 1989, Morris, 1968). Although an unlikely field from which to inform the analysis, ethology can contribute insights into the theory and practice with children with special needs. For years, ethology remained a science that dealt strictly with instinctual behaviors of animals. Then, the renowned primatologist Jane Goodall (1971, Peterson, 2006) single-handedly redefined a field long dominated strictly by the scientific method. Goodall's decades of field observations of chimpanzees in their own environment demonstrated to the scientific community that primates were not just subjects for experimentation, but were *individual beings,* possessing both individual personality traits and cultural affiliations. Despite resistance from ethologists who had regarded her as an amateur—which, in fact, she was—Goodall's data proved unassailable. Given her years of persistence, working in primitive and dangerous conditions and often in complete isolation, she began to unlock the secrets of primate behavior. Considering the precision of her field notations, the hours of filmed evidence, and the sheer longevity of her study, her work could not be ignored. Her naturalistic method of totally *immersing* herself within her subjects' lives enabled her to redefine her field, with reverberations felt in anthropology, paleontology, and the evolution of mankind. Unconcerned with the canons of the scientific method, Goodall was able to approach the phenomena before her with fresh eyes. Untrained, naïve, utterly obsessed with her subject, Goodall was perhaps the "Outsider Scientist."

Nikko Tinbergen (1983) was notable for his pioneering efforts to link animal and human behavior, after working with his own autistic grandson. He viewed autistic children as being profoundly shy and yet possessing an innate inquisitiveness, attributes he also found in the animal kingdom. Tinbergen's method included luring the child beyond isolation without directly engaging or pressuring interaction, but through long periods of co-habituating, which intended to draw individuals out of their shell. Be it chimpanzee or autistic child, according to Tinbergen, one needed only to activate the individual's innate sense of curiosity so that an activity or interaction was *irresistible,* an apt analogy to the stimulation of the art environment.

Another seminal ethologist, Konrad Lorenz, indirectly contributed to the psychology of creativity. A free-wheeling eccentric, who with Tinbergen earned the Nobel Prize, he eschewed experimental research methods. Lorenz literally immersed himself in his subjects. Most notable was his work on "imprinting," demonstrating how infants can bond with surrogate mothering figures. Adopting a gaggle of orphaned goslings, Lorenz was followed around by his imprinted geese, which had bonded with him as though he was in fact their mother. He unwittingly proved that there is an "innate window" in development in which attachment is not just a matter of gender or even blood, but of nurturance (Lorenz cited in Hess, 1977, Tinbergen, 1951).

Lorenz and Tinbergen also first described the useful concept of "supernormal releasers." These are visual configurations that have such a powerful impact upon the viewer, that they can "release" innately driven behavioral responses. Lorenz described exposing a goose to a larger-than-life cutout silhouette of a hawk. Despite its obvious fakery, the goose consistently ran for cover. Thus, exaggerated stereotypes of images, whether fake or real, can elicit almost identical reactions that present a compelling, behavior-altering visual impact. In nature, escaping just from an *image* of a hawk may contribute to the survival of the species. The evolutionary psychologist Deidre Barret (2010) has found that supernormal releasers permeate contemporary culture; from the improbably huge breasts and unattainable bodies of media stars to saturated advertising of junk food, which Barret asserts has contributed to childhood levels of obesity never before seen. However, not all super-stimuli are calculatingly manipulative or elicit destructive responses. Applied to this case, supernormal stimuli took the form of self-identification with heavy machinery, releasing a hyper-focused theme that was elevated to iconic status. His vehicles provided not just an outlet for expression but almost certainly afforded the young man a sense of self-mastery and protection.

Outsider Aesthetics

The Outsider Art aesthetic is characterized by the intensity and fidelity by which self-taught artists strive to articulate their inner world-leading to imagery of compelling private visions and a visual record of alternative realities (Cardinal, 2004). Plotting the colorful history of Outsider Art, John MacGregor (1989) traces back works created at the eighteenth century Bethlem Royal Hospital in London. During this period of the Enlightenment, a more sympathetic view of mental illness was just taking hold, permitting some artistic expression within the patient population. From within the notorious old "madhouse" (formerly known in 1271 as "Bedlam" hence the term in today's vernacular) came anonymous cell-wall scratched designs, such as elaborated cosmological formulas, to the later paintings of Richard Dadd, whose fine art became a sensation in Victorian England. While studying these works which are preserved in the Gutmann-Maclay Collection at Bethlem, I was struck how hallucinatory yet technically articulated Bosch-like imagery could coexist, if not flourish, with the artist/patients' debilitating insanity. The Romantic ideal of the "mad genius" had been visited and revisited throughout art history, from Blake's visionary painting to Lord Byron's feverish verse and later, the sub-culture of madness cultivated by Dada and Surrealism. Louis Sass (1992) describes the link between madness/genius, Romaniticism and modernism as thus: "an unmooring from practical concerns, allowing consciousness to drift in unexpected directions, coming to rest in strange orientations" (p. 127). Each of these elements are core constructs in formulating the Outsider aesthetic.

Seizing upon these interrelationships, in the 1950's modern artist Jean Dubuffet combed the asylums of Europe for art of psychiatric patients, then later collecting the work of eccentrics, shut-ins, naïf's, and eventually the art of children. He freely appropriates these works as source material for his own art as well as forming the basis for his anti-establishment philosophy of art. His collections had an important influence upon the modern art world, and from his efforts the aesthetic philosophy of his term L' Art Brut continued to gain traction.

There is, however, no pedagogical method attached to dealing with the Outsider Art problem, indeed, to develop any strategy that seeks to impact upon the art or the artist would constitute an oxymoron. The Outsider canon is more predicated upon celebrating the artist's untouched autistic or even psychotic state, with its most inventively bizarre works being coveted by critics and collectors of the art form. Disturbing these delicate forces by fostering any curative intervention might contaminate, normalize, or, in Dubuffet's term, be "asphyxiating" to the Outsider artist (1988). However, celebrating the "bizarre" in the Outsider aesthetic runs the risk of negating the artists' profound pain and suffering. Such blind indfference could perhaps lead to the exploitation and commercialization of vulnerable Outsiders, an issue that has serious ethical ramifications.

To approach the Outsider "conundrum" then, requires that the art specialist must somehow balance these interests. Using the most cautious of interventions, the art specialist seeks to preserve and respect the child's unique artistic worldview. As an educator, however, the art specialist's mission is to also foster growth, meaning pathology is decidedly *not* romanticized or celebrated. Instead, a method of unobtrusive interventions respects the artist's unique vision, all the while assisting children in adapting to the exterior world around them.

THE EARLY WORKS: APPROPRIATION AND SUPERNORMAL RELEASERS

We can immediately put the Tinbergen/Lorenz concept of supernormal releasers to work in our discussion of R. J.'s earliest work. His drawings were probably created for years, perhaps in the thousands, though none of the earliest examples survive. These precocious drawings of heavy construction vehicles are assumed to have reached supernormal proportions for the child. Their massive scale, enormous power, coupled with the noise of grinding transmissions and revving engines all constitute an overwhelming dose of stimulation. Compared with his small, fragile home, they certainly dwarfed the boy, the local population as well as limiting contact with others outside the community.

Figure 2.1   R. J. *Untitled.* No Date. Graphite, 12 × 17 inches, photograph by Dawn Henley

R. J.'s perseveration upon these vehicles thus went beyond the process of recording interesting objects. Invoking these iconic forms perhaps released *magical,* even *talismanic,* experiences that were essential to surviving his isolative world. Figure 2.1 presents a sample of one of the early "portraits" drawn in the free-art sessions set up by Ms. Dawn. This example is one of R. J.'s many pictures of garbage trucks that rumbled around the construction yard. Realistically and faithfully rendered, this early work is drawn in a loose, contour style with his favored thick, dense 4B pencil. There is little distortion or imaginative addition beyond what is concretely *there.* The contour lines delineate the bulk of the form transparently. There is little reference to place or function and the scale of the truck scarcely fits into the pictorial field. The piece is part of an endless inventory of images, stereotypical and formulaic, with only minor variations, created without any comment. Only the boy's rapid flipping to the next page after completing each successive picture indicated the urgency with which they were created.

In analyzing this early work it may be fruitful to couple supernormal configurations with transitional phenomena. Consider another ethological phenomenon—that of nestling birds who compete for their mother's feeding. Studies have shown that it is the largest and reddest triangular form which the mother responds most readily to—thus this baby is apt to be fed most often (Tinbergen, 1951). By analogy, R. J. might have conjured the biggest and most powerful stimulus as a preferred object of attachment and means of sustenance. It is perhaps akin to being psychically comforted or fed on command. It is a powerful metaphor, the spectacle of trucks queuing up to receive or discharge their cement loads, or garbage trucks gobbling up everything in their path; the child becomes vicariously fed as well. As an illusion triggering supernormal reaction, the trucks made for big "medicine", providing a means of stasis not to be trifled with through careless intervention.

Thus R. J. was left to his devices: In the first four months 11 sketchbooks were filled of vehicular works—each slightly varied, but otherwise unchanged...

THE FIRST ELABORATIONS

Only in the fifth month was the first intervention made. Ms. Dawn sought to cautiously imbue these trucks with a modicum of life, and to animate and develop them beyond their stereotyped state. Thus a natural progression would be the introduction of color media—colored paper, felt marker, oil crayons were set upon the table, as always in a buffet style. However, in one instance the colored media was placed not on the table, but within R. J.'s work space, without comment. This was not simply an instructional effort, but was a gesture of co-habitation. Ms. Dawn had left the media as a kind of strategic "gift," in the Goddall/Tinbergian mold, one that could stimulate his curiosity, but within his private space. In ethology this is termed "provisioning," meaning the observer leaves food items, objects of curiosity, et cetera, to lure those who are shy out of their respective forests to encourage their interaction. In any event, R. J. was provisioned thus, yet remained free to ignore, reject, or incorporate the colored media without expectation.

Because trucks such as tractors, cement and sanitation vehicles naturally display loud colors and bold graphics, it was hoped that these elements would eventually be appropriated. Color materials were now routinely left in R. J.'s workspace. After three sessions in the fifth month, R. J. tentatively picked up several felt markers and began to quickly color in a cement-mixer. Despite his haste, he colored the body in alternating reds, yellows, and greens, then filled in the contrasting black wheels. His drawing (not pictured) appears only slightly more animated and forceful than the descriptions of his previous repetitive monochromes. Its line-work seems as tightly wound save for the logo-type graphics whose loosened linework enliven the piece. While still driverless, the color-work imbues the work with a slight degree of vitality—all without any behavioral repercussions.

Shortly after this momentous use of color, R. J. began to obsess less about coloring the vehicles than upon the markers themselves—elements of Outsider persona in its purest form. He began filling his pockets with them, hoarding and secreting them out of the room. It is often the case for those who for years perseverated on one particular stimulus to become unusually attached upon bonding with the new object of their obsession. Thus it is not unexpected that R. J. went from shunning anything out of the ordinary, to coveting these brilliant colors. Whether this was, again, a need to "feed" and nourish the psyche in the face of his extreme poverty or a residual impulse of past institutions (where it was a natural response to steal and hide prized possessions away), we shall never know. R. J. remained mute and expressionless in his intentions. However, within only five months of attentive yet benign support in the studio, his art had slightly *changed*.

SELF-BIOGRAPHY

Within the next month there came quickly another development. The first human figure appeared—a rendering of the driver of the truck (see figure 2.2). In this work, R. J. had reverted back to the earlier heavy-lined monochromatic style. Returning to monochrome truck profiles could be considered a step back or regression. However, bearing in mind the

Figure 2.2 R. J. *Untitled*. No Date. Graphite, 12 × 17 inches, photograph by Dawn Henley

"non-linear" trajectory of Outsider development, it would be premature to judge. For in this image, the truck is animated, well grounded to the road-bed, and is convincingly smoking down the road. The smeared graphite smudges blend perfectly with the billowing carbon emitted from the eighteen wheeler's exhaust. Despite the soft, difficult to sharpen 4B pencil, the first figure has been included—there is now a *driver*. He is no mere faceless cipher. In a few deft strokes R. J. captured not just the trucker's profile, but his subtleties such as a billed cap that cast a darkened shadow over the facial features. An elbow bent arm rests casually out the window. As a kind of postscript R. J. included a thumbnail study of the truck's rear, which for the first time, alludes to R. J.'s placing the truck in context. During his commute he almost certainly would have observed the tractor from both perspectives—which again conveys context and the first instance of personal narrative-from, "this is what I obsess upon" as opposed to "this is what I *saw*".

Then six weeks elapse without another human figure, all reverting back to tractor trailers (though two are drawn on colored construction paper).

It was also in the fifth month that R. J. began to first enter Ms. Dawn's personal space. He first approached her sometimes while holding out a piece of red tape as if to ask for this material. He would then hastily retreat back even before a response was given—an expression of shyness and ambivalence that Tinbergen termed "approach/avoidant behavior" (1983). By the eighth month, toward the end of the first school year, ambivalence over approaching his teacher had all but vanished. Ms. Dawn was sometimes surprised to find R. J. gently leaning shoulder to shoulder while she was busy elsewhere with other students. She also noted that R. J. appeared at her door each morning to check that she was there, a behavior the child psychoanalyst Margaret Mahler and her colleagues termed "checking back behavior" (1975). This relates to another related Mahlerian concept of "object constancy," meaning the need to insure that the significant other has not inexplicably vanished and whose presence is as predictable as a cement truck.

During the fifth month, R. J.'s drawing activity unexpectedly seemed to cease—notable, as it was the first hiatus to be observed. Could this be yet another potential regression? Unbeknownst to Ms. Dawn, R. J. had begun to make figurative sculptures that he kept strictly hidden away (again unpictured). In the Outsider tradition, he had begun to create in secret by finding, probably in the trash, plastic action figures that served as the core or armature of his figures. R. J. would then build up layers atop the plastic toy, ending up with a much expanded figure using discarded masking tape with chewing gum, toilet paper, and even masticated mashed potatoes, the figure grew in bulk. Hence a three inch action figure would be enlarged to nine inches, taking the form of different characters. R. J. often carried these with him, stuffing his pockets and revealing them only when in private. He finally permitted Dawn to learn of their existence only because he needed more material to finish the detailing. He coveted the colored plastic tape that only she could provide. Given this material, R. J.'s sculptures morphed into highly refined figures. One of the few to survive the scrutiny of Dawn (yet was also ultimately destroyed) was that of a policeman finished off in blue and black glossy art tape.

I have described in Henley (1992) how the art specialist may not just be regarded as a person to relate with, as much as the *supplier of material.* To attain this material, however, required that R. J. divulge his secret figures to Ms. Dawn, so that she could meet his needs. She did so obligingly without question (as with the markers, he stole further stores of this tape material as well). The tape seemed more important as a creator of clothing and accessories than to personify the person: from the uniform blue shirt, to black cap, to the belt containing various police items such as handcuffs and gun. A radio was sculpted out of tape as well and attached to the uniform's lapel using a fine wire bent around a pencil to give the cord element a coiled realistic effect. The figure itself was somewhat stiff in demeanor, with a strange face and disturbing mouth made from depressing a pencil point into the tape, leaving the mouth in a permanent "O." Its expression was also somewhat goggle-eyed, as though it too was surprised at its creation.

After years of endless vehicle drawings, a 3-D life polychromed figure was a welcome respite, despite the strangeness of their process and appearance. Whether their creation lay in regression or progression is a matter for debate. I believe however that however primitive, the figure signified his newly established relationships and positive introjects, which referenced an enhanced attachment to those who were positive in his environment. At school, several teachers figured prominently. At home, his grandmother. In the community, perhaps it was the policeman, a strong male role model that remained missing from his life. Whatever the significance was, R. J. had departed from cement-mixers, and began to evoke significant figures—truckers, policemen—all the while becoming more approachable in the studio.

However, the switch to sculpture brought with it certain peculiarities: he refused to have them displayed or discussed. They remained private little dolls pocketed by R. J. for weeks on end until they slowly began to disintegrate. Perhaps in the tradition of a Teddy, whose ear has worn away from months of incessant stroking, the figures assumed the role of transitional object, not quite an internal idea, yet not fully *out there.*

Eventually most figures slowly eroded and were discarded—their magical power somehow exhausted and thus disposable.

Autobiography and Sublimation

Damasio (2010) states how R. J.'s burgeoning self-awareness can be described from the neural-developmental paradigm. Damasio refers to building the "core-self" to the extent an individual can evoke memories and hold mental imagery in a coherent pattern that is connected to the causative object (p. 212). This capacity was first observed in R. J.'s recounting of the tractor-trailer and its driver. Damasio's "autobiographical self" goes further, requiring a level of consciousness that indicates that a significant part of one's life has come into play (p. 169). Such a developmental milestone becomes a kind of line of demarcation, demonstrating that the artist can now retrieve feelings, memories, and experiences through constructing a personal narrative. These figurative works contrast sharply, with the cement mixers that were static and void of context. The next series of works indicated that the autobiographical capacity had begun to evolve.

This watershed moment came when R. J. reconstructed a dramatically disturbing experience that had recently occurred in his neighborhood (see figure 2.3). R. J. recounted directly to Dawn in his halting, monosyllabic

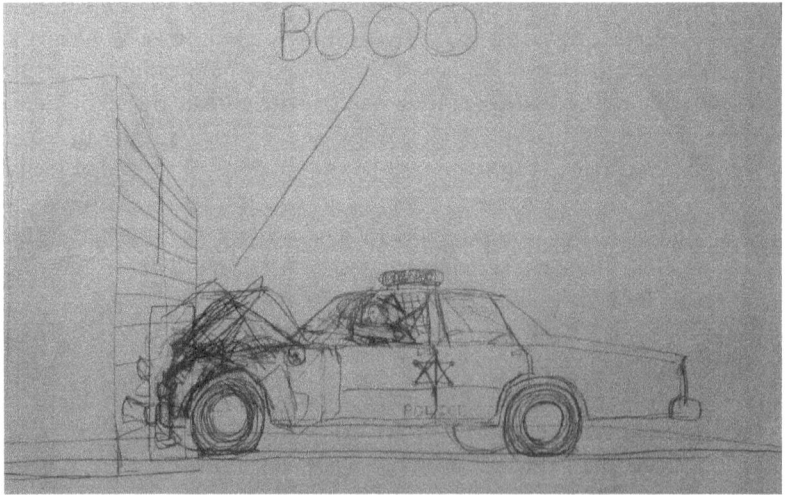

Figure 2.3   R. J. *Untitled*. No Date. Graphite, 12 × 17 inches, photograph by Dawn Henley

style what he had seen on the news: a Chicago police patrol car that had crashed. It is perhaps the first image that is driven by a personal narrative, one that evokes something of both inner emotion and external reportage.

The recollection of this experience is remarkable . The drawing is realistic, without peculiarity, or undue distortion. Treatment of the line-work is loose and appropriately agitated. The flurry of tangled lines comprising the crumpled front end is at once brutal yet elegantly defined, suggesting a violent release of force and kinetic energy. The crash wall stands in stark contrast—its sparse contour lines drawn in perfect perspective. It towers above, as though impassively observing, while absorbing the full force of the crash. The officer expresses intense human emotion which was first for this child. He is depicted during the moment of impact, whiplashing forward, howling in shock and pain. Also included was some terse text—with the capitals "BOOO" scrawled at the top. The text, which is large and looming, perhaps alludes to an abbreviation of the word "boom." Or, taken at face value, "BOOO" is perhaps a reference to the scariness of the collision. Regardless of its ultimate meaning to the artist, it is the first image that suggests that Damasio's hierarchal level of autobiography has been achieved.

It is here that we are also poised to witness the boy's capacity to experience and communicate both inner and outer reality, as R. J. had begun to give form to deeply held emotional states. This includes the unconscious process of projection, in which the collision and resulting trauma might have been perceived as a *dire fear* that such violence could happen to him or his loved ones at any moment. As chaos reigns on the streets, the world becomes dangerously unpredictable, yet perhaps also quite exciting. Thus confronting such a harsh reality may have evoked a sense of ambivalence. This element embodies the postmodern ethos, as contradictory feelings can coexist without the need for their tidy resolution. Cops race through the streets chasing criminals or madmen, ending with violence and trauma. R. J. or others in the community might have had little sympathy for the police as dangerous high speed chases often end up hurting those they aim to protect. In addition, inner city police are sometimes perceived as forces of oppression, more often avoided than sought out as an agency of protection. Yet R. J.'s depiction seems to empathize or at least identify with the pain of the officers. Perhaps his earlier police sculpture also reference officers as a positive introject of solace and protection.

Such mixed feelings, social realism and dynamic draftsmanship each contribute to the dramatic tension of the work. As an image of sublimation 'par excellence'. It is a work of graphic narrative, explosive emotion and stunning detail. Its multiple references, both overt and symbolic, give the viewer an enriched, complex aesthetic experience.

Whatever discrepancies exist sit side-by-side with unresolved issues lending a strong visual and conceptual element to the narrative.

Kramer, who visited and observed the child working on a later drawing, witnessed how he doubled up a piece of drawing paper and taped it together lengthwise—the first instance where he intentionally altered the scale of his work. With the paper now elongated, he drew a block-long fire in the neighborhood. In this panoramic work, he depicted multiple vignettes of people, firefighters, and their equipment as they fought the fire (See Henley, 2001 for illustration). Always one to improvise and add events as they unfolded, Kramer added this vignette a few days later in a lecture to the Art Institute of Chicago. She described the partially completed drawing thus: "For a child of such limited means to create such a complex composition with expressions of pain, fear and heroism, without unduly distorting form or content, is an achievement worthy of sublimation" (1988).

Appropriation, Elaboration, and Self-Narrative

The last series of works—considered R. J.'s mature style—were landscape images that began to be appropriated from the long and tedious bus commutes to school. These first urban landscapes of highway scenes obviously constitute a remarkable departure from his early work—just nine months earlier.

Figure 2.4 is again drawn in thick 4B graphite, and depicts a six-lane freeway divided by a wide, black-shaded median. The scene is notable because the earlier versions of his highway-scapes depicted roads that were devoid of cars. In this piece, however, vehicular traffic was included in the composition. The commuters are composed with a curious symmetry, evenly distributed in an orderly line. The traffic is shown moving along briskly—a rarity for Chicago clogged roadways. The roadwork is complemented by a complex array of urban development along the frontage roads, including overpasses, factories with logos, railways, and a reference to a salvage yard—its crane dangling a junked vehicle. Intermixed is an entanglement of power lines, billboards, water-towers, and other utility infrastructure, all of which enliven the composition. Above floats a sky of billowy clouds, loosely sketched in contour line, adding a feeling of lightness to the contrasting density of smudged black lines.

All told R. J. is working with increased awareness of his environment, almost certainly drawing now from personal observation. The smudged 4B graphite conveys the atmosphere and mood, as the black exhaust of the trucks and the overall grime of the scene can almost feel inhaled. One can sense the clamorous industry, the rumbling of trucks, now in dynamic

Figure 2.4   R. J. *Untitled*. No Date. Graphite, 12 × 17 inches, photograph by Dawn Henley

action. The perspective appears to be from an elevated position, perhaps from an overpass portion of the highway. This perspective creates a sense of distance from the experience. By elevating the scene in vast sweeps of landscape, we sense a mastering of the experience, virtually confirmed by the coherence and authority of the composition.

R. J. is now in and out of the picture—elaborating upon his experiences with the "observing ego" that is required for self-biography to evolve. After having attended the opening of his first exhibition, his newfound capacity of autobiographical narrative seemed to reach its apotheosis. The show was held at an exclusive gallery in the "Gold Coast" section of Chicago. The gallery owner had magnanimously taken down his million-dollar impressionist paintings and instead charitably handed the space over to a group of talented children with special needs. Picked up at his home (we were able to see R. J.'s home conditions firsthand), he was in awe of arriving downtown: fêted by gallery goers who were fascinated by his work, served finger sandwiches, all with a soft violin in the background. Several works were bought, not as a charity, but by Outsider Art collectors, who predictably preferred his earliest and most obsessive truck-works. To receive the attention and then money for his work had to be unimaginable to this sheltered child. So it is understandable that he would commemorate the experience of what turned out to be the most memorable self-autobiographical work to date.

Created the following Monday after attending his opening, R. J.'s drawing of the gallery experience was undoubtedly profound, almost overwhelmingly so for the child. The work, however, recounts not the exhibition experience, but curiously, the ride home with us from the opening while in our car.

R. J. began by choosing the ubiquitous markers left about the art room, trying in vain to capture the view from inside the car and how the headlights washed over a darkened night sky. He then grew frustrated and abandoned the piece—perhaps the stakes were so high that he *had to get it right*. Ms. Dawn silently responded by offering a more fitting technique—rather than coloring wide expanses of paper in marker scribbles, she handed him a sheet of dark blue paper. She showed him (on a separate paper) how the blue paper could stand for the night sky while darker tones of the interior of the vehicle could be overlaid in pencil. He then began to draw himself from the vantage point of being in the front seat of the car. He faithfully depicted his knees protruding into view, registering a perspective of looking out the windshield into the highway night beyond. Damasio explains this as a neurological/perceptual shift—a "visual mapping" where visual properties of shape, color, movement, depth, as well as the component of feeling, produce a "blended" multidimensional visual scene (p. 260).

R. J. then ran into trouble trying to delineate the transparent shine of the headlights. Ms. Dawn again intervened by introducing white chalk. She broke a stick in half and showed him on the same scrap of blue paper, how to use the side of the chalk in light strokes to convey this lighting effect. He again quickly adopted this technique and seemed pleased with the results—his ride was now properly and believably illuminated.

The significance of this first-person account cannot be underestimated. It formed the first reference to the artist himself—that he is firmly *there*. No longer mired within an inner world of inanimate obsession and not just a passive observer, but he is now "in the driver's seat," recounting a personal passage—a developmental culmination Damasio refers to as the "reflective self"—a state where "etched brain circuits" produce not only mental representations that imitate reality mimetically, but also symbolize one's actions and objects within the context of the individual's feeling states (p. 290).

At this moment of optimum development, R. J. perhaps *ceased* to be an Outsider. The work curiously lacked the driven obsessionality of his earliest works. Standing on its own aesthetic merit, it seemed accomplished but otherwise quite unremarkable for a sixth grade boy. But for the artist, the picture might as well have constituted "The Odyssey." It attempted to "fix" in real time and space what might otherwise have become evanescent—perhaps little more than a dream (Naumburg, 1943, 1973). Being transported from the glittered lights of downtown, back to the beleaguered south side, presents an obvious metaphor: That of a passage: An archetypal journey as mythological as in any storied fairy-tale, blending a narrative rich in illusion and reality.

During this dark and quiet ride to his home I found myself reflecting upon the evolution of R. J.'s artistic journey. Had his gift become diluted or excessively normalized, thus robbing him of his unique gift? Was he in peril of being in touch with deepened emotionality? Did he now expect commercial success? Had we balanced his interests? These ruminations were abruptly halted when we arrived at his home. We could discern R. J.'s sense of relief at finally being dropped off. My soul-searching eased as R. J. clearly was relieved to be back now in his familiar environs. Back with Grandma, in his cozy room, with his window that looked out upon the eerily night-lit yard, back beneath the highway we had just traveled. He was again within his comfort zone. Greeted by his kindly grandmother, who could have scarcely imagined his magical evening, he was offered some sweet potatoes. He glanced up at us and smiling sheepishly, mumbled to Grandma, "Already et . . . ."

Note

1. R. J. was referred to as Darius in Henley (2001).

References

Barret, D. (2010). *Supernormal stimuli: How primitive urges overran their evolutionary purpose.* New York: Norton.
Bowlby, J. (1969). *Attachment, Vol. 1.* New York: Basic Books.
Cardinal, R. (2004). *Marginalia.* Zwolle, The Netherlands: Museum De Stadshof.
Damasio, A. (2010). *Self comes to mind: Constructing the conscious brain.* New York: Pantheon Books.
Dubuffet, J. (1988). *Asphyxiating culture.* New York: Four Walls Four Windows.
Eibl-Eibesfeldt, I. (1989). *Human ethology.* Hawthorne, NY: Aldine de Gruyter.
Flax, J. (1990). *Thinking in fragments.* Berkeley, CA: University of California Press.
Goodall, J. (1971). *In the shadow of man.* Boston: Houghton-Mifflin.
Hartman, D. & Zimberoff, D. (2005). Trauma, transition and thriving. *Journal of Heart-Centered Therapies, 8,* 3–86.
Henley, D. (2012). Knowing the unknowable: Towards a multidisciplinary approach to assessment in child art therapy. In A. Gilroy (Ed.), *Discourses in art therapy assessment* (pp. 40–54). London: Routledge.
Henley, D. (2007). Art therapy and the multiply-handicapped deaf child. In E. Horowitz (Ed.), *Visually speaking* (pp. 110–130). Springfield, IL: Charles Thomas.

Henley, D. (2004). The meaningful critique: Responding to art from pre-school to post-modernism. *Art Therapy: Journal of the American Art Therapy Association, 21,* 79–87.
Henley, D. (2001). Annihilation anxiety and fantasy in the art of children with Asperger's syndrome and others on the autistic spectrum. *Art Therapy: Journal of the American Art Therapy Association, 39,* 113–122.
Henley, D. (1992). *Exceptional children exceptional art.* Worcester, MA: Davis Publications.
Henley, D. (1989a). Nadia revisited: A study into the nature of regression in the autistic savant syndrome. *Art Therapy: Journal of the American Art Therapy Association, 6,* 43–56.
Henley, D. (1989b). Artistic giftedness in the multiply handicapped child. In H. Wadeson (Ed.), *Advances in art therapy* (pp. 262–272). New York: John Wiley.
Hess, E. (1977). *Imprinting.* Stroudsburg, PA: Down, Hutchinson and Ross.
Kramer, E. (1988, November). On sublimation. Lecture given at The School of the Art Institute of Chicago.
Kramer, E. (1971). *Art as therapy with children.* New York: Schocken Books.
Lowenfeld, V. (1957). *Creative and mental growth.* New York: Macmillan.
MacGregor, J. (1989). *The discovery of the art of the insane.* Princeton, NJ: Princeton University Press.
Mahler, M., Pine, F., & Bergmann, A. (1975). *Psychological birth of the human infant.* New York: Basic Books.
Morris, D. (1968). *The naked ape.* New York: McGraw-Hill.
Naumburg, M. (1943, 1973). *Dynamically oriented art therapy.* Chicago: Magnolia Press.
Peterson, D. (2006). *Jane Goodall: The woman who redefined man.* Boston: Houghton Mifflin.
Sacks, O. (1995). *An anthropologist on mars.* New York: Vintage Books.
Sass, L. (1992). *On madness and modernism.* New York: Basic Books.
Selfe, L. (1977). *Nadia: A case of extraordinary drawing ability in an autistic child.* London: Academic Press.
Tinbergen, N. (1983). *Autistic children: New hope for a cure.* London: Allen and Unwin.
Tinbergen, N. (1951). *The study of instinct.* Oxford, UK: Oxford University Press.
Wexler, A. (2009). *Art and disability.* New York: Palgrave MacMillan.
Winner, E. (1982). *Invented worlds: Psychology of the arts.* Harvard, MA: Harvard University Press.
Winnicott, D. (1965). *The maturational processes and the facilitating environment.* New York: International Universities Press.
Winnicott, D. (1957). Transitional objects and transitional phenomena: A study of the first not-me possession. *International Journal of Psychoanalysis, 34,* 89–97.

CHAPTER 3

HOW DO YOU GET TO PROSPECT AVENUE?

TIM ROLLINS

> *We gotta get out of this place*
> *If it's the last thing we ever do*
> *We gotta get out of this place*
> *cause there's a better life for me and you*
> *(Mann and Weill, 1965,*
> *recorded by the Animals)*

AFTER OVER 30 YEARS OF EXPERIENCE working inside and outside schools in distressed neighborhoods all across the United States, I believe now is the time for art educators to come up with an alternative to the idea of the alternative. I've got a testimony.

Come with me and take a mental flight to Studio KOS, our group's "downtown" studio on West 26th Street in the Chelsea district of Manhattan. It is a crisp and clear and cloudless day on September 11, 2001. Rick Savinon, a member of the Kids of Survival team since he was 13, and I are finishing paintings for a nearby gallery exhibition due to open on September 21 and we are already stressed. The first plane, then the second plane, hits the World Trade Center towers while we are on our way to the studio, which faces all the way south. We see everything and, yes, we feel true shock and awe.

Our studio has industrial windows facing south. To our right and left the studio is scattered with two paintings, both inspired by the literature of William Shakespeare. The first is generated by *A Midsummer Night's Dream*. The imagery consists of hundreds of strange and imaginary flowers that we made with children all over the city in various schools and after school programs and community centers. The floral elements are painted in vibrant, even joyous, colors with watercolors and inks on Thai mulberry paper, collaged on a grid of pages taken from a music score. The music is the Overture to *A Midsummer Night's Dream* written by a young Felix Mendelssohn at the age of 17. In addition, there are 21 works on paper made with animal blood on large book pages taken from a folio of Shakespeare's *Macbeth*. So here you have it. Rick and I look out the gleaming large windows to our south: total, diabolical destruction. To our left is wildly innocent beauty. We look right. We look left. More than ever before, we realize what side we are on.

We stay in the studio watching and waiting because we know we must bear witness. Rick opens the window to get some air. The wind blows north from a place now called Ground Zero and it hits us. The smell, the odor, is indescribable. I know it from somewhere, but how? We know the acridity from somewhere... burning garbage from the town dump in my little hometown in rural central Maine where I grew up dreaming of being an artist someday? Close, but no. I ask Rick, whose face is sunken with sadness (9/11... what a birthday gift). Rick looks right at me. "Tim. Don't you remember? That's what the hood always smelled like—back in the days."

Let's now travel to September 11, 1981: "So, how do you get to Prospect Avenue?" It is hilarious how one simple question can transform a life. Nilda, the school secretary on the other end of the phone, is helpful. "Let's see... you live near Gramercy Park in Manhattan, right? Your best bet is to take the 6 train at 23rd St, then transfer to the uptown 5 train and keep riding until you get all the way up to Prospect Avenue Intermediate School. Number 52 is only six blocks from there. Just ask for I.S. 52 on Kelly Street. Everyone in the neighborhood knows it. Oh, by the way... good luck." That was a weird thing to say, I thought.

It is another crisp, clear, and cloudless day near the beginning of the public school year. On the subway train barreling north to the South Bronx, I'm wondering how I got to all this.

In 1975, at the age of 20, I ventured to New York City from central Maine with hardly a penny to my name. I came to study as a transfer student with artists such as the composer John Cage, and the conceptual artist Joseph Kosuth. Keith Haring was a classmate. Soon, I became Kosuth's studio assistant and I was meeting and hanging with folks like Robert Rauschenberg and Andy Warhol as well as many politically conscious and socially activist artists and musicians who made up the furiously energetic and innovative scene at the time. After graduating from the School of Visual Arts in 1977, I studied art education and political philosophy at New York University, dedicated to John Dewey's (1934) powerful idea that education was "the total work of Art." After graduate studies at NYU, I fully took on the masochistic act of becoming a full-time art teacher for adolescent special education students with the Board of Education of the City of New York. For two years I worked with a program efficiently titled *Learning to Read through the Arts,* which served four different schools in five different—and tough—neighborhoods throughout the city. I traveled to the schools by subway with all my materials. Mondays, I was in the Lower East Side of Manhattan. Tuesdays, I was in Bed-Stuyversant in Brooklyn. Wednesdays, I was in Jamaica, Queens, and on Thursdays, I was in the South Bronx near what was then called *The Hub on Third Avenue.* Teachers were off on Fridays, so we were without union rights, and the program could pay us what they wanted to without benefits.

Still, I loved the work. I was enthusiastic and determined. The kids were very excited to have reading skills integrated with the hands on dynamics of art making. I also appreciated the opportunity to visit a diversity of neighborhoods, no matter the dangers seen or unseen. Most of my friends in the New York art world rarely ventured north of 23rd Street near my home.

During this time I helped found an exciting activist artists' collective, Group Material, in a storefront on 13th St in the East Village. At the time there were like-minded groups (ABC No Rio, Collaborative Projects, Fashion MODA, PADD, Artists' Meeting for Cultural Change, and others) springing up all over. What is important to realize is that spaces and co-ops like Group Material were deliberately created to pose an "alternative" to the many so-called established alternative spaces (Artists Space, Franklin Furnace, the New Museum, P.S. 1, and so on). At that moment, many of us felt that these alternative spaces were essential showcases for emerging artists, who needed first exhibitions before being absorbed by the ever growing and now voracious commercial art market.

Group Material exhibitions were unique then. The shows centered on a philosophical or social theme. "Alienation," "Consumption," and "Community" were most successful. One ad hoc exhibition was impelled by the media obsession with the murder of black children in Atlanta. While planning the show, I was conducting my Monday workshop in a bunker-like school building on Stanton Street in the Lower East Side. One of my younger kids, Lamont, had arrived late to class. He was wearing his Baptist church suit with a large, folded green ribbon pinned to his right lapel. Explaining his tardiness, Lamont described the special service and rally at his local church seeking answers to the Atlanta child murders case. And that was it, the "Eureka Moment." I scrapped my planned lesson, asked to double my workshop time to one and a half hours, and asked the 12 young participants a question: "Who is killing the kids?" Using the materials I had, we spent the entire workshop time making drawings and paintings on standard 14 × 24 inch school-grade paper. The room was silent. The concentration was intense. The results were unconventional, varied, and strange. These were disturbing images, unlike anything else the children had produced. After seeing their work, the Group Material members wanted to exhibit them. Still doubtful, I showed the works on paper to my friends and mentors, the great painters Leon Golub and Nancy Spero. While some other folks immediately dismissed the paintings as social work or just "children's art," these two mentors had another take on the work. "Kid," said Leon, "you're really onto something here." That encouragement was all I needed. I would pull the piece together and show it at the Group Material headquarters space on East 13th Street as part of the upcoming *Atlanta—An Emergency Exhibition,* opening in May 1980.

I returned to the Lower East Side school the next Monday to prepare for the exhibition. We pinned small green ribbons, like the one Lamont wore the week before, to the upper right side of the works. At the Group Material space I then simply butted the sheets together in a grid of 24 drawings—like a ferocious and arresting quilt of concern. Two weeks later, the renowned critic Lucy Lippard (1981) wrote about the installation with a special note. That was it. I knew that I was really onto something.

With my days dedicated to the *Learning to Read through the Arts* program, I wanted to have a less peripatetic teaching situation. While I enjoyed the support and mission of the public junior high schools I engaged with, there was something very magical about the South Bronx site and situation. Something was happening. I could sense it well.

In the summer of 1981,[1] George Gallego, the principal at the South Bronx site, saw me in action with my students and attempted to recruit me for his school, Intermediate School Number 52 in the Longwood district. I was honored, particularly because I was so young. But I was also apprehensive. At that time the Longwood neighborhood was considered one of the most dangerous, drug-infested, and physically devastated communities in the world. My friends thought that I was crazy to even consider the offer. Still, I had great admiration for this principal who had been born in Puerto Rico and raised in the Bronx community, only to return to contribute his vision of rebirth with very difficult and stressed youth. This was an administrator who walked the walk, and was a mentor to me. And so I did what so many of us socially conscious white folk do. I agreed to visit the school for two weeks as a temporary visiting artist-teacher to help create a functional arts program, and then return to my comfort zone, congratulating myself at gallery openings and cocktail parties for years to come. George agreed. Here I am, on the uptown number 5 train sliding toward a place so hopefully named Prospect Avenue.

The number 5 subway train goes underground all the way uptown until it hits the Jackson Avenue station. There it emerges from below the earth up onto an elevated track where the light of day strafes the graffiti strewn cars inside and out. I wasn't fully prepared for what I was about to see. The popular media had a long-running field day with images of the South Bronx as a burned out wasteland, an urban nightmare, and mainstream America's worst fears made material—literally concrete. The next stop after Jackson was Prospect Avenue.

The irony was painful. Stepping out of the train onto the crumbling platform . . . there it was: that anxious odor of tar, ash, and trash that Rick recalled on that day of 9/11. The cold autumn wind blew through the rows upon rows of empty shells of burned out buildings. The ruins were wheezing. Walking toward I.S. 52, I found myself silently quoting scripture. "Though I walk through the valley of the shadow of death, I will feel no evil . . . " Thank God I committed to only two weeks!

I could hear the sounds coming from the massive school building[2] two blocks away. Even before I opened the large metal entrance doors, I knew I'd be walking into pandemonium. Once inside the foyer hall, two security guards were screaming and powerless as swarms of kids were running up and down the stairs pushing each other and yelling and laughing at the top of their lungs. I'm directed straightaway to the Main Office to sign security sheets and for other paperwork.

George bounded out of his office to the main desk with a long grin on his face. Several secretaries, including Nilda, seemed pleased but concerned at my entrance. "OK everybody, pay up!" George yelled. They all made bets that I wouldn't show once I got a taste of the streets of Prospect Avenue. George was proud that I had, and was even more delighted to let me know that he had found a room for me. I realized how difficult it must have been to find a classroom when I learned that the entire top fifth floor of the school building had been closed and shut for years, waiting for repairs and renovations. Because of overcrowding, hallways and even some bathrooms had been refashioned as classrooms.

It was an honor to be provided with Room 318. It had been recently abandoned by the previous art teacher, who stopped showing up to work without an explanation. George was also thrilled that I had a sink, although without waste plumbing. The water from the faucet had to be collected in an old spackle bucket and dumped into the boys' bathroom across the hall. The room was large by most standards but had only a few long tables, four or five student desks, and no windows. The windows had somehow been knocked out and were now replaced by sheets of crude plywood with surfaces covered in even cruder graffiti tags in large black ink markers. Most intriguing, though, was the classroom's ceiling. It must have been 20 feet from the floor, festooned with graffiti made from what appeared to be large sticks of vine charcoal. I asked George, "How the hell did the kids get all the way up there to make the drawings?" George shrugged. "Tim, the previous art teacher didn't have much control of the class, obviously. One day the better artists in the room found the long wooden poles used to pull the large upper windows down to get some air during the early summer weeks. They used masking tape to attach the fat rounds of charcoal to the ends of the poles and made their marks on the ceiling that way." I thought how Matisse, in his last days, would have appreciated this. "George, you know if your students are this diabolically creative, perhaps we have a chance to make something special here."

I returned the next day for my first "demonstration" class. I asked for an hour and a half session with the special education sixth- and seventh-grade students most interested in art. There were no materials, so I brought what I could: two reams of 8.5 × 11 inch copy paper, number 3 Mongol pencils already sharpened, a boom box, and a collection of early hip-hop cassette tapes (Grandmaster Flash, Afrika Bambbatta's Zulu Nation, and others).

The kids ran down the hall at the 10:00 A.M. bell toward the huge metal door of Room 318. Then came the Bam! Bam! Bam! Opening the door, there they were: twelve 11- to 13-year-olds rushed in and took the seats at the one long table I had arranged in the center of the classroom. I took my place in the front of the group and we instantly started scanning each other's faces, body languages, and demeanors. It was clear that I was fresh meat and could be in serious trouble here. Luckily, I had experience working with this age group, so I immediately put on what I call my "death mask" face—emotionless, hard, mysterious, and a little strange and scary. I introduced myself as an artist who likes working with young artists, not kids. I had one request. In the next hour or so, I asked everyone in the classroom to make the best drawing they had ever made in their lives ... now. I dropped thick stacks of copy paper in front of each of my 12 angry kids. They looked at me as if I was a crazy, then they looked at each other to catch a group consensus. I started playing the tapes—pretty loud; it helps the concentration of adolescents. And without hesitation or protest, they all began drawing, drawing furiously, bent over the sheets of paper like a row of hyperactive monks. All the while I march from left to right and back again along the row. I hold onto my death mask countenance but, in actuality, I can hardly contain myself. The drawings were so surprising, detailed, literally fantastic, and fundamentally "out there." The kids drew and drew and revised on their own. One image led to another that led to others until the workshop period completely evaporated.

When our time was up, everyone checked out everyone else's creations and there was elation in the air—not a lot of talk or analysis, but just a strong satisfaction with what we made in 60 minutes. While waiting for the dismissal bell, one of the alpha kids, Roberto, wanted to speak. "Mr. Tim, can we ask you a question?" "Sure, if it's not personal." "Are you going to stay or are you going to leave us like everyone else?" Ouch! What a little manipulator, I thought to myself. "Well the deal with Mr. Gallego is that I would be here for two weeks, then I probably have to go." Roberto said, "Mr. Tim can we ask you another question?" I'm steeling myself. Death mask face is getting tighter. "Go ahead." "You're a good teacher. Will you stay?" What followed was one of those ten second silences that feel like an hour. And what followed that was the utterance of the one word that gets us educators into so much trouble: "Yes."

I said yes not to play the hero, or to submit to self-congratulatory self-sacrifice. I said yes because I felt something extraordinary would develop in this broken-down classroom. I made a declaration of independence to the kids who would soon become my kids, some for life. "I'm going to stay not because I'm such a nice person or a do-gooder. I'm staying because while I know we will be making art together, something deep down in my soul is telling me that we will be making history together. I mean it. What do you think? Do you believe me?" Everyone in the group started looking at one another, some laughing nervously. They thought I was crazy. Still . . . Roberto finally answered. "Make history? Hell, yeah!" So, it was on.

Some people think that in the early 1980s I just hopped on the number 2 train and headed uptown to volunteer my services to poor brown children in need—the missionary model of community engagement that everyone is too comfortable and familiar with. Instead, after those first days at I.S. Number 52, I was clearly on a mission not of my own making. Looking back, I feel that our ragtag group, which would soon evolve into *The Art and Knowledge Workshop* and the art making team of KOS (Kids of Survival), was born not from benevolence but from desperation and a righteous anger with the conditions of the school system in the South Bronx at the time (see figure 3.1). This project would be working within and without the system, simultaneously transforming the usual arena of low (or no) expectations into something far more effective, meaningful, and beautiful.

Upon accepting my position as the art teacher for the special education students at the junior high school, I immediately demanded to reset the caliber of the art making and learning experience. I asked that art become a major subject for the students, who would meet with me daily. In exchange for what was first considered an outrageous demand, I developed lesson plans and an original curriculum that integrated writing,

Figure 3.1 Untitled photograph of Tim Rollins and KOS 1988, photograph by Tim Rollins

reading, cultural and art history, science, and current events with the making of artworks. Simply put, I found it unethical to teach 12-year-olds how to paint when a shocking number of them could not spell the word "paint." There would be letter grades given, daily journals maintained, slide lectures, quarterly exams, and exhibitions in and outside of the school, no matter what.

As a group, our first assignment was to clean up and repaint Room 318, transforming it into a working studio called *The Art and Knowledge*

Workshop. A boom box blasted music into the room while we worked. I moved much of my personal art and literature library onto a large communal table in the back. Still, the general school environment outside our large metal door remained chaotic and oppressive. The third floor of the school was officially called *The Learning Center* (a nice way to segregate the special education students from the rest of the school). The kids called it Loco City.

On my first day of teaching, an administrative assistant handed me the following school supplies: two strips of staples (no stapler), 12 Mongol number 2 pencils, 12 paperclips, two pieces of chalk, and one eraser. I was told that I could order a modicum of art materials, but I had to go through a Board of Education vendor (no regular art supply stores would accept their purchase orders) in order to expect delivery in about six months. Other than that, we were on our own. The classroom furniture was old and inadequate. We put together the small traditional tables to create long rows of surfaces suitable for a large Thanksgiving dinner. We took the plywood off a few windows, allowing for some natural light to enter. We persevered. I contacted programs like *Artists' Materials for the Arts* (pretending to need materials for my own work, which wasn't actually a lie since this had become my own work), friends, and looked out for specials and scraps from art stores.

After several months, however, it became clear that it wasn't enough to create an oasis in a large institution so inhospitable to learning and creating. The daily annoyances were constant: the ridiculously brief classroom periods, interruptions by the minute, intercom announcements, knocks on the door, late arrivals, early dismissals, the roaring jet planes taking off from LaGuardia Airport, and the invasive loud chimes from the Episcopal Church next door, always shattering any quiet to be found in the already raucous neighborhood. Instead of bells to signal the change of class periods, we had what sounded more like a long-enduring banshee of a factory whistle. Beyond physical concerns, more bothersome was the mediocracy of the school culture. Condescending, well meaning good intentions were all around: lots of high fives, backslaps, and "good jobs!" as praise for even the slightest accomplishments. Kids who showed up on time and never cursed out the teacher were assigned to classes for the gifted and talented. Students who did the opposite were placed in special education. I eventually found the complete lack of high expectations and rigor (and the open contempt by those instructors, administrators, and social workers toward anyone who challenged the low standards) exasperating.

After my first year of acclimation, something had to give. The sense of need and necessity was still present in our space (by now referred to as the "refugee camp" by other staff members). Instead of running toward burnout, my students and I reclaimed a sense of possibility, even adventure. We required what John Dewey would have called a new "organization of energies" toward a more genuine learning through art. Always frustrated by my kids' disinterest in reading except for Marvel Comics,[3] one day I decided to experiment. Inspired by the oppressive school environment, I brought in a vintage copy of *1984* by George Orwell. I provided the workshop participants (we no longer wanted to be identified as a "class") with stacks of 8 1/2 by 11 inch standard white copy paper.[4] Once armed with the paper and the softer Number3 "Black Warrior" pencils I bought for everyone, I asked my young artists to listen to the story I'd be reading aloud, all the while drawing whatever came to mind. Reminded of the great Symbolist artist Odilon Redon's rejection of illustration for what he called "visual correspondence," I told the group not to describe in imagery what I was reading, but instead draw anything that the tale reminded them of in their everyday lives. A little puzzled at first (I was as well, acting on this hunch), everyone began drawing as I read. As I continued reading aloud, I found myself really getting into it. And as I was really getting into it, the kids were really getting into the making of their drawings. The strangest images began to appear, like the magic of photographs emerging from the developing tray: large pyramids of stones with sad, resigned eyes, clocks with hands approaching the stroke of midnight, pulled down window shades, piles of earth (or perhaps bullshit), and copies of prints from an old George Grosz monograph pulled from our ad hoc art library. Then one of the kids had an idea. Could he draw on a page from my book? I resisted, but he was adamant. Right on time for us, we had our first collective "Eureka Moment": drawing on the book page, on literature both handed down to us and yet so often denied to us by history. A conversation was initiated between a 12-year-old from the South Bronx and one of the greatest authors of all time. What would happen if we expanded this idea both literally and metaphorically?

The next day, I bought two cheap paperback copies of *1984,* and on a larger sheet of rag paper I picked up on sale. I used some leftover Elmer's glue to adhere a perfect grid scaled about 24 × 36 inches. I selected some of the most mysterious and evocative pencil drawings from the previous day's workshop session. I then cut away the transparent cellophane from some dusty, unused, and discarded library book covers.[5] Using a fine point Sharpie permanent marking pen, I carefully traced the kids' drawings onto the clear sheets. I borrowed one of the school's only working overhead projectors and transferred the drawing onto the grid of book pages I'd prepared. It worked. Discovering the surface of pages

I'd made, the kids wanted to paint them in right away. We began with a few old acrylics. The result was so odd, striking, and exciting that we all decided to go larger—far larger. By the next week we were working on a grid of book pages measuring about 5 × 10 feet, with transparencies made from drawings agreed upon by a loose committee. With a rolling utility cart, we could reduce or enlarge the images, spending a significant amount of time and care in the composition of the composite painting.

Everyone was thrilled with the finished work called "Ignorance Is Strength" (after George Orwell), although many teachers and the principal didn't appreciate the critical irony of the title.

By coincidence, soon after finishing the large painting, I received a phone call from a friend, the art dealer Ronald Feldman, who I knew through my contacts with artists Joseph Beuys and Conrad Atkinson (one of my mentors), both represented by his gallery in Soho. He was organizing a group exhibition along with the popular art critic Carrie Rickey. The theme was "1984." Knowing that I had curated several shows of emerging artists as a director of Group Material, he wondered if I knew of any young, new artists who he should consider including. I immediately gave him some names, but then something crazy took over. "Actually, Ronald, I know of some very young artists who have made work that would be perfect for your show... the junior high school kids from my class here in the South Bronx." Silence. I knew that he was thinking of the often cloying "children's art" usually restricted to exhibitions in the lobby of the neighborhood bank; handprints made in the primary colors with tempera paint. School Art. "Well, it's a long shot, Tim, but why don't you bring something down and I'll take a look."

The next week, Roberto and I took the graffiti-plastered number 2 train from Prospect Avenue down to Canal Street. We have our Orwell painting rolled up. It's after school and heading into rush hour, so we're holding the long roll up over people's heads hoping to get the work to the gallery on Mercer Street in one piece. In the gallery, an assistant asks us to unroll the painting on the floor and announces that Ron will be out in a minute. We wait anxiously, and I wonder if it was a mistake to bring Roberto along, perhaps sparing him the disappointment if the work is rejected.

Out comes Feldman, silent as he looks... and looks. He looks now with his hand on his chin. "Everybody, come get a look at this," he summons his staff and grins. Roberto starts laughing. "Tim and Roberto, this is fantastic and we're going to make it a centerpiece for the exhibition." This would be the first exhibition of our collaborative painting.

Back in the South Bronx, the group wants to have a team name. We brainstorm for days, mostly with awful ideas such as "Kids from the Streets." In desperation, I decided to offer a 20 dollar bill to whoever came up with something usable in time for the exhibition at Feldman. Modifying earlier attempts, Franklin suggested "KOS," for "Kids of Survival." Everyone loved the acronym, which sounded un-childlike and arch, like FBI, CIA, or KGB (or KKK as Franklin, who was African American, loved to remind us).

About 12 of us all went to opening in Soho. I had permission from parents, but I did not notify the school from fear of their usual trepidation and interference. The painting was a hit with the art world crowd and while there were no buyers, the work attracted much positive critical attention in the press and earned a large reproduction in the *Village Voice*. Leon Golub was right, after all. KOS and I were onto something. Soon after, Leon recommended our work to the Barbara Gladstone Gallery in Soho, in which we had a group show, called *Social Studies,* of artworks with explicit political content. But this time the participating artists were major figures in the contemporary art world— Leon Golub, Nancy Spero, Jenny Holzer, and Eric Fischl. This was "big time," and we knew we had to make an important statement. For almost a year we had been working on a large-scale painting inspired by the comic novel *Amerika* by Franz Kafka. While we had made several paintings after 1984,[6] we had tired of the sensationalistic, semi-macabre imagery of these works. I will never forget the day when one of my most troubled kids, Eric, asked "When can we make something beautiful?"

The visionary last chapter of *Amerika,* "The Nature Theatre of Oklahoma," features a scene in which the novel's protagonist, a teenager named Karl, is recruited by a utopian commune called *The Nature Theatre of Oklahoma.* The collective operates on two major principles: "Everyone Is Welcome!" and "Everyone an Artist!" Since this sounded so much like the working creative ethos of our KOS team, we adopted the story to inspire a new painting.

Arriving at an arena to sign up for the Nature Theatre, Karl encounters a group of participants dressed up like angels, aloft on tall pedestals and playing spontaneously on long golden horns. Symbols of voice, freedom, affirmation, and perhaps confusion and rage, the image of a cacophony of golden horns resonated. I asked the KOS members if they could portray their individual spirits and songs in the form of a golden horn, what might it look like? The constellation of wildly original forms was painted on a large grid of book pages (our signature method by now) in beautiful, glowing metallic paint (see figure 3.2). *AMERIKA I* (after Franz

Figure 3.2 *AMERIKA*. 1988. Watercolor on book page, photograph by Tim Rollins

Kafka) was a breakthrough for us, and well received in the *Social Studies* exhibition. The well-regarded critic Grace Glueck (1988) gave it an especially enthusiastic mention in a review in the *New York Times,* and the work was acquired for the prestigious permanent collection of the Chase Manhattan Bank.

Soon after, things at I.S. Number 52 began falling apart. George died of stress-related colitis. A succession of incompetent replacements arrived, who dismantled the scheduling system I had worked so hard to put in place. Instead of six classes of 12–14 special education students a day along with the after school program, I was ordered to have 30–40 kids for only two periods a week, with my special education students "mainstreamed" in art—regulated to a table in the back of the room. Order was almost impossible to maintain. During one especially raucous session (materials were no longer provided so I was resigned to use only the copy paper and pencils I could provide), Roberto started singing from the "special table" in the back of the room.

> "We've got to get outta this place!
> If it's the last thing we ever do!"
> I remembered the tune. It was the song from the 60s by the Animals.
> "Robbie, how do you know that song?"
> "Don't know. Just heard it somewhere and I remembered it. It's how I feel about this class!"
> That was it.

Using the money we had earned from the sale of the *AMERIKA* painting as a deposit, and receiving initial support from the National Endowment for the Arts and many artist friends and local community groups, we moved *The Art and Knowledge Workshop* in 1984 to the Longwood Neighborhood Community Center five blocks away from the madness of the junior high school. The workshop and KOS were now housed in a safe haven—a gymnasium of an old, abandoned elementary school that had been saved and renovated by the city in collaboration with community nonprofits. Unlike the isolation insisted upon by the public school, we now had organic, vital working relationships with many of the local organizations that are now active in the coming renaissance of the neighborhood, especially the Bronx Council for the Arts and the Longwood Historic Community Association. I continued to teach full time at I.S. Number 52 for three more years. Working as a Board of Education employee during the day, I continued to work with my most dedicated young artists almost every day after school and on weekends in our spacious, secure, and bell-free studio.

Free from the restrictions of the local school, by 1987, the work of Tim Rollins and KOS was exhibited and acquired by museums and permanent collections worldwide, allowing KOS opportunities for college scholarships, world travel, and independence. As of 2011, our work is in the permanent collections of over 95 museums, including the Museum of Modern Art in New York, the Tate Modern in London, and the Museum of Contemporary Art in Basel. Many of the original KOS members have gone on to colleges like the Cooper Union, the University of Pennsylvania, Stanford University, the School of Visual Arts, and Bard College, becoming artists in their own right while maintaining ties to the KOS project and family. I continue to work and live in the neighborhood, just a few blocks from Prospect Avenue.

SOME THOUGHTS

Self-satisfaction and congratulation are not enough. What seems most important at this juncture in arts education is to strategize ways and means to influence those forces and energies that can effect change in current public school culture. Art outside of the classroom is essential, and surely more convenient. But all of my instincts as an artist, educator, and citizen impel me to devise plans that will have *The Art and Knowledge Workshop* begin or renew partnerships with public schools in distress. In recent years, we have worked as visiting artists in public schools from Philadelphia to Milan, allowing us to demonstrate methods in which art is not used as a recreational activity, but as a powerful means to general knowledge.

Our alternative pedagogy is *not* to offer an alternative, but rather to do everything in our power to respectfully advocate for positive pedagogical change in art education within the so-called mainstream classroom, especially in the public schools. It is time that progressive, proactive, and experienced arts professionals with sustained community presence effect much needed change in attitudes and expectations. Many of us—artists *and* educators—toiling in the fields of the public schools have proven track records of success. We know what works and what doesn't with our students, especially in neighborhoods like the South Bronx. The KOS experience has inspired dozens of gifted and challenged young people to develop their own careers in the visual arts, literature, performance, film, and installation throughout the United States and abroad. I am prouder, however, of those members who followed me into education, teaching at colleges such as Columbia University and the University of California at Berkeley. Still others chose to give back by taking positions in the local public schools.

Successful and striving arts educators can make classroom changes, changes our students need and deserve. We must begin to take the schools back from the inept, the cynical, and the clinical. Let's revise that old Animals' song to "We've gotta get *back in* this place if it's the last thing we ever do."

NOTES

1. The program ran through the summers.
2. The school building is one of the great structures that Snyder designed throughout New York City in the early 1900s.
3. Through Marvel Comics I came to art and literature as a kid back in rural Maine. X-men was my favorite.

4. This is 1982 and the school still used mimeographs for reproducing worksheets. I "liberated" several reams from the supply room for this project.
5. The sheets were donated by the school librarian, who, like many others in the school, believed that the art teacher can make something out of any kind of trash—in this case she was so right.
6. These paintings were based on *Frankenstein,* Dante's *Inferno,* and Faulkner's *Absalom, Absalom!*

References

Dewey, J. (1934). *Art as experience.* Merion, PA: Barnes Foundation.
Glueck, G. (1988, November 13). Survival kids transform classics into murals. *The New York Times.*
Kafka, F. (1927). *Amerika.* New York: Schocken Books.
Lippard, L. R. (1981, June 24). A child's garden of horrors. *The Village Voice.*

CHAPTER 4

Young and Disabled in Harlem: Making Art Like It Matters

Alice Wexler

> *Most empathists held that bodily feelings were projected outward from the perceiver onto the art object. Current neurophysiological findings, however, suggest that the work of art writes itself on the perceiver's body... The sensation (in bones and muscles, in the being) that the empathists wished to explain—of the union or communion between viewer and object, listener and musical work, reader and poem—is real, not illusory or only metaphorical. They simply lacked physical models that could account for it. Yet now we can understand that the arts affect at once our bodies, minds, and souls, which themselves are aspects—processing modules in the brain—of an individual that apprehends as one.*
>
> (Dissanayake, 1995, p. 185)

ELLEN DISSANAYAKE HIGHLIGHTS A THEORY THAT MAKING ART is a biological response to a need to "write ourselves" onto the surface of the world, and to find there the material manifestations of both yearning and completeness. Those symbols act as a feedback loop between internal and external realities. Bill Richards turned this theory (30 years before Dissanayake's writing) into praxis after an event as a graduate student at Indiana University, long before working with adolescents with physical disabilities. In a drawing course he taught for nonart majors, he was perplexed by an unresponsive female student who had never made art before and was not interested in trying. Richards did what he could to stimulate her interest, but without success. On a cold morning (the class started at 8:00 A.M.), Richards asked if anyone might like to travel to a farm outside

Bloomington. The only hand that went up was the recalcitrant girl's. Perhaps her interest was piqued because she lived on a farm. The students piled into cars and spent the chilly day drawing outside. Returning to the classroom, the students displayed their drawings for critique. Among the drawings of landscapes, fences, and trees was a magnificent drawing of a cow. "Who did this?" Richards wondered out loud. The girl's hand went up. This incident changed his life, as it appeared to change hers. She began to care for her appearance, which had been disheveled, and participate in the coursework. Richards was dumbfounded. It was confusing to him and the students that she had, in her first drawing, bypassed what Richards was trying to teach.

> I was trying to teach the students an understanding of the formal and conceptual aspects of drawing and she bypassed the process by going directly to making authentic art. I came to realize that processes could be taught but not creativity, and that my function, when not teaching a process (e.g., figure drawing), was rather to make a context for creativity to flourish and to provide encouragement and the necessary evaluation of the work.
> (B. Richards, personal communication, August 7, 2011)

Richards describes her drawing as "Picassoesque." The drawing tools, rather than an obstacle, were a vehicle for visualizing a deep knowing and love for the subject. Released from the indoctrination and conditioning of the art world, Richards was now happily free-falling in unknown territory.

In 1989, Richards initiated a studio with the assistance of Susan Weeks and Dr. Barlow on the seventeenth floor of the Harlem Hospital in New York City and called it the Harlem Horizon Art Studio (HHAS) because of its panoramic view. It became a respite for children languishing in chronic hospitalization or potential harm after school. Once the evidence showed that art could repair bodies and minds, it was undeniable that something was happening that defied rational proof.

In the early years of the studio's opening, most of the adolescents were male. Young men are generally more susceptible to violent crime and drugs than young women. Young women have other roadblocks, such as early and unwanted pregnancy. But in Harlem, poverty, which is two and one half times higher than in white communities in the United States (DeNavas-Walt, Proctor, & Lee, 2005), and inadequate resources, especially health care, touch almost everyone's lives. In low socioeconomic Black communities, wholesome foods are a rarity while unhealthy foods are ubiquitous. The community is also more likely to be exposed to environmental toxins. All these disparities factor into the high morbidity in Harlem.

Not having a safe place to play, the young men ended up in the wrong place at the wrong time—in crossfire or oncoming traffic. Several adolescents needed wheelchairs, others were treated for broken bones or neurological damage. A few boys had reached a plateau in their recovery and were written off by the medical community. As word traveled that an oasis of art making was under way on the seventeenth floor, neighborhood youngsters came as friends who although not having physical disabilities, shared the same unavoidable risks in the Harlem streets.

CAN CHILDREN BE SELF-TAUGHT?

Richards is not certified in either art therapy or art education. His experience as an artist convinced him that artists cannot be taught. He holds the same expectations for children-as-artists, and so treats them with the same professionalism. Under Richards and his assistant Bryan Collier,[1] the studio ran like a well-ordered ship, a routine carefully laid out for first-comers and old-timers. Because the children were not told what to do, they needed to invent their own iconography. Richards supplied support, encouragement, art materials, and sometimes personal and professional advice, but he would not interrupt children while at work. Rather, through subtle behavior and often cryptic comments, he encouraged them to find their own style and content. Richards reserves judgment about their ability and patiently waits for a visual breakthrough that usually comes in the form of an abrupt change of iconography or graphic style. Children are given the same directions whether they are neighbors, outpatients in wheelchairs, inpatients attached to IVs, six-year-olds or 16-year-olds.

The outpatient and community children joined the in-hospital painters after school, getting to work on a painting in progress or thinking about beginning a new one. Some children were fairly new to the studio, having come with one of the more seasoned artists and still testing their talents. Newcomers began by painting with watercolors on paper and, depending on their level of serious work, graduated to canvas and acrylic. The children were not, however, trained in the useful tools of perspective, color theory, or figure drawing—all that is commonly taught to young people who aspire to become artists. Nor were they guided toward the visual expression of unresolved issues, or digging into unconscious material.

Because Richards's approach falls outside art education and art therapy, the children's artwork is more closely aligned with the idiosyncratic work of *Art Brut,* a genre named by Jean Dubuffet in 1945, the precursor of the term *Outsider Art* coined by Roger Cardinal in 1972. Both art forms are characterized by the artist's need to communicate emotions that cannot be expressed within the orthodoxy of the art world. Isolation, illness, or lack of education motivates the maker to express the ironic condition of living outside social conventions. The strangeness of the Outsider's spontaneous visual iconography is often foreign to the rest of us who are well versed in social conventions, have a complete set of limbs, and a full complement of senses. But the Outsider's spontaneous gestures and utterances translated into paint either slowly or instantly chip away at the social devices we use to hold back the world.

From the panoramic windows of the art studio, downtown Manhattan can be seen in the distance—it is tantalizingly close. Yet the young Harlem artists, living only miles from Chelsea and the sophisticated art schools throughout the city, have inherited the unorthodoxy of the Outsider artist. Their vernacular does not come from the formal ideas and concepts of the university, but rather from the life changing experiences that have made them even more separate from the mainstream. Perhaps because of this separation, their artwork has the same power as Art Brut to make us look deeper into our own compromised reality.

Ironically, from the early years until today, the children's work has received discerning attention from a segment of the art world. Several children have earned professional status by exhibiting in Manhattan galleries such as Ricco/Maresca and the architectural firm of Kohn Pedersen Fox, the Jamaica Arts Center, and the Low Memorial Library at Columbia University. They have also sold their work to corporations and collectors. Their artwork, however, cannot be considered a product of the art world, even though critics, dealers, and curators have given a nod to it. It is not validated by the system that has created the formality of modernism, the bricolage and appropriation of postmodernism. Even though Nathan Knobler says testily that "they are not members of a tribal group living on another continent. They are not psychotics or visionaries" (as cited in Richards, 1994, p. 24), they might as well be, given the remote possibility of their acceptance into a foreign world.

HHAS art is not grounded in artistic, historical, or contemporary connoisseurship but instead arises from the youngsters' bodies, minds, assets, and limitations. Paint is transformed and reorganized to conform to their ideas, and often to their anguish and loneliness. A response in the body is then activated in the way that Dissanayake described earlier. The visualization of those ideas resonates in children whose nervous systems imitate the integrity of their images.

This response in the body might also be compared to Rudolph Arnheim's isomorphism (1966), a theory of aesthetic empathy based on the premise that emotion is not separate from perception and cognition. Our internal body-self, and the materials that we use to concretize it, affects our external body-self, setting a new integration between the two and with the world, in the Laingian (1990) sense of ontological security. With our emotions, perception, and cognition, we embody the materials that shape created works, and set in motion a chain reaction that affects our bodily experience.

Abraham, Brook, King, and Louis were among the early, mostly male, artists at the studio whose stories will be told throughout this chapter. Abraham, Louis, Chappell, Gregory, and Jason became known as the *Five Young Painters,* the title of an exhibition of their work in 1990 at the prestigious Ricco/Maresca Gallery (see figure 4.1). They reveal how many variables factor into their success, each artist bringing his own physical condition, personality, and support system. Depending on the characteristics of each, they experience greater or lesser autonomy and dedication to their craft. Abraham describes how the studio's baseline philosophy allows children to capitalize on their inherent strengths.

Figure 4.1 *Five Young Painters.* From left: Gregory Smith, Louis Donaldson, Abraham Daniel, Jason Butler, seated—Chappell Williams. 1990, photograph courtesy Ricco/Maresca

> We're not taught! The only teaching we have is spiritual teaching—like encouragement and positive vibes. We take everything from within and then we let it out... Once you do something consistently for a while you grow with it, because it's yours. It becomes part of you. It becomes kind of instinct—like a reflex.
>
> (1993, personal communication)

Children can make sense of their experience when they find their own language. Independent of theories, formulas, demonstrations, or other secondhand ideas, they find the *rightness* of visual language. The body's storehouse of experience then becomes a reliable resource for artistic ideas.

HOW IT WORKS

Many of us have witnessed how images communicate directly without an intermediary, embodying deep feelings in their tangible forms. I would argue that the directness of images can be dramatic when it transforms the chaos of inner reality into coherency. Intact senses must be aligned for transformation to take place. This phenomenon might be called homeostasis, or self-organization, which sometimes happens when viewing and making art. The artist, however, might not be conscious of this deeper process. Although the visual transformation of material happens consciously, the visceral transformation takes place unconsciously inside the body. This art making experience requires the intensity that comes from "seeing for the first time," and why Richards doesn't teach technique, which might look good, but circumvents total immersion in painting. Allan Kaprow (in Kelly, 2003) describes Pollock's directness and simplicity that transformed his marks into a kind of holy presence.

> The crudeness of Jackson Pollock is not, therefore, uncouth; it is manifestly frank and uncultivated, unsullied by training, trade secrets, finesse—a directness that the European artists he liked hoped for and partially succeeded in but that he never had to strive after because he had it by nature. This by itself would be enough to teach us something.
>
> (p. 7)

Richards uses the term *art of necessity* to describe this heuristic form of art making. He requires focused, sustained, and self-motivated behavior from the children for his method to work. While these qualities do not insure "good art," they are nevertheless the grounding for self-actualization,[2] hard-won for young Black males in the streets of Harlem, and more so for young Black males in wheelchairs.

Abraham

When I met Abraham in 1992, he was 15 years old. His constant presence as well as his availability and openness about his work contributed to the serious and positive atmosphere in the art studio. At that time Abraham was living with his mother, stepfather, and two brothers in Harlem and leading a relatively independent life; a scenario that was unimaginable only a short while before. At the age of nine, he took the dare to climb a four-story scaffolding. Neurological damage from his fall left him in a coma for a month and in a wheelchair for several years. However, he never accepted his life as a quadriplegic, and his supportive family and love of painting led him to a recovery that his doctors thought impossible. In response to their prediction that he would spend the rest of his life in a wheelchair, he said, "Yeah, that's what they told my mother. But you can't live by the expectations of man because man is going to fail every time" (personal communication, 1992).

The story of Abraham's "miracle" spread throughout the borough, and the press came often to visit and document his recovery. For example, *U.S. News and World Report* stated:

> The most dramatic [breakthrough] involved the 15-year-old Abraham who after falling 3 stories from scaffolding spent a month in a coma and awoke a quadriplegic. Under Richards's guidance, Abraham managed to control the violent shaking of his hands sufficiently to paint. As he improved, his teacher provided larger challenges, larger canvases. When one afternoon, Abraham found himself unable to reach the top of a canvas, he stood up. He pushed the painting, put down his brush and walked to the bathroom.
>
> (Horne & Siedes, 1992, p. 54)

This story was told and written about endless times. Abraham was studied, interviewed, and most importantly, became an adolescent object of desire for many of the neighborhood girls.

Debra Morris, Abraham's home attendant from 1987 (one year after his accident) until 1995, described how, just prior to his recovery in 1990, Abraham would "break up his wheelchair all the time." He was demanding his imminent freedom. In a 1992 interview at HHAS she said:

> Yeah, I was there. I remember when he was making the sky. He was mixing the powder blue and I was holding him by his back, giving him a little bit of support, and then he sat down and he said, "Now what are we going to do with the sky?" because we had this big open sky here, right. And then

he says, "I know what I'm going to do," and then he start, and I says, "Abe, what are you doing?" right, and he's making this rainbow, he's making this beautiful rainbow in the sky and then he came down with this powder blue paint that he had, and he start making this spirit, you know, and it was so beautiful. It just took my breath.
(D. Morris, personal communication, 1992)

Abraham stood (and later walked) to complete his *Liberation Painting,* the painting that would become a symbol of his freedom. The image of Abraham standing to "reach for the sky" as he painted his *Liberation Painting* is both ironic and poetic, and about hope and freedom. He stood up to paint a rainbow in the empty sky and dressed himself as Superman, his arm shielding his mother. His message is that not only can he walk, but that he also has the ultimate freedom of flight and superhuman strength.

But first Abraham had to overcome severe spasticity,[3] leading to an inventive way of ordering his artwork characterized by a protracted and erratic application of paint. After about six months he was able to paint from his wheelchair, usually with a helping hand to hold him in place. Richards often said that he took forever to get the paint from the palette to the canvas and back. A patch of paint would emerge from his brush onto the canvas, and then radiating shapes building outward brought into focus an ambiguous but readable image. His yearning for visual order was so steadfast that he was able to complete unified and forceful paintings. Visions from comatose dreams after his tragic fall became subjects of his paintings, compelling him to confront physical and psychic barriers. Tenacious acts like these changed the children's bodies as they submitted to their longing to be known. In 2010, at 32, Abraham wrote about his life before and after his fall.

> With no sense of fear, I did not think I would get hurt from the things I used to do. Unfortunately, my bad behavior caught up with me at the fourth story of a building. I descended from a scaffold, landing on my head, damaging my cerebral cortex, and losing a lot of blood. People thought I was surely going to die. I was comatose for thirty-three days, hospitalized for one year and six days, and wheelchair bound for six years. Still determined to be as healthy as young children my age, I decided to go back to school. Although difficult, with lots of perseverance and dedication I achieved scholastic greatness.

In an article in the *New York Amsterdam News,* Kenneth Meeks (1990) quotes Abraham: "I tried to be steady . . . but my hands would shake, and my fingers would wiggle when I held the brush. But now I'm as calm as the letter C" (p. 41). He was, as Kay Larson (1991) wrote, "an island of intense concentration" (p. 37).

Tim Lefens (2002) in his book *Flying Colors* also captures these moments of intense concentration not expected from severely physically disabled young people who cannot walk, talk, or hold a brush. This population is the last frontier in the humane treatment in institutions. All over the country, says Lefens, children are treated as less than fully human—"To let it go on means our country is not whole" (personal communication, May 2011). Lefens, who is also a painter, broke though barriers with a strategy called Artistic Realization Technologies (ART).[4] He began his work in room 333 at the Matheny School in New Jersey, constructing a studio for the residents, who until then had lived without communication (most could not speak). He describes the astonishment of walking into room 333:

> I got slapped awake, the full power of life I thought was gone for good reappearing with startling intensity. The vanity of their bodies ripped away from them, the singular driver of the human spirit stood clear, intact, burning with a curious fire. I could see it. The students could see that I could see it, and signaled back to me with their eyes.
>
> (pp. 118, 119)

The children at HHAS and at Matheny School are in a hyper-focused optimal state of control (Csikszentmihalyi, 1990). This "optimal state" occurs when psychic energy is aligned with realistic goals and matching skills. Many assume this population to be first, unable to have such lofty goals as to "speak" through visual symbolic communication, and second, to have skills that bring them into being. Morris remembers Abraham's battle with jittery hands: "He wanted to do it. That's what it is. He wanted to do it. He wanted to put that paint on that canvas. He wanted to tell us something, and boy he's really saying something now" (1992, personal communication).

Many factors were responsible for Abraham's self-activated recovery. First, he longed to defy statistics and alter what others believed to be the inevitable. In addition, he was quadriplegic, and therefore the possibility of ambulation, although slight, was within the realm of reality. However, as Morris tells it, nothing before his encounter with HHAS changed his prognosis. Abraham describes himself before the accident as "a regular guy like everybody else, but more determined and strong headed." He left Rusk Institute with slurred speech, spasticity, no hope of improvement, and coming out of a "state of shockedness." He wanted to be independent, and he was angry and stubborn. But when he came to HHAS, he says, "I found out it was all right to have some help."

BROOK

Children with spina bifida, such as Brook, must make inconceivable efforts to focus. Brook's perceptual problems relate to hydrocephalus, the accumulation of excess water in the brain as a result of the disruption of spinal fluid at the opening, or lesion, on the spine. Thus spina bifida creates complex neurological and associated problems. Given his perceptual problems, and that painting was not his medium of choice, his symbolic representation did not inspire psychic changes apparent in the other artists. He came to HHAS as a five-year-old, and then returned years later as a teenager with limited ability to conceptualize visual order.

While it is the job of adolescents to make sense of their lives, many youngsters, like Brook, must also try to make sense of life in a wheelchair. Brook is not one of the lucky children to have two parents, or even one. Because his mother was legally unfit, as a six-year-old he was assigned to his grandmother. His grandmother, however, was also caring for Brook's two sisters—one being the mother of two infant girls—two brothers, and two school-age nephews. Brook's lack of adequate care at home, combined with his perceptual limitations, reduced his ability to care for himself. An attendant was finally placed at their home by the Children's Aid Society, and she remained with them until the children were returned to their mother in the Bronx in June 1997.

At 13, Brook was making the critical transition to high school and grappling with the issues that come with early adolescence. Many adolescents in the United States experience identity crises as an outcome of puberty and the transition into adulthood. The awakening of self as a separate identity simultaneously awakens the fear of difference and deformity, real or imagined. Embodying the teenage nightmare is unimaginably painful for teens with disabilities. Peer relationships at this transitory age between childhood and adulthood are significant. Because of the simultaneous need to separate from parental control and the fear of that separation, young adolescents seek each other's help. For the adolescent with profound disabilities the anxiety that comes during their development into adolescence is layered with complexity and frustration. The crucial socialization during this transition is mostly nonexistent. Brook's life, for example, leaves little room to make independent choices. His most basic needs must be organized and planned. The artistic choices offered in the art room are therefore indispensable to a baseline of freedom.

The presence of neighborhood children, often brought by rehabilitated youngsters to the art studio, created an inclusive environment for young adolescents who rarely have contact with both able-bodied and disabled peers. Brook's circumscribed life left rare opportunities to form deep relationships, to go on a date, and to be alone without an adult. His home attendant became a trusted and empathetic listener, a substitute for the relationships he lacked with peers. But his sexual curiosity remained unfulfilled.

Although often couched in dialogue about their artwork, the young artists' search for purpose and identity pervaded their lives. The day after rapper Biggie Smalls was shot and killed, Brook worked on a drawing that became both a tribute and a way of processing his feelings.

> I live in Harlem, one of the toughest places to live in the United States... Harlem. And part of Harlem, the way I live is full of thugs, drugs, bang bang bang, shoot em up, shoot em up. My painting is a way, a door to walk out of, a way out of all this bang bang bang, shoot em up, I'm a gangster, you're a gangster. That's my way of walking out. I walk out of "I'm a gangster, you're a gangster" lifestyles through my paintings.
> (Brook, personal communication, 1997)

Rap music is one of Brook's obsessions—fantasizing himself as a rap artist. His verbosity, characteristic of spina bifida and ironically called "cocktail party syndrome," endears him to adults but can alienate him from his peers. His fluid and poetic conversational style and ability to transport himself into alternative worlds make his fantasies seem real to him. Brook fantasizes that he, too, is big and bad. As a 13-year-old in a wheelchair, he says that the art studio saved him from harm:

> Art keeps you off the streets and it shows that you have more talent than that gang bang material. It shows that you have another side. Before I came to the art studio I thought that I was big and bad, and I can do this and I can do that. But now that I'm in the art studio I feel beautiful. I feel I can release a side of me that I haven't released before.
> (Brook, personal communication, 1997)

While his imagination is active, Brook's visual-perceptual damage limits his making of appropriate symbols. His visual repertoire consisted of hearts and other stereotypical images. According to Richards, many of Brook's paintings had promising beginnings but he is stymied by a lack of qualitative judgment, such as to instinctively know that a painting is finished and not overworked.

Brook's story presents a complicated issue concerning the effect painting has on a perceptually impaired youngster. Brook benefits from the studio's shifting perspective from alterity to creation. He compensates for his lack of visual acuity with his verbal talent, and discussions about how his artwork intersects his passion for music and language. The studio provided a forum for his active fantasy world and, at the same time, presented the challenging task of translating it into physical form, however rigid it might be. In a conversation in 1997, Brook reflected on his growth.

> When I got here in the art studio, it was a whole new world... Let's just say that I wanted to be independent because the art studio shows you a whole new world from tube land. Before I came here I did not want to speak to anybody. I used to stay in my room all day: I would not even speak to my mom sometimes. Since I got to the art studio, let's just say I love to talk. The art studio gave me a chance to expect the best of myself.
> (Brook, personal communication, 1997)

It's uncertain how much his neurological limitations will impede his artistic development or how much his artistry contributes to his life as he gets older. In 1997, Brook was engaged in the process of visually exploring and communicating experience. His greatest benefit from his participation in the studio has been his new interest in living his life. Before coming to the art studio he self-admittedly avoided effort of any kind. The complexity of his emotional, social, and physical problems, and his inability to take responsibility for them, made him a passive young man. But after joining the art studio in high school, he began to see himself as a survivor. He saw his future as "an independent man with a lot of cash." At one time he was a remote observer of life, rarely interacting with peers. The last time I saw Brook he was at a high school Christmas party dancing in his wheel chair, moving his body to the music with his classmates.

KING

> It pushes me. It pushes me to do stuff that I got to do. Some kids when it comes to doing stuff, they don't want to do it cause it's too hard, but you can't give up. One part that I don't like about my class is when they do their test they just skip over and guess. But me I just take my time, and whatever score I get, I don't care because I know I tried my best. If the words are too hard for me I just sound them out, try to do my best. It's not about winning. It's not a race; it's just that you have to take your time. Take it day by day, and it's hard, take it day by day. It's not easy in class or out there.
> (King, 1996, personal communication)

Conflicted emotions tug at King's psyche. In 1996 he was a ten-year-old with cerebral palsy about to enter middle school. In his early days at

HHAS, he worked unhampered by the demons that would later take over as he approached an unknown future. The first time he was given a canvas he painted a wolf. "Bill said I was the fastest painter because I finished it all in one day" (King, 1996, personal communication). But later, King became a procrastinator, and finishing a painting was gut-wrenching. He might work on a painting all afternoon only to cover it with gesso at the end of the day. Richards coolly observed his frustration, giving him the space to work out his angst.

The young artists learned to use their obstructions as the raw material for art making. But first they needed to know that they would not get instant gratification. Lifetime goals such as self-actualization are not subjects of typical discourse on the Harlem streets. With the high mortality rate for Black males, long-range plans and contemplation of the future are consciously or unconsciously not conjectured. Dr. Barbara Barlow, then chief pediatrician at Harlem Hospital, defined a term that she coined, "psychology of determination," as achievement through prolonged effort. The artists defied the "very difficult odds by reaching out and using every bit of strength they can in order to heal themselves" (1994, personal communication).

Once King was a loner, but in the art studio he became a dynamic presence. Richards called him "slyly aggressive. He taunts and teases a lot of the other children and kind of ribs them and tries to get under their skin. He used to be very quiet and very introspective" (1997, personal communication). He was born prematurely with a twin who didn't survive. He was diagnosed with cerebral palsy spastiocoigia, which means that his lower extremities are more affected. Early in June 1997, I visited King at his special education, barrier free[5] school in upper Manhattan. It was the first in the borough. Unlike the rest of New York State, in which the Board of Cooperative Educational Services (BOCES) provides vocational and "special needs" services, New York City designates special education services in levels of modified instructional services (MIS). Some children in King's school, who did not need academic assistance, were in regular education programs and pulled out for occupational therapy (OT). Walking was part of King's physical therapy (PT) plan, and he could walk a few feet on a level surface with short rests. His physical therapist, Betsy Crawford, explained that he is "household ambulatory," but with an energy costly gait pattern, so he must monitor his endurance. His walker is designed so that he can sit and rest. His biggest problem, she said, was his distractability, attending to everything at once. According to Crawford, walking is time sensitive; if he doesn't take advantage of the opportunity in a youthful body, his older body will have more muscles and height that will cause more difficulty resisting gravity.

> We're trying very hard to keep him focused on that goal that we established in the beginning of the year when he got a new walker and new braces.... The contractual agreement we have with him is that every morning when he comes into school he is supposed to leave his wheelchair at the entrance of the hallway where he's left off by the bus, transfer out of his seat into his walker, ambulate into the lunchroom where he has breakfast, and then ambulate to the elevator and go to his class.

She has noted that when his paraprofessional is absent, King will manipulate the situation so that he doesn't have to walk. This information was a clue to why he wrestled with painting, his inability to make a commitment to an image without succumbing to distracting thoughts and self-created doubting. The difference between his struggles at school and in the art studio was that when painting, King was solely responsible for the goal and its outcome. This put him squarely in confrontation with his distractability. King described how at first he imitated other children's drawing styles: "I used to copy off of Kisha, but now I have my own ideas so I just draw them." His "wolf painting" was likely the first work that was his own, which might have begun a cycle of self-doubting. "When I painted the wolf painting I said I messed up, but then Bill encouraged me to keep going" (1996, personal communication).

King has a winning personality, and he gets along well with adults and peers. However, although not seen at the art studio, he had tantrums and other "manipulative" behaviors at school. I witnessed his lashing out for the first time at PT when a new classmate arrived with cerebral palsy. While much shyer than King, he was more self-reliant, which created ill-feelings in King. The new classmate could take his braces off, which were more complicated than King's, while King had negligible success with his own. "That has become a volatile source of focused discussion for King. He can easily lose his temper if he hears his classmate's name.... He perceives his needs as being taken care of rather than doing it for himself" (B. Crawford, 1997, personal communication). His contentiousness and competitiveness might have been another impetus in his then fairly recent distractability and self-doubt.

Crawford calls his fragility, lack of self-esteem, unwillingness to take risks, and power struggles with adults, the most troublesome aspects of his life, which interfere with therapy and the ability to motor plan in order to execute his physical body in space. In the art studio, King knew that he must "do it for himself," albeit in a community of positive peer pressure. His voluntary participation was the important distinction, which precluded expectations of how he was expected to function as a disabled person within a non-disabled world.

The pressure for children to walk, even though painful and frustrating, is an example of Ableism[6] and stigmatization—wherein people are treated as categories rather than as individuals. Ableism stems from notions of normalcy perceived by the dominant "abled" group: seeing is better than not seeing, hearing better than not hearing, and walking better than not walking. These unquestioned beliefs arise between the medical model, which suggests that people with disabilities should be cured, and a sociopolitical orientation to disability that acknowledges disability as a failure of social systems (Blandy, 1995). As Lennard J. Davis (1997) says, it not so much a problem of disability as it is a problem of how normalcy is constructed "to create the 'problem' of the disabled person" (p. 1). Crawford, for all her obvious good intentions, did not hear King, particularly when he screamed out during one of his rigorous PT sessions: "You can't feel my pain." I venture that within this simple but fully awake statement is his awareness of being other, of being sexually unwanted, of fear for the future, of wanting acceptance as he is, without adult-made contracts and goals.

LOUIS

> At Harlem Horizon Art Studio, you know, they didn't teach you. It's your inner thoughts...
>
> (Louis)

Louis, along with Abraham, was the first of five young men to join the studio when it opened in 1989. Like the many young males caught in crossfire by hanging out on the streets, Louis was shot in the abdomen. He was with his brother who did not survive, and consequently Louis suffered from survivor's guilt. He was brought to Harlem Hospital for rehabilitation, but after five surgeries he wouldn't eat, sleep, or talk; in effect, he was dying. Dr. Barlow asked Richards to entice him to the art studio that was just starting up. Miraculously, he was enticed. Contemplating about that time he said, "I could paint better from out of my bed than from in my bed, so I looked towards getting better than feeling sorry for myself." At first, weakened, he left his bed for short periods on crutches, and within a short time he was hooked on art. "Things that hit me inside just came out."

Louis brought to the art studio the notion that art is a set of rules and conventions. Because he failed art in school he spent the first months at HHAS trying to conquer the techniques that eluded him. In 1992 he was 21 years old. Looking back he said, "At that time they had rules and regulations, so when I came to Harlem Horizon I could just free up my soul; I could just relate to the canvas more than I could, like, relate to a person." Like many of the young men, Louis feared making the mistakes and enduring the failures of his past because he did not fulfill the expectations of the curriculum. Richards describes the process that children with previous art training must take as the breaking down of inhibitions to the point where "they're not thinking about making mistakes. When they have the confidence that they can really do what they want to do, then they can take the painting anywhere they want because they believe in themselves" (1996, personal communication).

Bryan Collier, assistant director of HHAS for several years, minored in art education, but he was disillusioned by the stagnancy and impersonality of how art was taught in the public schools.

> You can see it in the kids that they are bored. They had their formulas for projects to stimulate these kids and keep them interested. The kids didn't pick up on it because it was something that was coming from the top rather than the individual student.

Collier called HHAS "the missing link" that he was searching for. Witnessing how children work in a freewheeling format and their resultant products, he was compelled to ask why he made art, why people made art. From the standpoint that there are multiple individual reasons, he was able to encourage children to believe in "that voice that speaks to them, and you ask them to look within that source to make art" (B. Collier, personal communication,)

In 1992 Louis defined what Collier called "the missing link" in the following way:

> Bill only showed how to control one's self-determination. He never brought anything to us. We weren't taught anything like a curriculum in school. We were taught that curriculum is in ourselves; in our artistic conception. The art program is built on self-expression because art is within everyone. It's like a singer who goes out and sings. He gets something from the audience because they know what he's feeling.

Louis was admired for his naturalist paintings of forests and animals. He was a former veterinarian's assistant so he had a love and respect for animals. He also said that they are neglected, so if he paints them people "will have more consideration for animals and life. When you paint from the heart, then it enlightens people." His first major work was called *Garden of Eden,* which brought this love to his work. He painted it with another youngster, Chappell Williams,[7] which began a series of collaborative works. He said, "When you collaborate it's like when two

Figure 4.2 Louis Donaldson. *Brook's World*. 1990. Acrylic on canvas. 58 × 80 inches, photograph by Alice Wexler

minds meet. See, you don't know what that person is going to paint, you just have to move with what he's doing." He said that he did the work as a form of "togetherness, two artists just meeting, just expressing feelings on a canvas." A solo painting of Louis's, which was acquired by the hospital, is a work in four parts that he originally did as a series. Richards put them together, and he was amazed.

The children's work "speaks" to us because it makes palpable their desire to tell us something. Louis said that painting was a way for people to know who you are, and "if everyone were an artist, we would know what everyone is thinking." Painting gave him a language to show his love of animals and nature. Painting also became the common denominator between the children. Their deepening relationships neutralized anxiety about their physical and social limitations, and were replaced with poetic representations. One of Louis's major works is entitled *Brook's World* (see figure 4.2), a five foot by seven foot canvas included in the exhibition *Five Young Painters*. It was a tribute to the "inner world" of his paraplegic friend, the young five-year-old Brook.

An Interview with Bill Richards

This account of HHAS would not be complete without a review of what, how, and why Richards conceived a way to work with young people "outside of the mainstream," free of the social and educational pressures that are constant reminders of their marginal position in the social order.

Before teaching for 15 years at Moore College of Art in Philadelphia, he was invited to start an art program at the Youth Study Center, a house of detention for young offenders in Philadelphia. With a master's in painting and a minor in art history, he had never been an art teacher, nor was he certified in art education. His ideology about "non-teaching" was formed by his student's "cow drawing" mentioned earlier, his artistry as a professional painter, and bearing witness to youth who, if treated as professionals, would perform as such. The young people, ranging from six to 18, waiting for sentencing or a placement in another institution, were showing signs of creating serious artistic production. It was here that he was able to fully apply what he learned as a graduate student at Indiana University. Many years later, after becoming disillusioned with academia, Richards was invited to participate in the newly formed Injury Prevention Program at the Harlem Hospital, spearheaded by Dr. Barlow. His thoughts turned to the youth program in Philadelphia. Here might be an opportunity to fulfill the potential of the same un-prescribed program that he once started but could not see to its completion. At the same time he was also disillusioned with an ever increasing commercialized art world.

> So the critical thing for me was the possibility of finding or creating a situation where art can be utilized in a way that's really positive ... where it's totally unrelated to the hype and hoopla of "making it," of commercialization. I was totally cynical, and in the art world there isn't much room for cynics. ... So that's where I was in the beginning.

In 1992, I was beginning research for my doctoral dissertation. Upon entering the studio I realized that, like Collier, I had found "the missing link" to art education. Seeing the evidence resolved many doubts I had about art effecting long-term change. The following are segments of the interview that took place in 1994, during a second round of observations.

> *Wexler*: Were your expectations fulfilled?
> *Richards*: I never have a lot of expectations, so I didn't try to fathom what was going to happen other than I knew it was going to be beneficial to a lot of kids. But I didn't know how good the paintings were going to be. It was sort of a research thing in a way. I was curious to see how good they would get, how long they would sustain it. It's ongoing. We still don't know what's going to happen to Abraham, Gregory, and Orville: whether they will sustain it, whether the drive is strong enough to sustain this for ten or 20 years. We're providing them with certain tools

and connections so that if it's within them to sustain it, the opportunity is going to be there.

Wexler: Do you think their goals to become a better painter is what is healing, or do you think that it is some kind of dynamic that happens as they are working on their paintings—something internal that comes about, or a combination of both?

Richards: It's probably a lot of things. One of the things that I've thought about is that the making of a painting is a process involving organizing elements that creates some sense of wholeness. I think that one thing that may occur is that this business of making wholeness becomes a process that the body then seemingly imitates. So you're making something that is total and whole and unified and the body is trying to do likewise.

Wexler: You said before that you do not teach: you encourage. What exactly is your philosophy?

Richards: Before the age where making decisions that are going to affect your future in terms of what you want to pursue, whether that age is 18, 19, or 20 years old, up to that point you should have the freedom to explore things without being bombarded with the sensibility of a school system that may be totally alien to your own. So any kind of teaching involves a sensibility that is formed by one's own past experiences and affinities, and what you have worked out, rejected, and selected. That may have some relationship to some children but certainly it won't relate to all of them.

Wexler: How do you feel about the kids seeing artwork in museums?

Richards: This is a big question, and all the art people want to know, and feel that they're not being educated artistically. For example, a professor from an art university who wrote an essay in our catalogue is concerned that the kids are not being educated, that we're not teaching them history. My response was, "when you look at their paintings do you feel dissatisfied? Are the paintings not full?" "Oh no, the paintings are great." If the paintings are great why is there a criticism of the method? It's incongruous to criticize the method if the results are great.

Wexler: But do you think being aware of the art world has value?

Richards: I don't think it's necessary. Walking down the street may have value but, is it necessary? It depends on where you want to go. Early on I thought that when the good painters get bogged down, then I'll take them to museums. But they never really got bogged down. I was curious to see what their response was to Thorton Dial and William Hawkins, two self-taught Black artists. Their exhibition was not of great interest to them. They were interested in knowing how much money they were making. Louis picked up on the signature of Hawkins, the way he wrote around the borders of the painting, and he incorporated that in his work. He also picked up on some of the collage ideas. But those instances did not have a great impact.

Wexler: How should "teachers" be trained to work in this setting?

Richards: I think the best training is experience and becoming an artist. It's not technique that needs to be known, it's not teaching methods, it's the kind of person you are and how much you know about your craft and creativity, and what you can bring to the situation that's going to enable you to understand what's important and what's going on before you. It's not something related to the format and a preestablished plan. For example, the idea that the National Endowment for the Arts advocates is ludicrous. They put out a publication after they had a blue panel commission assimilate all the high ideas about the teaching of art called *Beyond Civilization* that is about the sequential development from the first grade to the twelfth grade, so that an informed twelfth grader has all these pieces of knowledge about the making of art. It's a guide for schools on developing their curriculum. I applied to the National Endowment for a grant and we were rejected this year. The person who came here to do the site evaluation wanted to know if she could become a volunteer here. So we got the highest recommendation and we still didn't get the grant. So after I got rejected I was livid and I called and got excuses like, well, they didn't know if we were really community oriented. And our grant said we had three exhibitions a year in the community and we're located in Harlem Hospital: you can't be more community oriented than that. So she said, "well, you are having a show in Japan, we would rather have it in the community." So I said that we're doing both. Then she said the real reason is because you're not training these children to be professional artists. And I said, "that's right, we're not. We're not training them because they already are professional artists." And she said, "Oh, no, they're children."

CONCLUDING THOUGHTS

What began as a humble undertaking (in the first session in 1989, Richards was a volunteer with five children in attendance) evolved into an internationally acclaimed art program that benefited thousands of young people. The studio was soon sustained on close to 100,000 dollars a year in grants with a staff of four (two salaried and two volunteers). By the end of Richards's tenure he had mounted over 40 exhibitions. Most significantly, the hospital was witness to the youngsters' improved health and the production of saleable art. Efforts were made to emulate the program in other areas in this country and abroad.

During the first decade, the studio compiled an extensive bibliography enumerated with honors, awards, and grants, extensive media coverage that included newspaper and magazine feature articles, and numerous television segments. Thus, the exemplary artwork, in combination with improved health, explains the fascination with the art program, aided by the "Harlem mystique."[8] The art boldly emerged from the emotions and experiences of the participants without teaching or input from outside sources. The art expressed its necessity to be, thereby initiating bodily transformations, highlighted by a quadriplegic regaining walking mobility.

Postscript: Where Are the Children Now?

Orville Anderson arrived at the studio in 1991 and has virtually never left. While in high school he learned to paint by watching Bob Ross on channel thirteen before getting "debriefed" at HHAS. He never graduated high school, but at 37 years of age, he is the coordinator of the art studio, and Abraham, now 33 years old, is his assistant. In May 2010, Abraham and Orville exhibited their work in a group show called *Breaking Down the Walls* at a gallery in Kingston New York. Abraham and Orville traveled by bus and train from Harlem with Abraham's mother, siblings, and his siblings' children. He has not been painting but writes poetry and plays chess when he's not assisting Orville. Richards has been looking for a studio for the two young men to share that would be easily accessible (walking distance) for Abraham. Orville continues to paint in the studio and at home in the Bronx. He wrote the following about his work.

> I developed what is now my unique yet powerful style. I use my paint and poetry as a tool to express my inner character. My landscapes of the Jamaican ocean shore and countryside express the beauty in my homeland. My abstract artworks show some of the frustrations which have haunted me, such as the death of my father in 1984. Many of my paintings express my love of birds, children, family, and God.

Orville struggles to keep the studio afloat. The hospital's affiliation with Columbia University ended several years ago, and along with it much financial support. The long-term grants have dissolved, and the hospital can no longer supply the studio with paints and other materials. As a result, children have dropped away, and the outpatient and community children no longer attend. As of this writing, Orville has seen but unable to contact Louis and King. Louis was registering for courses at Columbia University in 2010, and Orville spotted King in the subway. So far, Brook is not locatable.

Notes

Sections of this chapter were reprinted with permission from the National Art Education Association, RESTON VA. Alice Wexler, *Painting Their Way Out:*

Profiles of Adolescent Art Practices at the Harlem Horizon Art Studio.(2002) 43(3). pp. 339–353.

1. Bryan Collier was the director of HHAS for two years after Richards left in 1999. He is working as an artist and an illustrator for several children's books, producing 25 so far. A few notable books are *Martin's Big Words, Visiting Langston,* and *Rosa.* After his tenure at HHAS, Richard's went on to create and direct the Fine and Performing Arts Program at the Northeast Center for Special Care in Lake Katrine, New York.
2. I use the term "self-actualization" as Mike Rose (1989) uses it in *Lives on the Boundary:* "When years later, I was introduced to humanistic psychologists like Abraham Maslow and Carl Rogers, with their visions of self-actualization . . . it all sounded like a glorious fairy tale, a magical account of a world full of possibility, full of hope and empowerment. Sindbad and Cinderella couldn't have been more fanciful" (p. 18).
3. Abraham continues to battle with spasticity. His right hand is still severely spastic, his left arm is 30 percent contracted. His left leg is similar to his right hand, and he says that his "right leg is the only perfect part of my body."
4. A few years ago Tim Lefens was diagnosed with retinitis pigmentosa, and he is now legally blind. He says, "Don't get weepy for me, it's been scary but I can still paint. The thing I want to tell you is how, when I was lowest, way down there, pretty close to giving up, it was the kids and young adults I worked with who lifted me up" (http://www.philia.ca/cms_en/page1350.cfm).
5. Barrier free means that there are no barriers to access, as in providing ramps, elevators, and railings to enable children who need assistance to move easily throughout the school building.
6. Thomas Heiher (2002) defines ableism as devaluing the child as a result of his/her disability to the extent that society perpetuates the values of the dominant group.
7. Chappell Williams was a paraplegic, and one of the five boys who began their work when the studio opened in 1989 (made famous by the exhibition entitled *Five Young Painters* at the Ricco/Maresca Gallery in New York City in 1990). He arrived a few months after Abraham and Louis. He was also one of the studio's only abstract painters, and an avid reader. His dreams of becoming a football player crushed after he was shot in the back while leaving a party in Harlem.
8. Richards describes the "Harlem mystique" as "The aura related to a rich cultural history embedded in a region of social significance" (personal communication, September 21, 2011).

References

Arnheim, R. (1966). *Toward a psychology of art.* Berkley and Los Angeles: University of California Press.

Blandy, D. (1995). Assuming responsibility: Disability rights and the preparation of art educators. *Studies in Art Education, 35*(3), 179–187.

Cardinal, R. (1972). *Outsider art.* London, UK: Studio Vista Press.
Csikszentmihalyi, M. (1990). *Flow.* New York: Harper Collins Publishers.
Davis, L. J. (1997). Constructing normalcy. In L. J. Davis (Ed.), *The disability studies reader* (pp. 9–28). New York: Routledge.
DeNavas-Walt, C., Proctor, B. D., & Lee, C. H. (2005). *Income, poverty and health insurance coverage in the U.S: 2004.* U.S. Department of Commerce, Economics and Statistics Administration, and U.S. Census Bureau.
Dissanayake, E. (1995). *Homo aestheticus: Where art comes from and why.* Seattle, WA: University of Washington Press.
Five young painters from Harlem horizon art studio (1990). New York: Ricco/Maresca Gallery.
Heiher, T. (2002, Spring). Eliminating ableism in education. *Harvard Educational Review*, 71(1), 1–33.
Horne & Seides. (1992, March 30). Reaching the neediest kids with painting and dance. *U.S. News and World Report.* p. 54.
Kelly, J. (Ed.). (2003). *Essays on the blurring of art and life: Allan Kaprow.* Berkeley and Los Angeles: University of California Press.
Laing, R. D. (1990). *The divided self: An existential study of sanity and madness.* New York: Penguin Books.
Larson, K. (1991, January 7). The art of healing. *New York Magazine,* pp. 37–41.
Lefens, T. (2002). *Flying colors: The story of a remarkable group of artists and the transcedent power of art.* Boston, MA: Beacon Press.
Meeks, K. (1990, February 24). For injured kids at Harlem hospital painting is therapeutic. *New York Amsterdam News,* pp. 1, 41.
Richards, B. (1994). *Renewing the spirit: Paintings from the Harlem horizon art studio.* Warminster: Cypher Press.
Rose, M. (1990). *Lives on the boundary: A moving account of the struggle and achievements of America's educationally unprepared.* New York: Penguin Books.

CHAPTER 5

THE ART OF LIVING AND DYING: LINDA MONTANO

LINDA WEINTRAUB AND ALICE WEXLER

PERFORMANCE ARTIST LINDA MONTANO'S ART is based on mutual experience and acts of healing. Her work is not unidirectional. Rather both performer and audience participate in a blended engagement in art and life. Montano's career might be defined as disrupting the bifurcation between audience and performer, art and life, art and nonart, commodity and gift, self and other. Montano descends from artists who intentionally ruptured the traditional art gallery and proscenium stage with their attendant audience, and thus redefined the parameters of the artistic encounter. Since the late 1960s artists such as Montano, who witnessed the high voltage social upheavals in the United States—in race, gender, religion, and war—have responded by profoundly broadening art beyond aesthetic and formalist boundaries to include the events of the world (Tucker, 1986).

Montano and other performance artists in the 1960s and 1970s, such as Yves Klein, Chris Burden, Spalding Gray, Paul McCarthy, Dennis Oppenheim, and Adrian Piper, broke ground in the art world by creating new art forms that "raise philosophical, moral and ontological questions rather than aesthetic ones" (p. 28) directly through their lives and bodies. The new genre of performance art, which Allan Kaprow called "lifelike-art" in its heightened awareness (in opposition to "artlike-art" in its separateness), discarded the object as intermediary and its commercial intent as commodity. " . . . lifelike-art-maker's principle dialogue is not with art but with everything else" (as cited in Tucker, p. 85).

Montano's work, since she arrived on the west coast when the new genre of performance art led by Allan Kaprow was in full swing, has been about attention, endurance, risk taking, control, spirituality, life process, and time. In *Choices* (1986), she talks about the element of time in her work. "It's used to extend, differentiate, frame and change experience... It's the difference between a two year and a twenty year marriage" (p. 66).

In this chapter, Linda Weintraub and Alice Wexler respond to interviews with Linda Montano in 2004 and 2011. In 2004, Weintraub witnessed Montano's care of her dying father that she transformed into the joyful work of performance. Seven years later Weintraub and Wexler visited Montano to return to her thoughts about her father's death, and the impact he made on her life and art.

Linda Weintraub's Introduction to Linda Montano

Performance artist Linda Montano has not waited to die to be reborn. Her rejuvenation is inspired by her father's illness. Montano is his primary caregiver, monitoring his physical and metaphysical condition as it evolves moment by moment. Her art is a record of his physical decline and their synchronous spiritual awakenings. He is her teacher, but this is an ecological lesson for us all to learn. Linda Montano's father is 91 years old. He enjoys his meals and wheelchair trips to the village. Three years ago he began painting. Sometimes he creates works of stirring beauty. They are spare, Zen-like, mysterious. It is also true that Linda Montano's father has lost the ability to speak, walk, feed himself, and dress himself. Seven years ago Montano says she heard voices beseeching her to return home to care for her aging father and prepare them both for the inevitability of death. Five years ago she declared this experience a work of art. I requested an interview with Linda Montano to gather information about this art piece to accompany the section of my book, *Avant-Guardians: Ecology and Art at the Cultural Frontier,* which deals with degeneration and death. Instead, she revealed a joyful (she used the term "ecstatic") revitalization of her own life and career. She may be his caregiver, but her father has been her teacher. The new wellspring of creativity and soulfulness that he exhibits, Montano believes, stems from his lifelong spiritual practice within the Catholic Church, but also from the loss of his discursive faculties. His spirit seems ultimately liberated. The only end point she discussed during our interview was the "death" of the pioneering role she once played in the art world as one of the originators of performance art in the 1960s. But her art is being revitalized by the teachings that she is receiving from her father. Once, Montano says, she felt like art's leftover, a waste product of a bygone era. Now she is being "recycled." She is transformed. Her work seems, once again, timely, innovative, and compelling.

Linda Weintraub's Reflection on the 2004 and 2011 Interviews with Linda Montano

Dad Art, the subject of the following interview, was not yet a completed work of art when I visited the artist, Linda Montano, and her ailing father in 2004. Over time, this friendly visit has been reclassified as "professional." Conversations are now interpreted as "interviews" and casual observations are subjected to "art analysis." This change in status is generated by Montano's formidable artwork in which Dad served as her subject, muse, inspiration, and collaborator. What I experienced during that visit was an ongoing work-in-process that had no known termination date or anticipated outcome.

As in all her "performances," Montano utilizes art to augment, release, and concentrate healing spiritual energies. Although her therapeutic interactions sometimes generate videos and drawings, her reputation as a seminal figure in contemporary feminist performance art is earned through the intangible medium of the human spirit. Montano is sustaining the legacy of healing through art she inherited from her mother and grandmother. She comments, "Throughout their lives, they consistently transformed pain into beauty. They were models of transformation, transcenders; pioneers who knew how to find a way out of suffering through art" (R. Nobel, February 12, 2011, personal communication).

Meeting Montano's Dad took place in her childhood home. She had returned there six years earlier to act as his full-time caregiver. I observed the tasks that occupied each hour during my visit and imagined them being repeated, day after day, totaling entire years of effort. Yet instead of enduring the dispiriting drudgery of this routine, Montano invested each act with the aura of a sanctified ritual—including tying a bib around Dad's neck, wheeling him toward the Refrigerator, and spoon feeding him his mid-afternoon yogurt snack. When Montano installed Dad at the kitchen table covered with blank sheets of paper and placed a brush in his trembling hand, she radiated an ecstatic glow.

Montanto's maverick career as a performance artist reverses the conventional protocols of both therapy and art. Unlike therapists, she summons the healing power of art to serve her own needs, not just those of a client. She diverges equally from most artists by including herself as a foremost member of her art audience. From the start of her art career, she attended to her psychological state as if it belonged to another, explaining, "In the beginning I was in such pain and in such a narcissistic mindset, that I had no idea there was anybody but me in the universe. At that time my work was totally self-referential" (R. Noble, February 12, 2011, personal communication).

In *Dad Art,* Montano explores the multifaceted nature of art therapy. *Dad Art* is the collection of watercolors that Montano's father painted as the creative finale of his life. *Dad Art* is also a film. This remarkable collaboration between the artist and her father presents the footage taken by Dad. It displays a video camera as an art therapy tool. The camera enabled Dad to communicate as he declined, and Montano to manage her emotions after he suffered a stroke. She explains, "I could hide in back of it to shield myself from the pain of Dad's minute-by-minute decline. My terror and sadness would be masked" (L. Montano, 2011, personal communication, Retrieved 2011, http://www.lindamontano.com/). She filmed him being fed, bathed, taken to the hospital, dying, dead, and being buried. *Dad Art* is also a three hour performance in which the film is shown as Montano sings love songs and several collaborators provide grief counseling to audience members. Ultimately, *Dad Art* is an intimate exploration of the "greatest mystery," death. Montano explains that tending to her father enabled her "to practice states of transformation while I'm still living" (L. Montano, 2004, personal communication). She discovered that approaching death emits a "vibrational frequency" of great beauty (R. Noble, February 12, 2011, personal communication).

"Art/Life Counseling" is the term Linda Montano uses to refer to her honored art practice of over 30 years. The words "art" and "life" do not refer to the "life" of the people or the "life" of the era. They are specifically the life of the artist as she forms her identity, matures, and awakens. One such Art/Life Counseling project that factored into *Dad Art* lasted from 1984 to 1998. During this time Montano conducted counseling sessions once a month in the window of the New Museum in Manhattan. During these sessions she discovered that examining the consciousness of "the other" was a powerful facilitator of self-healing. "Art allows for this kind of personal embrace. It allows for the exploration of the subconscious in public" (R. Noble, 2004, personal communication). Therapy provided a means to pursue her own spiritual progress.

This self-directed use of art therapy characterizes Montano's current performance art project. In this instance, she is being restored and empowered by embodying Mother Teresa of Calcutta, the internationally renowned nun and humanitarian who was awarded the Nobel Peace Prize for ministering to countless poor, sick, orphaned, and dying people. Montano's urge to minister arose long before she learned about Mother Teresa. Questions like "How can I be just like Jesus?" (R. Noble, 2004, personal communication) became lodged in her consciousness during childhood. While other girls were dressing like movie stars, Montano was dressing up like the Virgin Mary and giving Necco wafers to her playmates. As a teenager, she entered a convent as a novice with the Maryknoll order to become a "Holy Girl" (R. Noble, 2004, personal communication). Although she did not complete this training, she retained its goals but transferred them to Art/Life Counseling.

Montano could not have anticipated that she would come to share Mother Teresa's appearance as well as her mission. Montano developed the unfortunate similarities after she contracted a debilitating illness called dystonia. She reports that she was "pretzeled from her head to her feet like a corkscrew, face all puckered in pain" when she heard an inner voice saying, "I feel just like Mother Teresa...and thought, I guess Mother Teresa looked like this too, because she's short and looks all stooped over and spasmed and has to take care of all 9,874,987 people who are dying, and festering with leprosy and drooling with deformities?" (L. Montano, 2011, personal communication, Retrieved 2011, http://www.lindamontano.com/).

Once again, Montano summoned the healing power of art to attend to her own afflictions. She borrowed Mother Teresa's model of Christianity and applied it to her Art/Life Counseling art practice. Montano covers her twisted body with the distinctive habit of the Missionaries of Charity, Mother Teresa's order—blue stripes on a white robe and white cloth head covering. She moves slowly among busy Manhattan pedestrians, holding a handmade cross, inviting them to join her in a gentle, saintly, one-on-one interaction. Often she is accompanied by a collaborator "bodyguard," who, by protecting the "Mother," lends an air of authenticity to the performance, as does an audio track that includes singing, bells, and the voice of Mother Teresa. People of all persuasions pause, bow their heads, and seem to be renewed by this brief encounter. Her motive, however, is not purely altruistic. Montano explains, "...making believe I am holy for three hours and giving nice blessings to people is a great job, helps me forget my sick-self and it seems appreciated by 99% of the people who suspend their belief for a while and play art with me" (L. Montano, 2011, personal communication, Retrieved 2011, http://www.lindamontano.com/). In this manner Montano resurrects her Catholic upbringing. Christ and the Saints taught her not to waste suffering.

Ultimately, Montano exposes the art therapist's dual capacity—to be healed as they heal. Montano acknowledges this by admitting that her psychological and physical challenges pushed her so far "into a level of transcendent creativity that I became my own art therapist. I learned how to fix me!" (R. Noble, February 12, 2011, personal communication).

Alice Wexler's Interview with Linda Montano, April 18, 2011

The Art of Nonverbal Communication

I entered Linda Montano's house in Saugerties on one of the first sunny days in April after an unusually hard winter. She approached me from the shadows of the heavily draped living room. I faced a life alert with intensity, wisdom, and intuitiveness. I felt, as I do from people like her, that my own life was being sized up. We walked out into the sun in the back of the house that she had lived in since age six. Although I anticipated that she would play the role of psychiatrist, in a kind of role reversal, she made herself comfortable on a lounge chair, stretching out to the sun but covered with cloth in a way reminiscent of her role as Mother Teresa. I abandoned my list of questions as we talked about autism, a "disability" that interests both of us. My interest in autism is in education and scholarship. Montano's interest is in the authentic moment of performance, and the guilelessness of many classic autists[1] is disarming to her. Because of the atypical neurological wiring of autistic people, they abandon past and future and live in the here and now. Their moral and intellectual purity, which frees them from "the dirty devices of the world" (Sacks, 1995, p. 260), is the effect of their dis-attachment to the symbolism of language. The abstraction of language, on the other hand, allows the speaker to represent what is not true.

Montano is particularly interested in the judgmental brain, the critic that appears to be turned off in the autistic mind. But before continuing, I concede that this statement, like other speculations, is not meant to deny that multiple ways of being autistic exist. Underneath the social construction, autists have complex and layered relationships with the world and society (Biklen, 2005). Thus, being "present" does not necessarily mean context free. The quality of presence is often attributed to autists who cannot speak. Therefore, the observer must infer from his or her own cultural and biological context what appears to be going on. Nevertheless, the way that autists *appear* to perceive and interact with the sensory world is profoundly different from people with typical brains. So, what this unique sensory experience suggests is a different relationship with the world and society that is not driven by the concerns that prevent concentrated presence.

The present moment, which might be the default experience of autism, has meaning for Montano as a performance artist. Arguably, presence, or living in the moment with its concomitant authenticity, is equivalent to enlightenment in the world of performance art. Additionally, her current interest, as she says, is with the brain, "because I now have a brain injury (dystonia), and the judge brain, and the analytical brain, the brain of word and critique is not operative."[2] She compares this condition to contemplative practice, to a kind of holiness and a sacred gift, which is the other side of cultural, social, and abstract knowing. The gift of presence, she says, also means the autistic loss of what we "typicals" consider essential.

It wasn't Montano's speechlessness that led her into an empathetic engagement with autism. Rather, she says, "the artists who are leaning toward the creative quadrant of the brain are hanging out with the underdog, hanging out with the black sheep, or the one who slips into the well of darkness, of purgatory, and suffering and victimization. So, those are our brothers and sisters."

Montano must nevertheless feel a kinship with autists, who have to use ingenuity to find a relationship between their internal language and the external world. She senses the contradiction of turning her struggles into art because, while they are acts of survival, they are also the products of being socially and culturally aware, of narcissism, of careers, and of media that are not in the frame of the autists she admires. This dilemma was only one of the many soul searching "undoings," filling in the blanks, as well as fixing and learning from what wasn't done that preoccupies her work.

> What I'm trying to talk about here is the word authentic, and how ruined... it's so easy to get ruined as someone of the world, by jealousy, competition, money, career. "How did I do? Was that a good performance? Gee, I wish I hadn't done that ending. I always know she's there because she laughs so loud, she just wants a gig. A person over there is asking for a grant, and she's selling her archive." What I'm talking about is the challenge to be present and authentic: when we really are cognizant of the dark, and our darkness, and the weakness of others, and the pressure to communicate creatively when the other brain is casting either a spell of judgment, criticism, critique, or greed. So some people have escaped that, and we mentor from them.

Her speech was now slow and stumbling, then racing, searching for the correct words; in effect, she was her authentic self. I thought of performance artist Anna Deavere Smith (1992), and her search for the authentic in language. Her theory is that in faltering speech, "when syntax changes, when grammar breaks down" (p. 53), the self emerges. There was some irony in making this comparison (which I will continue to make in the next several paragraphs): Smith being a wordsmith and a more scripted performer, a believer in finding the authentic in language. But how, and if, language reveals depends on how we use it. It can be worn like a mask, it can be *designed* to reveal, or reveal who we are not by design, but as a kind of momentary lapse of self-editing. "Over time, I would learn to listen for those wonderful moments when people spoke a kind of personal music, which left a rhythmic architecture of who they were" (p. 36). Looking for what's underneath the discursive meaning of language is what ties Montano and Deavere Smith together, although the former abandons spoken language for the communication between souls, and the latter uses it as an entry point to the soul. Also uniting them is their search for, in Deavere Smith's words, the uncomfortable places, thereby developing stamina in being where they don't belong. "Belonging" in Deavere Smith's life meant "leaving safe houses of identity" (p. 24), in her case the Black neighborhoods of Baltimore. For Montano it was the patriarchal church. "I would call these places that are without houses crossroads of ambiguity" (p. 24). Most people live in safe houses, Deavere Smith says, and even if they leave them they'll find safety in a new identity. Certainly, Montano's life is replete with ambiguities of all kinds. Her identity is as fluid as her access to the characters she adopts and discards, and then returns. She learned intuitively that the arts could be used transformatively, and she can accept the many ambiguities of her identity through the transformation she finds more sacred than her childhood religion. She exchanged Christian ritual for the ritual of becoming and acceptance.

> Acting is the furthest thing from lying that I have encountered. It is the furthest thing from make-believe. It is the furthest thing from pretending. It is the most unfake thing there is. Acting is a search for the authentic. It is a search for the authentic by using the fictional as a frame, a house in which the authentic can live. For a moment. Because, yes indeed, real life inhibits the authentic.
>
> (Deavere Smith, 1992, p. 8)

Like Montano, Deavere Smith became an artist in San Francisco. It was the 1970s, a time full of change and promise. Both women claimed their place in this dynamic time of changing cultural signs and symbols of race, gender, sexuality, and religion. Montano found her "religious" symbol, the chicken: "the woman was not allowed on the altar, but women are allowed on the altar of art, or the stage, and the sermon on the street." Growing up in segregation all her life, Deavere Smith's life was opening in San Francisco. She set out from here to discover the soul of America, the "American character" through words, in its language, "to get below the surface—to get 'real'" (p. 12). In San Francisco, Deavere Smith found Shakespeare, the key to breaking through the accepted rhythms that restrict humanity. Montano literally found her voice in the multiple personalities that she had stored, which later became a serious investigation that she called "creative schizophrenia," culminating in the video *Learning to Talk* in the mid-1970s.

Whereas Shakespeare was the source of Deavere Smith's epiphany and entry point into her signature one-woman performances, Montano was bred in the Catholic Church's miracles, mysticism, and transcendent thinking, which she says was the perfect forum for a conceptual artist.

> ...and I am convinced now that I was rehearsing my subsequent performance role as I knelt in church for hours praying, asking plaster statues to talk or to forgive me. I'm also convinced that the images that I internalized then are those which appear, reappear and shape my work even today.
> (Montano, 1981)

AUTISTS ARE OUR (SPIRITUAL) MENTORS

Judith Bluestone's (2005) description of autistic behavior is reminiscent of the psychic knowing of a sensory deprived ascetic that both interests Montano's work and defines her early silent life. Bluestone's own behaviors as a classic autist were driven by an atypical sensory-motor experience that disallowed socially expected sustained attention and communication. She understood intent energetically rather than from verbal communication, and waiting until the end of a sentence was pointless and at times painful: "the pragmatic me says 'what a waste of my time' and the sensorialy overwhelmed me says 'I have other things to spend my energy on. I don't need to play this silly game'" (p. 75).

Perhaps Montano feels a kinship with the autistic engagement with subtle energies that Bluestone compares to the mysterious system of energies in quantum physics: other energies in addition to the visual, olfactory, auditory, and proprietary. Bluestone describes herself in a constant state of interaction with other forms of energy: gravitational pull, biometric pressure, temperature, and general hyper/hypo-stimulation. In her work with people with autism she finds that they experience a different and deeper reality. She theorizes that most people in technological societies experience life as particles. Most people on the spectrum, on the other hand, are more sensitive to waves. She explains waves as the energy surrounding an object, how it is organized and her relationship to it. She thus experiences the object's energy, not the object itself, as a living thing with either a menacing or a protective influence, and thus she is affected by the environment in a way that others cannot perceive. It might not be too far afield to make a comparison between Bluestone's experience of the world as "objectless" and Montano's disengagement with objects as a former sculptor (described later in the chapter). Her development as a performance artist led her to concentrate instead on the effects—environmental and contextual changes—produced by our relationship with objects and each other.

Like Montano, Judith Bluestone also saw the cosmic purpose of autism. Bluestone was endlessly asked what she thought was the cause of the epidemic-like increase of autism. Asking what might be the purpose was a better question. Parents preoccupied with trading in their two-year-old BMW for a new model are now worried why their child would not hold their hand with affection.

> What those of us with autism are doing is giving the world a wake-up call... What is humanity? What is the purpose of our existence? Is it material possessions or is it our connections to one another? We can buy anything except the eye contact and the smile. You can't buy it, you have to earn it. You earn it by being a little afraid, and a little uncertain, and trying and finding out, how do I connect?
> (J. Bluestone, May 28, 2008, personal communication)

Similarly, Montano says:

> The universe is shunting us into the convent and into the monastery, into a sacred place when everything is being pulled from under our wings, and under our feet. The climate is in rebellion, and food is in rebellion... everything stripped and denuded, forboden and forbidden and fright. I'm not being negative, I'm just being real and honest. And it's really like, wake up to one's own compassion or die.

Montano now celebrates the fact that she was nonverbal until late in life. Rather than a neurological disorder, her lack of speech was imposed by the culture of her family, which was religiously austere, disciplined, and purposeful. Her brother and sister do not corroborate what Montano remembers: growing up in a spirit of psychic communication.

> We did not discuss, we did not address verbally, at least I don't remember that we did. I would stand on my bed and time travel, and from seven on went to church, morphed into this deeply silent child. Silence was good, but I ended up in the hospital because I vomited every morning on wallpaper in my parent's house I didn't know how to say, "someone's stepping on my coat, the cloakroom is too filled." I stopped vomiting when I was finally able to tell my parents what was going on.

Words were dangerous, unreliable, not to be used. But Montano transforms the painful and destructive into art. She practiced speaking in 1975 when it became apparent that she *could not* speak. Her entry into language was formalized in front of a camera with the video *Learning to Talk*. Growing up with non-English-speaking Italian grandparents, she learned "persona-morphing...changing my consciousness by changing my accent." Persona-morphing was the buffer that made possible the transition from stillness to language. It was at the same momentous time that she left her husband, Mitchell Payne, for composer Pauline Olivieros.

> ...and I sat in front of a camera for a year, speaking in different accents. It was almost like a multi-personality phenomenon.... I became seven different people. When I left my husband I started speaking in accents because I couldn't be me, and then I morphed it into art.

In school, Montano talked when necessary. She became instead a reader: psychic reader, tarot reader, and "people reader." And she had music: both parents were musicians. But her home was monastic, nevertheless, and her daily rounds of church-house-grandmother reinforced the danger—real or imagined—of talking.

> The church feeds a kind of punitive reason not to talk...the whole sin, fear, guilt, triumpherat was being stressed, certainly not the love, compassion, resurrection. So the crucifix not the resurrection...that gave me another reason not to talk. Maybe I would sin and go to hell. So it drives one into a kind of poetic, fantastic, imaginative, creative, whatever brain is not the thinking brain, vocation.

A BACKGROUND OF MONTANO'S LIFE

Montano was born in Benedictine Hospital in Kingston, New York, January 1942. A rumor or story circulated in her memory that no one knew her mother was pregnant. She was pregnant in winter and she wore a heavy coat over a thin body. "The sentence that I remember is, 'Linda, everyone was shocked when you were born.'" Montano ruminated about this important piece of memory and how it played out in her adult philosophy.

> I'm a real believer in rebirthing, what happens in utero, what happens before and after utero. So maybe there is something to petting the mother's stomach that is an important piece in the pre-birth process, and the anointing of this fetus of this child. Maybe it is important that people give women the affirmation of pregnancy. So maybe my mother didn't receive a lot of that.

Montano calls the details of her life a "performance art puzzle," each detail having significance in the psychology and artistic formation of the artist. She was born during World War II, her parents survived the depression. She was born on a Sunday morning. Her parents drove from their home in

Ulster Avenue in Saugerties to the hospital in Kingston. She imagined that it was cold and snowing, that the family doctor delivered her before going to church. It was 7:35 in the morning and people were sleeping. She is one of four children, the second born. She has a sister and one brother three years older, and another brother 11 years younger. She became the latter's surrogate mother by choice. Looking back now, she says, "I thought he was my child." Her mother was extremely creative, she sang in her dad's band. Her dad played trumpet and drums. Her grandmother lived around the corner, two streets over, and she walked over every day. Nan was a "performance artist" weighing 350 pounds. She was nonverbal, as Montano was, and "made art from sunrise to sunset. She was extremely eccentric, like a big Zen monk. I hung out with her all day. So church and Nan were my formations, and my mother's creative spirit." In an e-mail to Jennie Klein, her collaborator in *Letters from Linda M. Montano* (2005), she says:

> I truly believe that for each of us, family is our fodder, our diving board, our memory bank, our first story, our image maker, our reason for doing, our magnetic talent maker, our mystery to solve and blood to honor. The way this is de-scrambled in each artist's work is unique to his or her individual vision.
>
> (p. 4)

After high school and a year in college, she went into Maryknoll Sisters Convent for two years "because the persona that most inspired her was that of a 'holy girl'" (p. 18). She spent most of the hours of the day in silence, with the exception of chanting "ecstatically with over 300 nuns," one hour of recreational talking at the community room, and the occasional art project. Silence did not lead to Catholic holiness, nor did the art projects lead to new heights as a nascent artist. Rather, communing in silence was the seed that unfolded what was to become Art/Life. An insightful nun said, "Go and be an actress, Sister Rose Augustine" (p. 90). She left weighing 80 pounds.

> I came back, and the same doctor who delivered me, I'm sure it was him, and he said "well what does she want to do," and my mother said, She wants to go back to school, so he said, then send her back to school. And that was the only therapy I got for being totally mad, totally insane.

PERFORMANCE ART

> Art is not lofty, it never was lofty. Art was meant to challenge and to bring people into connection with themselves. And that can be painful, ugly, and difficult.
>
> (Sims, in Wallace, Weems & Yenowine, 1999, p. 85)

When Montano talks of the paradoxes of her life they make existential sense. Her work has the potency of both performing and living at the dangerous borders of psychological and physical endurance, like walking to the edge of the abyss and back in eternal return, her life illuminated in the burden of eternal return (Kundera, 1984). "But is heaviness truly deplorable and lightness splendid?... The heavier the burden, the closer our lives come to the earth, the more real and truthful they become" (p. 2). Montano's mission from birth was to make lightness out of burden.

Montano entered the Catholic Church searching for the holy girl, but instead began her life as an "art saint," and the germination of conceptual, confessional, and ritualistic performance art. In 1981, she used her ascetic experience of self-starvation at Maryknoll in a video called *Anorexia Nervosa,* interviewing five women, including herself. Without moralizing or judgment, she "de-medicalizes" and makes manageable the disorder in a symbolic act. "It has always been my personal belief that the themes that artists employ are born in childhood and that an artist's work explores, transforms, perpetuates, or makes the information from that time manageable via symbolic acts" (Montano, 2000, p. xi).

After returning to life, she enrolled in a Catholic College, and Mother Mary Jane became the mentor who encouraged and empowered her. Her senior thesis was a series called *Visitation* (Mary and Elizabeth embrace and both are pregnant), made of clay, wood, car parts, and plaster. In 1965, she went to Florence to study sculpture at Villa Schifanoia, a Catholic women's art school. In this school of Italian classical art, where she fabricated monumental torsos, heads, and crucifixes, she produced a "happening" at the opening of her Masters show. She brought "ten pieces of Italian junk" up to the roof of the villa, where participants assembled them into a sculpture by numbers. The final product was more provocative to her than her own sculpture.

> It was then that I began questioning the need for permanent object making. It seemed that the simple event of everyone assembling Italian found junk on the gallery roof was more engrossing, communal, exciting and a respite from the loneliness of the studio.
>
> (Montano, 1981)

Afterward, Montano went to the University of Wisconsin, Madison, and received an MFA in sculpture. It was the time of conceptual art, and the mostly male artists were making clean, hard-edged sculptures. She and two other women were in the patriarchal art department. She was in culture shock. Minimal art was overwhelming, at the opposite end of the spectrum of her life. She tried to work in plastics like everyone else for two years. But after visits to the agricultural school she turned away from plastics, and found that live chickens best expressed her internal and external temperament (Montano, 1981). She presented nine chickens for her MFA show, which included a "video of the chickens at their original site, a telephone at my home that answered with chicken sounds, a car loudspeaker that brought chicken sounds throughout the city of Madison, posters of chickens, etc" (Montano, 1981). For the next seven years Montano explored this image, leading her to work with duration, sound, repetition, and stillness.

> And I had just started yoga then in the 70s, and the yoga meditation theory was that there was such a thing as stillness, and then I practiced stillness as art in order to do it as life. The whole process was that art was always a rehearsal for my life, in a way to learn, and to cement into a daily practice, something that I couldn't do in life, so if I could do it in art maybe I could do it as life. So the chicken woman was the beginning.

With this event she began a number system that would continue to structure her work. She noticed that there were three chickens in three cages that were three by six feet. Sometimes she put six chickens in the third cage and three in the first, and so on.

> I realized later that my personal numerology for this piece and subsequent events were based on the Catholic concept of the Trinity.... The Chicken Show revolutionized my sculpture vocabulary and freed me from everyone else's definition of art that was not applicable to my needs.
> (Montano, 1981)

Chickens also became a metaphor of her relationship with the patriarchal Catholic Church, a battle that began in childhood. Her mother was a fighter and communicated without words the second-class position of women within. "And I knew the truth and I picked it up." I asked if she thought that disempowering women was an intentional act by the clergy.

> I think it's bigger than the clergy, and I don't know enough about women's history or feminism to talk to that, but I think it's just a total universal language of sexism and misogyny, and the clergy was also in collaboration with that.

Eventually, after moving to Rochester and marrying Mitchell Payne, chickens became ever-present in her life and art. She became the Chicken Woman—who was nun, saint, martyr—and the chicken became her "totem and twin" (Montano, 1981). Seven years of this work led to her philosophy of the inseparability of art and life. The image of the Chicken

Woman was distilled into large issues: "confidence, courage, stillness, endurance, concentration" (Montano, 1981).

THE GENESIS OF DAD ART

Montano's Dad learned not to "act Italian" because he grew up in an insular and prejudiced Saugerties long before it became an artistic community. Italians were one of the latest of immigrants: before Italians came the Germans and the Irish. He was called Wop, Guinea, and other pejorative monikers of the time. To offset his immigrant status he co-opted an aristocratic grace, business acumen, and priestly sanctity. Montano learned by watching him from afar. "He was also a musician, so he taught. By listening to music I learned to love music. I remember one thing he said. Listen to Ella Fitzgerald sing C above high C." From that one comment, she acquired perfect pitch.

The big change in Montano's relationship with her father came during his mid-80s when he became ill. Montano was in the regrettable, all-too-common position of academic censorship at the University of Texas at Austin's Art Department. It was her second tenure-track position, and she was in the final stages of the process. Her work at the university was state of the art, which ideologically throttled conservative academics. Questionable student performances, parental complaints, and finally, the objection of the university president sealed the final outcome.

This incident at the University of Texas was an indication of the social and political struggles erupting across America. The 1980s and 1990s saw American culture deeply divided by debates over social identity, public morality, communal values, and freedom of expression. A key focus in these polarizing discussions has been the role of the visual arts in public life (Wallace, Weems, & Yenowine, 1999). The authors of *Art Matters* reflect on the 1980s when controversial art peaked while the public became more and more apprehensive. It was the time of Andres Serrano's *Piss Christ* and Robert Mapplethorpe's sexually explicit photographs of gay men. And it was also during the early years of AIDS when public fear and ignorance of the illness, as well as moral judgment, was rampant. Added to the confusion of the unknown disease was the concomitant art that questioned sexual conventions. This highly charged atmosphere added to the significant emergence of censorship. Americans became socially and morally divided in a struggle for power that challenged freedom in the arts. Thus, censorship of sexually explicit artwork, the emergence of AIDS, and a more pluralistic society became vital themes in art that drove the art world (Oddo-Kelly, 2010). " ... something has changed: it is now very hard to recreate the feeling of safety and fearless adventure that was palpable in the early 1980s" (Wallace, Weems, & Yenowine, 1999, p. 22). The academy became the flashpoint of social, political, and moral polemics.

Montano confessed that she was not an academic. Similarly, Deavere Smith (2000) struggled with the contradictions between the academy and the theater. Academicians are often expected to hover over the surface of the complex content and feelings that the theater evokes. Deavere Smith calls this "cursory" education, "covering the material, whereas in theater 'we become the material.' In fact our job is to *un*cover the material" (p. 96). The same fears that gripped the public in her first performances about race riots are the same fears that create knee-jerk reactions to nudity, hetero- and homosexuality in academia. Where there is censorship, there is bound to be artistic urgency. Paradoxically, the intensity of fear and censorship surrounding art equals the public's unconscious or conscious need to experience it.

Montano left this collision course both personally and publicly, and instead followed an internal voice. "I was hearing, go be with your father, right around when this was all happening. I kept hearing this and hearing this, and came back." At first, her "job" was to drive her father to doctors' offices. At the same time, Montano unwittingly discovered Dad Art. They began a video project together. She videotaped them together and apart, having breakfast and watching television. This ritual was suddenly interrupted when he fell, hit his head, and had a stroke. As Linda Weintraub outlined earlier, for Montano the next three years meant taking constant care of her Dad.

> And it became this incredible performance of our life training, a teaching phenomenon, and it was unbearably wonderful. Anyway, I couldn't watch him suffer, so I got behind my camera and took videos. It's a performance film, I sing songs, I'm singing his songs and I have death counselors, and I have people coming up upstage writing letters to death. I felt that piece with my Dad that all my art had led up to that. Everything I had ever done, everything I learned, everything I ever studied, was a prelude to being with my father in his last seven years. And now I'm undoing and re-seeing and fixing and healing and he said "I'm not going to die until you're perfect."

I asked what perfection might have meant to her Dad. After some silence she said that it was his gift, his way of loving her, wanting her to mature in a certain way, to learn something that he thought she needed.

> Again, it was never expressed what he thought I was lacking that he needed to stay around for. It was all intuitive. It certainly has worked since I had to work so hard since he died, to clean up, open up, and change my ways,

and all kinds of things. . . . I think my dad's suffering was so hellish, and maybe that was the teaching. To maybe be ripped open in my heart, to be ripped, and to understand suffering.

It could be argued that the transformative potential of art is to turn suffering into a gift. That does not mean to numb the pain, but to use pain, to make it valuable. Montano's gift is to transform suffering into humor. At the time of the interview she was working on a video called *Hungry Survivors* with her editor, Toby Carey, whom she calls her alter ego.

> It's really about admitting and feeling our pain, and the pain of the universe, and then taking it one step further: the second step is creating a receptacle for the pain. So first is admitting the pain, creating a receptacle for the pain, and then transforming the pain through humor.

Montano calls Dad Art a regeneration of her work because of her confrontation with the most sustained suffering of her life, as she bore witness to her father's decline and finally death. It was reminiscent of the grief she felt when her ex-husband, photographer Mitchell Payne, was murdered. She calls these traumas food for art. The regenerative quality of this new work has changed her. She describes how in the past she was given permission to be a "bad girl" who made good art.

> We were always "permissioned" to make good art and be bad artists. That was our calling: to be punks—rotten, alcoholic, and addicted—because we're privileged, we're on the edge. It was a great calling, a vocation, and I think artists hang out in that underground because it is linked to that nondiscursive quadrant of the brain, great for art but not great for life.

Perhaps this transformation was what her father waited to see. Her vocation, she says, disrupted psychological maturity. "So, it was either being a jerk or to have semblance of compassion." Shortly after her father's death she developed a movement disorder called dystonia. But again she uses everything in life, and physical illness led to probably her most brilliant and culminating role as Mother Teresa of Calcutta (see figures 5.1 and 5.2).

> So why does that make me want to perform as MOTHER TERESA? How strange you might ask. All I can remember is that one day when in complete outright spasm, while I was pretzeled from my head to my feet like a corkscrew, I heard an inner voice saying, "I feel just like M O T H E R T E R E S A". . . . I guess Mother Teresa looked like this too, because she's short and looks all stooped over and spasmed and has to take

care of all 9,874,987 people who are dying, and festering with leprosy and drooling with deformities... And since I was so stooped over, miserable and in pain, I thought, why not use it, use the image, use my Catholicism, use my affection for Benares and my new compromised pitiful condition? How not to waste the suffering, we Catholics are taught, And since I have videoed myself in the guise of many personas throughout my performance art career like Bob Dylan, Lamar Breton, Doctor Jane Gooding and other gargoyle faces from my unconscious, I thought, why not "be" MOTHER TERESA???? Creative schizophrenia you might argue? No, it's recycling this great saint as art.

(L. Montano, August 13, 2011, personal communication)

Implications

Only when active artists willingly cease to be artists can they convert their abilities, like dollars into yen, into something the world can spend: play. Play as currency. We can best learn to play by example, and un-artists can provide it. In their new job as educators, they need simply play as they once did under the banner of art, but among those who do not care about that. Gradually, the pedigree "art" will recede into irrelevance.

(Kaprow, 1999, as cited in Kelley, p. 125)

Montano's performances are consciously enacted within a social and historical context by which she is shaped, but also transforms. With raw honesty, she performs as an active subject who invites bystanders to engage in active participation of dialogue and guided action, or praxis (critique and action). Paulo Freire (1990) calls *praxis* and dialogue the foundation of freedom and social justice. Freire's (1990) meaning of dialogue is not tactical, but rather an epistemological encounter and the examination and understanding of an object of knowledge in relationship to one's own history. Montano's work is a dialogic process in its search for the full apprehension of meaning. She searches for authenticity, accessing life through a sustained process of peeling through layers of the outer self, and the simultaneous documentation of this process through the interactions between symbolism and real life.

Performance art is a tool which assists artists to ecstatically feel/face Life/life.

(Montano)

The personal integrity that generates this kind of truthful art is, alas, many light years beyond contemporary American education. Critical curiosity is stifled by the often rigid methodologies of educators who invite

Figure 5.1   *Linda Mother Waits.* 2011, photograph by Tony Whitfield

Figure 5.2   *Linda Mother Giving Blessing.* 2011, photograph by Tony Whitfield

either memorized discourse or a predictable pedagogy of questions and answers (Leistyna, 1999). But it exists in Freire's *conscientization* (critical consciousness) and Maxine Greene's *social imagination, the possible, and what is not yet*. Both Freire and Greene's work is grounded in the self as it confronts the struggle for freedom and democracy. Greene's journey, however, is informed by the meaning, possibility, and imagination stimulated by an engagement with the arts.

Montano's performance art embodies Greene's *wide awakeness* in her excavation of religion, sexuality, and the art world for their hidden meanings. It is rigorous in its disruption of the known, the tacit, and the expected. While not an academic, Montano practices what Freire (1999) calls "epistemological uneasiness" (as cited in Leistyna, p. 48), which invites discovery, investigation, and reinvention of the world. The constant refining and reflection of her life that appears in her work inspires others to revisit what they "know" and ask similar questions.

Montano's work is profoundly educative in life and art and reminiscent of Kaprow's (2003) definition of the *un-artist:* "the offspring of high art who has left home" (as cited in Kelley, p. 230). Montano left the "safe house" of conceptual art at the University of Wisconsin, and found art in everyday life. Death, religion, love, and friendship are the objects of knowledge that she dialogically engages. But rather than a somber litany, she performs a ceremony of sacred representational play. She abandons nothing in her life. Everything is valuable, everything material for art, especially the binding of social and religious institutions. As she transforms everyday life into artful play, religion and social conventions lose their power to bind.

Notes

1. Autists: this term is sometimes used instead of "autistic people," or "people with autism."
2. Quotations that appear without a citation indicate that they are part of the interview of April 18, 2011.

References

Bilken, D. (2005). *Autism and the myth of the person alone: Qualitative studies in psychology.* New York: New York University Press.

Bluestone, J. (2005). *The fabric of autism: Weaving the threads into a cogent theory.* Seattle, WA: Sapphire Enterprises.

Deavere Smith, A. (2000). *Talk to me: Listening between the lines.* New York: Random House.

Freire, P. (1990). *Pedagogy of the oppressed.* New York: Continuum.

Kelley, J. (Ed.). (2003). *Essays on the blurring of art and life*. Berkeley and Los Angeles: University of California Press.

Kundera, M. (1984). *The unbearable lightness of being*. New York: Harper & Row Publishers.

Leistyna, P. (1999). *Presence of mind: Education and the politics of deception*. Boulder, CO: Westview Press.

Montano, L. (1981). *Art in everyday life*. Barrytown, NY: Station Hill Press.

Montano, L. (2000). *Performance artists talking in the eighties: Sex, food, money/fame, ritual/death*. Berkeley: University of California Press.

Montano, L. (2005). *Letters from Linda M. Montano*. New York: Routledge.

Oddo-Kelly, L. (2010). *Does censorship have the potential to impact the erudition of art education in America?* Unpublished manuscript. State University of New York at New Paltz.

Sacks, O. (1995). *The man who mistook his wife for a hat: And other clinical tales*. New York: Harper Perennial, Avon Books.

Tucker, M. (1986). *Choices: Making an art of everyday life*. New York: New Museum of Contemporary Art.

Wallace, B., Weems, M., & Yenowine, P. (1999). *Art matters: How the culture wars changed America*. New York: New York University Press.

CHAPTER 6

TRUTH, GOODNESS, AND BEAUTIFUL ART: SET FREE IN THE PENITENTIARY

PHYLLIS KORNFELD

> *Trust in the Inexhaustible Character of the Murmur.*
> (Andre Breton, 1924, Manifesto of Surrealism)

I UNDERSTAND THE MURMUR that Breton is pointing to as the quiet, ineffable knowing, not arising in the mind but stirring deep inside ourselves, which directs us to right and good action. It can be a reliably brilliant guide for the choices we make in all aspects of our lives, but only if we pay it constant attention and follow its lead. Not easy at all. It is a heroic struggle. As an art teacher I endeavor in as many ways as I can to teach people how to recognize and trust this unseen guide and allow it to move their hand and paintbrush. We all put a lid on that voice in a thousand ways. These obstructions have to be illuminated as soon as they appear so that we become familiar with them. Self-deprecation, for example, is one such hindrance to the release of the creative impulse. Not infrequently I have to remind someone that "there will be no self-deprecation in this class!"

Look at a page of doodling, say, your own or someone else's, and you can discern the exact spot where self-consciousness entered the picture. (It takes practice.) We have to shift our attention away from *me me me* to something we can see only when the evidence is on the paper. I've seen this shift, this happy release of goodness, depth, and beautiful art, occur many times in the 29 years I've been teaching art in prisons. How long it lasts depends not only on the individual, but also on the pressing external circumstances of incarceration in which it is striving to stay alive.

I have witnessed the same shift with people in my *Late Bloomers Creative Drawing Workshops*. When they identify themselves as "Late Bloomers," by signing up, they are already acquiescing to a stirring within. A good seed, I like to point out. They sign up in response to the promise of adventure into the unknown, and to a hunch, or a *murmur*, that the release of whatever it is in them that wants to get out is to be desired. The majority are upper-middle-class women, educated, experienced art lovers—imprisoned in a way, not by steel doors, but by ideas and conditioning. The tools and goals I have for both groups are the same. Success is most clearly measured by the fresh beauty of the art and its continuing evolution.

I've thought of myself as an artist since I was six years old, and became an art teacher at 25 when I earned a master's degree in art education. I tested the waters—for one year each—in elementary, middle, and high school, and then college. I remember feeling constrained, overworked, under-joyed, and restless. It wasn't for me. My next employment was with the Oklahoma City Department of Education. A small crew of artist/teachers designed and operated an experiential environment where fifth graders were bused in for the day and led through all kinds of hands-on art activities with bigger-than-life found materials, like climbing all over a mountain of bed springs while weaving designs in and out of the iron coils with colored rope and yarn. Shopping in surplus yards and creating the installations was fulfilling and fun for us teachers. It was an exciting and novel experience for the fifth graders. Herding the kids through it was certainly lively.

I next had the opportunity to be the art part of a team establishing an alternative high school. I was the entire art department, free to explore potential tracks for and with each boy and girl, using their passion for film or drumming or math—whatever it was—to fuel and direct their art. I was in a rush of creativity myself and could pass that energy along to a few young people, not of the mainstream, but rather self-defined as rebels and nonconformists. They wanted to take risks and were serious about their art—much of it strange and compelling. The school closed after its second year, in part because there was much consternation in the community over giving students too much "freedom."

In 1983 I was hired to teach painting and drawing to men and women incarcerated in state prisons—my introduction to the work that would be the passion of my lifetime. I met my first prison art class in a medium security men's facility in Lexington, Oklahoma. I entered through electronic heavy steel gates that rolled open before me and rolled shut behind me as I moved further inward until I was out in the sunny yard, hordes of blue-denimed men streaming past and around me in all directions. I knew that this was it—a strange-but-true sense of belonging I still experience every time I set foot in a prison. I waited in the newly designated art room for the ten men chosen to participate. They came in many colors and sizes. Several presented me with their inexplicably elegant drawings and sculptures made without benefit of an art program or decent materials. I was looking at art radically different from anything I'd ever seen. (I had never heard of Outsider Art, not in Oklahoma, not in 1983.) That this mystery came from, or through, these particular folks—uneducated, unworldly, untrained, not knowing—was confirmation for me that there is some thing or some place that is accessible to all of us, any of us, and *it* appears to already know which colors to use, where to put what, how things relate, when to repeat and when not, what is genuine and what is not.

Braulio Diez,[1] a 30-year-old from Vera Cruz, Mexico, was serving 20 to life for second-degree murder. While working as a migrant farmworker, he killed his foreman in a fight. Diez maintains that his so-called victim has been seen alive. He had been in for several years when we met. I learned that he had no visitors, no job, did not participate in programs, had no window in his cell, did not read or socialize. He spent "24/7" drawing pictures on the backs of inmate request forms, old calendar pages, and whatever trash paper he could get his hands on. His drawings overflowed with sweet and noble creatures, lush landscapes, and fabulous architecture. They are documents of ancient times and other universes (See figure 6.1).

Figure 6.1 Braulio Valentin Diez. 1983. *Untitled* (church of the roses). Mixed media on paper, photograph by Phyllis Kornfeld

Juan, a small, mute man, also from Mexico, had fashioned a miniature diorama of a parlor filled with chairs, lamps, tables, and a few dignified figures socializing as if at a cocktail party. His clay was black rubber caulking laboriously pinched from window frames, tiny bit by tiny bit, over many months. He painted the piece with latex paint he managed to acquire in lovely, subtle Art Deco colors.

INTENTION

> The most beautiful thing we can experience is the mysterious. It is the source of all true art and science.
>
> (Albert Einstein)

My intention, with every single person who shows up for art class, is to find a way to cut through fear and to discredit fixed ideas about personal limitations, about what art is, and about how art should look. I begin with the certainty that every individual has the potential within, right now, to bring truth and beauty out into the visible world. I'm an excavator. In digging for artistic gold I have to get the layers and layers of mud and rock out of the way. With some amazing individuals, as I discovered that first day in Lexington, the pathway had already opened. For them, all I did was provide supplies and protect the artwork and materials from the ever-present possibilities of theft, vandalism, and confiscation. I encountered another extraordinary field of creativity in two neighboring Massachusetts prisons years later. I did have to kick-start those artists, but not much. Their response was swift in coming and yielded a great many astonishingly fine drawings and paintings, much of it falling into the category of Outsider Art, with which by then I had become acquainted.

Arthur Keigney, one of the Massachusetts artists, was in for life without parole. He had been producing a steady stream of greeting cards, cartoons, and a few amazing soap carvings, for many long years. They were wry and innocent at the same time, and very funny. He insisted that his art was "retarded." Keigney joined the art class to learn how to draw portraits. I agreed to help him and, on a hunch, added the condition that he begin sketching scenes and people from his life. That was all it took. He made drawings and paintings with gusto and humor until he died in prison five years later. They were depictions of the old neighborhood, reform school, maximum security, punishment units, animated with clearly authentic characters, toward whom Keigney expressed a sort of affection. He knew intuitively how to arrange the components of his picture on the canvas and which colors to choose. The figures gesture in a real way, communicating with each other. Trash litters the streets and

Figure 6.2   Arthur Keigney. 1991. *The Booking Room.* Acrylic on canvas, photograph by Phyllis Kornfeld

mess halls. There is never a hint of self-pity and never a dull moment. His paintings are dignified even as they describe in detail the dregs of an awful life (see figure 6.2).

Most of the time, the breakthrough I'm aiming for requires various methods and implements with which to accomplish the blasting away. A good start is to say to a new person joining the class, "We are going to access that part of you that has *never been incarcerated*."[2] A stunned moment, and then I can see a small light in his eyes; he is suddenly conscious that such incomprehensible innocence in possible. In prison art programs, someone might attend once or twice, for several months, a year or two, or he might be so involved that he continues the program all the way to his release many years later. I have to try to make something happen immediately because I never know if I'll see this person again, and because I need to sustain my own excitement. When change does occur, the imagery is miraculously new and unself-conscious. I will never burn out so long as I witness (more often than not) the moment of "the big bang" all over again.[3] Someone who was fearful, tense, and awkward slips gracefully into relaxed concentration, fascinated by what is emerging. As I watch her draw, I might say, "The best part of you is in action right now."

In the early years I was careful never to hurt anyone's feelings. I taught that each person's drawing was as good as any other. I thought that self-esteem could be built by repeating, *yes you can. You can do it. Keep up the good work.* I look back on those practices as unsuccessful in promoting real change: not in the art and not in the person. Autonomy takes root when a man sees with his own eyes, in real time, that he has done a fine thing and created something beautiful. He holds the proof in his hands—"I can't believe I did this."

We all have some fixed ideas about ourselves that are obstructions to the creative impulse. I use the word "ego"[4] to refer to the part of us that says *I already know what I like and don't like, what I am capable of and how I am limited.* This part, the ego, ties us to what we think we already know and produces an art that is already known. Then there is another part of us, the mystery, the part that is not separate from all there is, where the creative impulse lives, eager to get out into action. When I look at the best of Outsider Art, I see the creative impulse thoroughly liberated, no ego in sight. As it courses through a human being, whether willing or helpless, it is informed, shaped, and colored by the particular influences that have formed the personality—a natural individuality rather than a collection of ideas.

From what I've seen, the creative flow is easily thwarted by how-to-do-it instructions, for example, a step by step guide to achieving balance in a composition. This achievement is completely intuitive in a naïve artist. Precise instructions offer security where there was fear. No risk required. I demonstrate technique and formal principles sparingly and judiciously. When I'm occasionally asked to impart the rules of perspective, I'm likely to say, "It will look more human, more natural, if you simply draw it the way it looks to you." Fortunately, all the folks who come to art class want very much to be there—usually they've been on a waiting list for months—and so they are fully cooperative (with a few exceptions). I'm trying to instill a preference for the unknown. I have to create an atmosphere in the art room that has no tolerance for the insistent who-I-think-I-am presentation. All the projects I assign force the practitioner to start off and remain in unfamiliar territory.

THE FIELD

> Art washes away from the soul the dust of everyday life.
> (Pablo Picasso)

Inside prison walls, the forces against positivity and creativity are relentless. The surrounding sounds, smells, sights, and coldness, crowd in on a human soul leaving no breathing space for something better to occur. When a thinking person begins serving his time, he searches for another kind of freedom—*they can lock up my body but not my spirit*. The art program is one of a very few options that can keep that spirit alive. Creating art, being around its creation, and looking at it on the walls, has an uplifting impact on everyone. The chance to learn, to make things, to work together, to create art good enough to give pleasure to others—these experiences lead to the development of better human beings.

The spaces in which the workshops occur are multipurpose rooms or sections of rooms. At the time of this writing, the art rooms are (1) a small school room that seats five, (2) the back end of the Catholic chapel, (3) a visiting room, and (4) a large space separated from the weight room by floor to ceiling glass windows revealing 30 men using the equipment, yakking, laughing, grunting. Incredibly loud and scratchy announcements blast out of the PA speakers several times an hour. Sometimes, in the visiting room/art room, at the far end of a very long table, small groups of correctional officers (COs) socialize over a meal from their lunchboxes, or a lone inmate sits across from his lawyer for a hushed conference. (I am not complaining, just setting the scene.) It is here that I ask people to focus, concentrate, slow down. There is little to be done about the physical setup—the men and I work together to find the best arrangements for seating and utilizing all conceivable surfaces for drawing, grateful for being given any space at all. We've used some of the funkiest tables imaginable, ancient card tables whose legs fold in—slowly—at the slightest pressure, and the men cheerfully make do. Good music soothes and stimulates. I can bring in a CD player. That is the outer environment.

The inner field—whatever forces determine choice and action (or inaction) in a human being—is where I can move more furniture around, so to speak. I have to build a firm structure, a fort, against the onslaught of negativity, of old idea—and worst of all—old tired images. This requires Rules—in an atmosphere suffocatingly thick with rules, I know, but these rules liberate.

RULES OF THE CLASS

I want you to know that you can become a true artist and make beautiful drawings. I promise that you will be able to tap into the same source for your art that inspired the artists you see in a museum, a book, or a magazine. Sound's good, doesn't it? All you have to do is follow the rules. You have to do exactly what I ask you to do. I think you will find that the rules express good common sense. They safeguard a sane, positive, absorbing hour and a half. We have so little time to accomplish a lot. We don't have time to speak personally. We don't have time to be negative. We don't have time to be casual.

Rule Number One—No Speaking Personally

Speaking personally is *what I like and what I don't like, where I've been and where I'm going, what kind of person I am, what I can do and what I can't do,* and especially, *how I feel.* What matters here is not how you feel, but what you do—what goes on the paper.

I first saw the effect of not speaking personally when I was on a retreat with Andrew Cohen in 2011, spiritual teacher and author of *Evolutionary Enlightenment.* People came from all over the world for a long weekend of meditation, teachings, and discussions. At the first meeting, Cohen asked the participants, for the sake of getting the most out of their time there, to please speak to each other only about what they came to learn and explore further. Or, be in silence. Focus and depth, new insights, collective discoveries, were the dramatic results. The ego was in hibernation. That is exactly what I want to foster here in the art room, in a prison, and unlike Cohen who says "please," I am insisting upon it.

Not speaking personally is radical surgery for the Late Bloomers as well, and myself, I must add. When the late-blooming artists want very passionately to transcend the old ways, they conscientiously follow the rule of not speaking personally. The impulse to announce, perhaps to your new art teacher, or your new colleagues, who you are, that is, how you want her and the others to see you, is strong and persistent. But what if you are not permitted to do so? If you cannot explain, "I've never done art before" or "I'm advanced, I do portraits" or "I can only draw stick figures," are you then undefended? Vulnerable? OPEN? This rule, not speaking personally, when consistently enforced, does absolutely lead to good art. I am wary even of "I'm a car person," for example, because, as benign as it sounds, it is another brick in the ever-hardening wall of self-image. I like to say, "There is no such thing as a car person. You are either a car or a person. Which is it?" He laughs and says, "I'm a person who likes cars."

Rule Number Two—No Negativity

You may not express negativity, like—*I can't draw hands, this is a mess, I am upset, depressed, not in the mood. I have a problem, a stomach ache, the weather stinks,* or even, *I had bad news from home.* You may not express negativity in your gestures or your face, about your art, or anyone else's—including slumping in your chair, sighing tragically, excessive yawning and stretching. Crumbling your paper and trashing it is negative. I know you are just starting out and you may forget once or twice, but if you don't follow these rules you can't be in the class. The no negativity rule does not necessarily apply to your artwork, unless it is a cliché, and then it applies.

Nine times out of ten, relief and good humor flood across a woman's face when she hears these rules. Prisoners live in close quarters with many unhappy people expressing their pain and anger aloud. I'm not making light of these real conditions, but of what use is it for anyone, including the vocalizer, to broadcast sadness. When someone in the art class blurts out something negative, the others jump on it before I do. *Hey man, no negativity.* They are good-natured about it, but we all know the consequences if it continues. Negativity stops everything cold. For example, listen to the difference between "I can't draw horses" and "I would like to learn to draw horses." The former slams a door shut. The latter opens to possibility. People are noticeably uplifted by a lovely slice of time that is free from negativity. When all attention is on the art, all else falls away. A new person came to class and asked me, "Do you wanna know why I joined this class?" I said yes. "Because I heard you don't allow negative talking in your class and I think that's awesome."

Rule Number Three—Don't Talk About Jail Business

Or anything else that isn't necessary, practical, or about your work. If something just went down, a shakedown or another disturbing incident, you can't bring it in here. It is understandable that you are upset, but it pollutes the atmosphere in the art room. The same applies to Late Bloomers. It's a good idea to sit quietly and then get out your pastels and freshen the atmosphere.

Practice

The position of the artist is humble. He is essentially a channel.
(Piet Mondrian)

Doodling

In a 1965 manuscript titled *The Place of Drawing in an Artist's Work,* Charles Burchfield wrote the following:

> It seems to me I have doodled all my life. I recall doodling on my mother's tablecloth when I was of grade-school age. Perhaps I was born with a

doodle pencil in my hand, the left one, in the same manner that a fortunate person is said to have been born with a silver spoon in his mouth.

(Burchfield's 2010 show at the Whitney included thousands of pages of his doodling—saved over a lifetime)

Years ago I gave a two day Creative Drawing workshop at a California prison for men with developmental, emotional, and physical disabilities. I was escorted by a CO and my host, the "resident" artist/facilitator, to what they proudly referred to as the "art department." It was, a huge sunny high-ceilinged space divided into three adjoining studios for fiber arts, ceramics, and painting and drawing. (It was a golden time for arts-in-corrections, especially in California.) While I waited for the men to arrive for the first session in the painting and drawing studio, I looked at some charcoal drawings-in-progress strewn about on tables and easels. They were studies of the same conventional still life. I flashed on the incredible potential for particularly interesting art that exists in this population. As the men began streaming in and finding seats, Anthony Aroz walked me over to his charcoal drawing and described his struggle to get the shadows right. I think I assured him it was okay to struggle.

I opened the workshop with a slide show of stunning artwork made by incarcerated men and women. My audience was mesmerized. This established my credentials, and their trust, needed for the next activity—doodling—which I defined as *Drawing Without The Mind*. The first key to successful doodling is to place your mind elsewhere, on something outside of your own thoughts that interests you so much you want to pay attention to it. In my usually ongoing art programs, doodling is solitary, practiced in the cells and dorms between workshops (or in the case of the Late Bloomers, at home). Doodling while on the phone is good, or listening to talk radio or daytime soaps on TV. If it's the TV, be sure to keep your eyes on your paper. (Listening to music is not useful—interpretation becomes purposeful, the arm dances, and you forget to slow down enough to watch your own next move unfold.) Here, in a weekend workshop, in a group all doodling at once, I had to be the compelling distraction. I directed the men to listen to me speak as they were doodling, to give my voice 100 percent of their attention. I served up funny and suspenseful anecdotes to hold captive the part of the mind that hinders doodling. Anthony stood up to doodle. I could see his energy grow more and more intense, and soon he was animating the paper with a charged line that could have kept a light bulb burning. In his words, "When I started drawing my nerves were jumping and I was excited to see my feelings and my thoughts come alive and my adrenalin was rushing through my veins like hot lava off the side of a cliff!" When it was time for the men to return to their units, Anthony clung to the table with one hand while the other was still electrified—an amazing vision of crashing stars and flying creatures. I kept track of his work over the next few years—color appeared with force in wild planetscapes. The explosion I witnessed had not flagged.

Everyone in my classes must doodle, with regularity and seriousness. Not doing so may jeopardize their membership in the art class. There is humor in my tyranny but everyone knows I consider it crucial. It's too bad that "doodling" is a sort of silly word connoting frippery and meaninglessness. I make it mandatory and try to sell it at the same time, occasionally handing out doodle rewards—much valued pre-cut mats, greeting cards, fancy stationery, a silver or gold colored pencil. The artists who take risks and stay open don't have to doodle but they usually do. Doodling becomes a stance, a willingness to allow something unknown to take control.

In the Outsider canon, exquisite obsessive doodling pours out of many artists, unbidden and with unstoppable force. For most of the people I work with, doodling takes effort and intention. It is a practice in the way that meditation is a practice with respect to developing a new relationship to thought. All manner of thoughts come and go without rhyme or reason, and they change nothing. You get up from your meditation cushion and nothing has happened, no matter what you were thinking. When you doodle, your thoughts are irrelevant, you can't give them credence. *Learning to draw without the mind* is best achieved using uninhibiting materials:

Cheap paper such as newsprint, or anything considered to be of little value. Worries about "messing up" good paper are deeply rooted.

Use a ballpoint pen: erasing is not an option when doodling. There is no right or wrong here—that would be a judgment call from the mind.

Move your pen SLOWLY. As people take notes on the doodling instructions, I direct them to write the word "slowly" in two inch letters. I must say SLOW DOWN every day in every workshop at least ten times. I gave a workshop, similar to the one in the California prison, to future art teachers at a mid-western university. After the workshop, a young athletic-looking man came up to me to share what had happened when he was doodling. He said, "I always do everything real fast and I was scribbling away and I thought, *well, wait a minute—I'm here, I might as well do what she says.*". He slowed down and suddenly found himself in a terrifying empty space. He said, "Wow, I didn't know anything!" His pen began to move and slowly filled the page. Everyone thought his page of doodling was especially beautiful.

When I am handed someone's latest doodling, the doodler and I look at it together. We point to where we can see that the mind was engaged and we point to the configurations that are strange and puzzling—these are the most touching, the most alive. *Where did that come from? I don't know*, a shrug of the shoulders. And doodling levels the field in a way. A person who is convinced that he can't draw sees beauty unfold at his own hand. A person who is convinced that she is really great and has nothing left to learn, is humbled, experiencing something inexplicable coming through her. Something deep is activated, and at the same time, relaxed.

As a person persists with the practice, his doodling often evolves naturally and goes somewhere new. Unintended imagery may begin to appear—faces and figures coming forward. Ronnie White was skilled in the clichés of jailhouse art when I first met him. He began to doodle—tightly packed tiny squiggles—and he watched with amazement as visions emerged. He called their source "the spirits of the night." Ronnie's drawings have graced book covers and illustrated text. His work is known in Outsider contexts and is legend, by way of the grape vine, in some prisons. Even as his mind participates in the process, it is evident that those spirits continue to guide him (see figure 6.3).

Figure 6.3   Ronnie White. 2001. *Spiritual Confrontation*. Ballpoint pen on matboard, photograph by Phyllis Kornfeld

Mystery Art

Fear of the blank page is real, but you can't sit there frozen forever. You root around in your own mind for a picture from your mental picture album, something you've seen or drawn repeatedly. The image is old before it hits the paper. Somewhere along the way I began to appreciate the value of a random mark on the paper. It makes the mental search for an idea unnecessary. All you have to do is respond to what you see.

A small cutout of an object pasted on a scrap of matboard might do the trick for the right person at the right time. Robert wanted to learn to draw portraits from photographs. I tried to show him how, but it wasn't working. His papers were ragged from erasures, the faces clenched, the hands like crabs. I couldn't bear it. "Here, do this" I said, and laid out a few cutouts—a Buddha, a cowboy hat, a mask, and a raccoon. He chose the raccoon, glued it in place, and easily proceeded to make a drawing with and around it. He knew what to do. He made a series of amusing collage/drawings that stood out for their freshness at a prison art exhibition.

I mentioned the fear of "messing up" good paper. I've seen people work themselves into a frenzy over a stubborn smudge of dirt. This is not a good omen for the ensuing drawing. Therefore I treat the offending mark as a fortunate head start for the art to come. A mat scrap with a handwritten name or machine-stamped logo on it, for example, is offered as a treasure, with instructions to make use of the mark.

The concept of "Rorschaching" comes to mind. I do not, however, use that word in the workshops lest people begin to fear psychological scrutiny. This pulling of images into focus has a mysterious quality, thus the practice is called Mystery Art. Most everyone seems to be familiar with the experience of staring at a stain in the ceiling until a face appears (you never can look at that spot again without seeing the face). I hand out photocopies of clouds, for example, to serve the function of the inkblot. People call them "cloud pictures," although the subject is not necessarily clouds—it might be ice cubes in a glass, or a mound of ice cream, enlarged to such a degree that what you see is blurry and unrecognizable. Once the suggestion of a face, figure, or other figurative image begins to emerge, the artist works directly on the photocopy, with black and white drawing media, to develop the figure, adding details, and to clarify it so that no verbal explanations are necessary. No one really knows with absolute certainty whether or not the figures she uncovered were already there just beneath the surface, waiting for her to make them visible. I don't discredit that notion, having experienced myself the stunning moment when a creative project arrives finally at the exact form that seems to declare that this was what it was always meant to be. Response, rather than the imposition of the ego, is a powerful weapon against cliché. I've had school teachers report that cloud pictures make copying nearly impossible. There are infinite variations. Place a wet teabag on your paper for a few seconds. Ask someone to step on your paper with their slightly muddied sneakers. Stare into a gnarled piece of wood or a branch of ginger.

It's good to keep people in suspense about what the next step will be. Feeling insecure in this context is a good thing. They are more open, which allows the desired release. The figures discovered are graceful and alive, unlike the frozen-front-facing-already-known figure many people tend to draw on a blank page. When this release occurs it is a demonstration to the artist that she is indeed connected to a part of herself of which she had not necessarily been conscious. Cloud pictures and doodling both have the effect that you can't quite take full credit for what happened on the page, and at the same time, you know it was you who did the work and made it beautiful. You learned how to slow down, pay close attention, and respond. You will amass a collection of visual ideas that you can use in further drawings—your own set of completely original images.

I ran a workshop for a program called *Inside/Out*, a semester long class composed of 20 women in which ten were enrolled in a university and ten were serving time in prison. We made cloud pictures. A few weeks later the following poem was sent to me, written by an anonymous woman who participated in the workshop.

THIS MIGHT BE A LOVE POEM
The art teacher handed me a vague and spotted photocopy
And told me to find the art within—
Miniscule images seen with artistic eyes and traced with pencil.
"What do you see in this dark area? Doesn't this look like it might be something?"
I did this obediently
As a student
But not as an artist.

Later, with my face against the warmth of your slow-beating body,
I grasped my teacher's lesson.
My artist eyes emerged:
I see birds in the hairs of your arm
Scores of birds, swooping and singing—That darker patch, that's the mother's body,
That wrinkle in your skin, the worm she feeds her young
Who line up to receive this treat except for that little one,
Formed by the longer hairs near your elbow, who flies up, up towards your face

Where your freckles, pores, and unshaven skin blend and contrast to reveal
Connect-the-dots-flowers
The tropical wide-open kind with petal of all shapes and colors, bugs
deep inside, and long
thrusting tongues tipped with yellow dust—
Pollen which is actually a speck of glitter,
Fallen out of my book and onto your cheek.
I gently blow it away; you open your eyes
And in that brief moment before you return to sleep
The flittering movement of your lashes over your eyes gives the impression of
Salamanders strutting around and around in their assertive gait, towards
the pool of your pupil.
Your body is a universe.

Collaborations

One day I gave everyone a piece of matboard to randomly muck up. My plan was a variation on the cloud pictures. At the next session, I noticed that most of the men had already anticipated what they were going to do with it next, having been well trained by me to search for figurative imagery. Instinctively, I moved to pull the rug out from under *already knowing,* and had each person give up his board to the fellow on his left.

> These will be collaborations.
> Write your first name on the back
> Stare at this for a couple of days until you know what it wants you to do—
> Do only one thing. One thing can be a single form repeated.
> Whatever you add must be ambiguous (define ambiguous).
> Whatever you add has to relate to what is already there, connected in some way. What are some of the ways it could be connected?

The next week the collaboration was passed along again. The list of names on the back of the board grew. We voted on whether or not a collaboration was finished. This practice too invites development. How do you know when a drawing is finished? I like the inherent movement—it keeps on going. The experience is *this is not mine; it belongs to everybody; it belongs to nobody; I have a responsibility to the others; I can't do my own thing.* Somebody cracks every once in awhile and cannot resist finishing it. The urge is familiar to all, but caring for art and caring for others usually wins out. Everyone has a stake in all the collaborations and together we keep track of the progress of each. Sometimes a piece goes too far and looks awful, a good time to learn about judicious subtractive drawing. Everyone agrees that the most beautiful of the collaborations transmits something larger than the sum of its parts.

My Practices

My practices are not structured weekly exercises but principles that guide my approach and response to Late Bloomers and incarcerated people alike. The primary goal is "out with the old, in with the new." There is always the possibility that innocence might be liberated. One way to trip up false ideas of self is by pointing out the universality of limitations. For example, everyone is afraid to try something new, everyone is afraid to finish her drawing because she might mess it up if she doesn't stop now. It isn't only you. If it isn't only you who feels that fear, then it must be an aspect of being human. Fear affirms that you are human and just like the rest of us. The capacity to choose is another aspect of being human. You can act in spite of the fear and finish your drawing. My seeming impersonality may sound cold but the practice actually creates a human bond that in turn creates trust. So when I tell the straight objective truth, which never has to be unkind, it is usually a version of "we-are-all-made-of-the-same-stuff." Fred, for example, did not take my "stern" comments personally because he knew that I would have had a like response no matter who the artist was who simply copied a poster he saw in a magazine. Here Fred tells us what he learned:

> In June 2003 I found myself in the County House of Correction. I had two and a half years of incarceration in front of me. For a 63-year-old man that's a long time. Now I must figure out what I will do with all this time. Most sports are out of the question for someone my age, cards, dominoes, chess and other board games can be fun at times but they don't offer the kind of reward or satisfaction I was looking for. I had to find something more. I heard there was an art class here. I always thought about art and drawing but I never took the time to pursue it. I thought maybe I can see if I have any talent. I always thought maybe I have a little. So I signed up. While I was waiting for an opening, I practiced drawing people and faces from magazines. When I was finally called to class, I was eager to learn, and I did with the help of my instructor. She displayed my work in the art room and the windows facing out into the corridor. My confidence and ability improved so much that I decided to try some "mall art" [copying commercial art from ads], which she sternly told me that this was not what she expected of me. She wants art from within you, the artist, not commercial art from another artist. Needless to say she refused to display the "mall art." A lesson well learned. Now I am trying to capture the life in

my pod here in this jail, it's an exciting project and if I take my time with it, I am quite sure I will produce a great piece of work. I look forward to the rewards a great piece of work brings. I will continue after I am released to pursue those rewards.

The drawings Fred made after writing the paragraph above depicted his housing unit, " the pod," and the folks who live there—playing cards, doing push-ups, kidding around. The drawings are as noisy and lively as the pod itself.

I practice censorship. Freedom to draw what you like is one of the few avenues to freedom available for a prisoner, but that does not include the freedom to display the drawing. The prison system regulates artistic subject matter. The only two artworks confiscated on my watch were a view of the yard and buildings from a second story window (might be an escape plan), and the depiction of a policeman shot and killed on the sidewalk. These were both quite good drawings, but I said that there would be no more of such depictions. If the workshops are to continue, we follow the rules.

I also censor for my own reasons. Sexually explicit art comes in distinct categories: sincere (and therefore good art) or arising from unsavory motivation (usually badly drawn). I support the good art, but do not show it. In fact, I'll ask the artist to wrap it in brown paper and I look at it later. I censor depictions of violence because they incite violence. The larger implication here is that the artist is responsible for the impact his artwork has on others.

Visual clichés are not permitted. I find it useful to name two or three, such as weeping eyeballs, skulls, spider webs, and bloody fangs. Everyone laughs and adds to the list, a not very long list. If you want to keep repeating these pictures that's up to you, but do it back in the pod. This is the *creative* drawing workshop. We are looking for something *new* to emerge. We need your chair for someone who will reach for the *heights* of *creativity*!

I discourage the expression of personal pain and victimhood. As long as the artist identifies himself as a victim, he will continue to believe himself to be helpless. The popular expressions of inner pain or love are overused, to say the least: a heart that is cracked, dripping blood, or pierced by golden daggers. The expression of love is also a heart, or hearts formed of flowers or kissing swans. People understand my anti-cliché crusade once they discover that there are alternatives. More than a few times a new person will breeze in and say, with good humor, "I know, I heard, no roses, no hearts."

Connections

> There is a place in all of us that has remained innocent, uncorrupted and untouched by the world. We have to locate that most delicate place, it's where we feel love—where tenderness and compassion arise, free from self-interest.
>
> (Andrew Cohen, 1991)

When a workshop closes for summer break, I assign projects to keep everyone from getting lazy and stiff. Last summer I handed out a short list: *doodle... collaborate... exhibit your work... teach people.* The spirit of collaboration is beginning to take hold among those who have been engaged in the collaborative projects that I continue to assign. People who live in the same housing unit are collaborating on their own initiative, drawing projects of their own invention. This reaching for connection is a positive action toward the survival of our human race.

An example of this realization inspired a creative Texas defense attorney to contact me a few years ago to ask me to testify at the sentencing phase of a capital murder trial. The defendant had already been found guilty. During the sentencing phase, the defense attorney presents arguments to show that a sentence of life without parole serves the greater good, as opposed to the ever-widening negative impact that results from condemning a person to death and executing him (For one thing, he may have children). I was to be an expert witness on the subject of art in prison. The defendant had made stacks of pen and ink drawings throughout his recently completed 14 years of incarceration. His subjects were cars and cowboys. The black and white images were tight hard-edged designs with a touch of Asian influence and a whiff of Americana. The defendant's record as a convict was free of misbehavior or infractions. He committed the homicide a few weeks after his release. The lawyer wanted me to speak about the ripple effect of positivity that occurs when one person is making art. He made it clear that he would not be arguing for the sake of the defendant, but for the good of others. In preparation for my testimony, I asked the artists in my long-standing workshops to think about the effect their art making has had on other people. The following are sample responses.

The effect on other inmates:

When he was down, one man told me, another man said to him, 'stick with your painting and you'll be all right.' He taught me how to paint trees. He in turn encouraged another guy to start painting and showed him what he had learned.

I finished a drawing in the day room, some guy came over, shook my hand, said, 'you keep on doing what you're doing.' He keeps asking me 'what you working on now?' It's a way to get along with each other.

I did this drawing of a Native American and the guy took it to Alaska. I got a picture in Alaska!!

Every head is a world. The way to know somebody—see what they made.

The effect on COs:

COs think we're less than they are, they get surprised when they see the work, see us in a different light—they say 'hey, you got talent.'

The effect on family and neighbors:

Someone on the streets sees my work, says it's a shame he's in there. It gives them an idea not to get in here.

It's positivity beyond the walls. It bridges rifts, rifts that occurred when I went to prison.

They send in a photo to get drawn, I send the drawing—they send a photo of the drawing framed and on the wall. It's a simulation of a society.

A man with four children sends home his handkerchief art. They ask for certain pictures. He said they hang his stuff all over the house and show it to their friends.

I make presents for holidays and birthdays—a picture for my brother reminding him of Vietnam, birds for my mother, places we've been to for my wife—a lot of connection.

An example of the effect on families was my own experience at a funeral service for Arthur Keigney, who died in prison at age 55. Except for a few brief periods, he had been incarcerated since he was 14. His six nieces and nephews asked me to display his paintings at the funeral parlor. The kids beamed as they led one guest after another by the hand to show what their uncle had created.

Getting back to the Texas case, the jury voted for the death penalty.

How Crystal Maintains Her Connection to the Human Race

Throughout her 27-year incarceration, Crystal Stimpson made things. She showed me her altars composed of tiny odds and ends, natural and plastic, so rarely found inside prison gates that they took on a sacred aura, which was her intention. During the years of the art program, she made unself-conscious full-of-life paintings that interwove images from the outside with images of her imprisonment: open roads confined by razor wire, the ceiling of a cell cracked open to a big blue sky. Later, in another program, she learned how to tool leather and when she was finally released, still on parole, she qualified for a good job with a reputable leather company. She also creates designs and does the tooling, on commission, for saddles and belts and women's purses. Sometimes she gets paid to decorate a shop window in her small town. "I can have a conversation with anyone, a banker or professor, and we can talk about the rose design he had tooled on his saddle, or the craft project his grandchild made. I don't feel like an outsider. My experience with art allows me to connect with all different kinds of people. Sometimes I can even teach them."

Exhibition

When Michael Iovieno was serving his time (he was released years ago) he had a constant itch to show his work. He assembled an impromptu "sidewalk" art show, laying out his small drawings in a row along the tier.[5] "Most ask, 'What is it?' Some look at me kind of funny. I played it off like I smoked a lot of pot before I drew them but I didn't. They've called it 'bugged-out shit,' which I like the label. Just to see someone struggle to make sense out of it is fun."

By the end of my first day as an art teacher in prison, I knew that this work had to be seen. It has been, and continues to be, shown in commercial and noncommercial galleries, in books and magazines, in the slide talks I give at universities and museums, in a traveling exhibit of the *Cellblock Visions* permanent collection. Here are a few comments from the guest books:

> We tend to forget that humans who do bad things are still humans with emotions and even remorse. Some of these artists show more passion and truth than any art student could ever do.

> This was one of the most affecting shows I have ever been to. The correlation and the CHOICE between creativity and destructiveness is so clearly illustrated.

> When I went to the display of penitentiary art, I was skeptical. I have never believed in special privileges for prisoner—they're in jail to do time—they shouldn't be able to enjoy themselves. Cellblock Visions has opened my eyes. The art was impressive. Now I think the prisoners are giving back something positive to society.

GIVING

One summer day at the prison in Lexington, Oklahoma, a crowd of inmates showed up in the yard wearing sparkling new white T-shirts with a blue and green logo of a running man. It said something like, "Inmates Run for Children's Cancer Hospital." That was the first time I had seen or heard of inmates given the opportunity to help others outside the walls. I thought that was brilliant, and never saw anything like it again, until recently. There are a few terrific programs scattered around the country where the prison and the community, or a university, work together on projects that contribute to a healthier life for the many, not only the incarcerated person and his family. The Community Partners in Action's Prison Art Program, a Connecticut nonprofit organization I work for, invites the artists to donate, if they wish, one or two of their paintings to a worthy cause each year.

During the 2008 presidential election campaign when Obama called for change, I considered the prison-industrial complex and its harmful ineffectiveness. When he spoke about crossing boundaries, I wondered how I might help expand the connection between the men and women in here and their fellow humans out there. When he suggested Martin Luther King Day for special volunteer projects, my friends and I produced an event benefiting local food banks. My part in the event was to organize a silent art auction. I asked the men and women in the workshops if they wanted to donate a work of art as a fund-raiser. They jumped at the chance. Someone said, "I know what it's like to be hungry." They were excited to give their best work. I watched the astonishment on the faces of the public. People were challenged to reconcile this jolt of spirit and level of excellence with the dark place it came from. The drawings were displayed on long tables and propped upright against the wall. They lit up the entire gymnasium and people were drawn from across the room. Some knew and loved art, others would not normally be viewing an exhibition. The bidding was lively, the bidders were passionate. This blending of people who would otherwise never come together contains the possibility for a better future. This is what art is born for. The artists were exhilarated and asked for more such opportunities. Hundreds of thousands of men and women just like them sit uselessly behind steel doors, year after year, to no purpose. They want to help. Millions of underserved and struggling Americans need help now more than ever. Art is a connector; one person to herself, one person to another, one person to a multitude.

An idea for a project occurred to me. Incarcerated men and women could donate their envelope art as a fundraiser for a worthy cause.

Envelope art is a long-standing connector in traditional prison art. Legal size envelopes, purchased from the commissary, are decorated, often elaborately, for the purpose of carrying letters to loved ones. I searched for a nonprofit that I thought would "click" with the prisoners, and found the Read Alliance that serves at-risk students in kindergarten and first grade by training and employing teens to provide one-on-one tutoring in literacy. I secured the cooperation of four prisons, two county jails, and one half-way house, along with a few individuals in prisons in other states. The "Call for Art" fliers were tacked to the walls of housing units and common areas. It read as follows:

> Incarcerated Men and Women Making Art for a Cause
>
> You can help. Donate an envelope!
>
> Decorated envelopes are being collected to be sold to benefit the Reading Alliance, (READ) a foundation serving at-risk kindergarten and first graders by recruiting and training teens to provide structured one-to-one tutoring in reading.
>
> The Art:
>
> No sex, violence, gang symbols, politics.
>
> No commercial figures or cartoons such as Mickey Mouse.
>
> No negativity.
>
> Do create designs that are original, uplifting, and beautiful.
>
> *Please do not include your name or inmate number. Your gift is anonymous, the highest form of giving.*
>
> A big Thank You for taking this step toward bettering the lives of your fellow human beings!!

The art came pouring in,—many masterpieces of envelope art, hundreds of sincerely joyful efforts, surprisingly few kissing swans—all effusing goodwill. We sold them at the Outsider Art Fair, February 2011. The display generated a lot of excitement and had a happy impact on those who came to look and to buy—so many commented on the thread of caring— from the prisoners to the art lovers to the teen tutors to the young children needing help to succeed in school. The art was wildly varied—explosive, delicate, funny, lovingly rendered, celebratory. I noticed envelopes by several people I had been struggling with to find just the right open-sesame, and here it was. They had no reason to hold back—after all, this was "only an envelope," and, it was a gift to a child!

WRAPPING UP

At this writing, a prison that I've been going to twice a month for 16 years is scheduled to close down very soon. It's the economy. Falling crime rates and conviction rates mean empty beds. Empty beds mean that a fully operating large facility is a waste of scarce resources. There are two "newish" men in the workshop here, the rest have been participating anywhere between six and ten years. They will be scattered and squeezed into other prisons around the state, some with an art program and some with little or no opportunities for creative outlets. A few of these men are nearing release, relatively speaking. Donald said to me the other day that he can finally see the light at the end of the tunnel—he has a year and a half to go. These artists, particularly the longtime class members, have been diving earnestly into the mystery, willing to struggle to bring it to light. They have come to love the adventure. We may have only a few sessions remaining in which to wrap up this art program. I want the men to find ways of sustaining the flow of very good art that has picked up its pace in recent years, and to spread it around.

Mark, who has been in the workshop for seven years, is steady and prolific. He was notified that he sold artwork in an exhibition for the third year in a row. I like how odd his work is—a few large ambiguous shapes, richly colored that glow and drift across the page, shapes that possibly have never before been seen on the planet. I wondered aloud, "What is it about your drawings? What are you doing that compels and even amazes people? Where are these coming from?" (The question arises freshly in me, so often, when each session begins and the artists lay out their new work for everyone to see.) Mark responded seriously, "I don't know, I just do whatever you tell me, that's all." Mark has completely given himself over to "whatever" I tell him because he has seen the proof, the lovely lively art that he and his fellows create. The pedagogy I've laid out here is not mine. It contains what came before and it contains the future. These men and this teacher, together for many years, have participated lovingly in a continuing and expanding evolution.

Andrew Cohen would ask those of us who came to his teachings to imagine that the future of the entire planet rested upon our own—my own—shoulders. (What would you do?) This seemed ungraspable although I sensed its huge implications. I can apply it, in a small way, to the life of a single sparkling new drawing and the extent of its impact. I want people to be responsible for the art they produce in the same way they need to be responsible for their words and actions. *It matters why you are making this drawing and it matters how you execute it. It matters what you do with it, and more than anything, it matters what you do next. You can make things better or you can make things worse with this ordinary pencil and piece of paper.* The final product does count. It either is or is not a manifestation of the mysterious, perfectly enhanced by the effort and care of the artist.

Wrapping up, in prison lingo, means completing your sentence. You are done with doing time. Thomas is close to wrapping up. I asked him what will have changed in him when he gets out because of art. He said "I learned to exercise my gift. I'll have a purpose."

NOTES

1. Wherever full names are used, they are true names. All others have been changed.
2. These three statements refer to concepts based on Andrew Cohen's philosophy of Evolutionary Enlightenment. For more detailed explanation of the terms see Cohen A. (2011). *Evolutionary Enlightenment,* SelectBooks.
3. Ibid.
4. Ibid.
5. A tier is a balcony, like a mezzanine, along the wall of a multistoried rectangular space, the cellblock. The prisoners call the ground floor "the flats"; the second tier is what would be called the "second floor" if it were an apartment building. Occasionally, there is a third tier. Each has a number of barred or closed cells along one side of the walkway. The cells face out either to a blank wall across the cellblock, or windows if the inmates are fortunate, or other tiers on the opposite wall. A prisoner has to pass each cell as she walks the tier to her own cell.

REFERENCES

Breton, A. (1924). *Manifesto du Surrealisme.* Paris: Simon Kra.
Burchfield, C. (1965). *The place of drawing in an artist's work.*
Cohen, A. (1991). *Enlightenment is a secret.* Larkspur, CA: Moksha Press.

CHAPTER 7

FOLLOWING THE SIREN'S SONG: SCOTT HARRISON AND THE CAROUSEL OF HAPPINESS

DOUG BLANDY AND MICHAEL FRANKLIN

FOR OVER 20 PLUS YEARS, the project now known as the *Carousel of Happiness* would call to Scott Harrison "like a siren's song." In terms of this chapter, the siren's song is a luring inner imaginal voice that beckons the artist to tenaciously follow an inner calling to final fruition. The long-term quality of Harrison's project and its cultural significance drew us to learn more about Harrison and his work.

The collaborative relationship between the authors goes back to 1986 when we were colleagues at Bowling Green State University. This current project joins together our mutual interests in community-based arts from the perspectives of art education and art therapy. Casually aware of Scott Harrison and his work, we both went to Nederland to learn more and experience the *Carousel of Happiness*. We instantly recognized the cultural and artistic significance of Harrison's project and decided to conduct this study.

Considering Harrison's *Carousel of Happiness* from an art therapy and art education perspective provides a unique opportunity to observe how the creative process unfolds from an initial idea over a prolonged period of time (Allen, 1992). The directed and sustained commitment to

Harrison's vision to one day build the *Carousel of Happiness* as a community gathering space is important to understanding Harrison's life history.

Harrison's story offers evidential confirmation for the importance of tracking a personal narrative, devotion to working with materials, and creating aesthetically engaging community-based destinations that inspire joyful and profound experiences. With deliberate and sincere intentions, Harrison has worked with his local community to create an inclusive environment that welcomes all ages on the developmental spectrum. In fact, this seems to be a significant part of the magnetic appeal of the *Carousel of Happiness*.

Since Memorial Day 2010, until the time of our interview with Harrison in February 2011, 70,000 people have visited the *Carousel of Happiness*. The short one dollar ride (free to those unable to pay) on one of the hand crafted wooden animals, while a Wurlitzer band organ plays, is a simple pleasure that results from a playful environment, beautifully carved objects, and the sensation of going around in a circle and watching perspectives change. Equally important is that the carousel encourages and contains both "joy and sorrow." Visitors, according to Harrison, often remark about memories that surface during their visit, how these memories hold dualistic content, and how fragmented recollections are soothed by watching or riding the carousel.

THE CAROUSEL AND ITS MAKER

Saltair Park, on the southern shore of the Great Salt Lake in Utah, opened to the public in 1893. Only 16 miles from Salt Lake City, this resort, owned by the Church of Jesus Christ of Latter Day Saints, was a popular family destination. Mormon apostle Abraham H. Cannon writing at the time described the park as being "a wholesome place of recreation" (McCormick, 2011). The park was also intended to be the " 'Coney Island of the West' to help demonstrate that Utah was not a strange place of alien people and customs" (McCormick, 2011).

Given that Saltair was to be the Coney Island of the west, it is not surprising that the owners of the park commissioned a carousel from noted carousel maker and carver Charles I. D. Looff. Looff was known as having manufactured the first carousel for Coney Island in 1876. In 1910, Looff delivered a four row carousel to Saltair. Period photographs show the handsome carousel located very near the lakeshore and adjacent to the train station bringing people to the park from Salt Lake City (*Saltair Park—Salt Lake City Utah,* 2011).

Figure 7.1   Postcard: Saltair Pavilion from Top of Roller Coaster

Saltair, at its peak in the 1920s, was attracting half a million visitors per year. In our possession is an undated postcard of Saltair with a view from the top of the roller coaster. The Great Salt Lake is in the background. The middle ground is dominated by the Saltair Pavilion with the Saltair Carousel clearly visible in the foreground (see figure 7.1).

In 1931 most of Saltair burned. However, the Saltair Carousel survived. Saltair burned again in 1951 and once again the carousel survived (Hopkins, 2006). In 1957 a windstorm struck the park, blowing the roller coaster into the carousel resulting in heavy damage to the carousel (Hopkins, 2006). It was rebuilt, but with only two rows of carousel creatures.

With the closure of Saltair in 1959, the Utah Park and Recreation Commission donated the Saltair Carousel to the Utah State Training School in American Fork. An article appearing in the February 4, 1960, edition of *The American Fork Citizen* describes the carousel as becoming part of a seven acre amusement park, called Fairyland, on the grounds of the training center (*The American Fork Citizen,* 1960). Fairyland was also open to the general public. Sixteen years later, an article in the July 27, 1976, *Desert News* described the rehabilitation of the carousel by staff and residents of the training school (Perry, 1976). Readers of the article learn that "there were 20 layers of paint on the horses," that some "of the horses dated from 1872," and "Saltair apparently opened in 1893, but it is unknown if the carousel is as old as the horses." (p. 10 A)

In 1986 the Utah State Training School sold the animals off the carousel to Charlotte Dinger who in turn sold the animals at auction. One of the original carousel animals can be seen today in the West Jordan Historical Society in West Jordan, Utah. Harrison, now living in Nederland, Colorado, heard from the truck driver transporting the animals that the carousel mechanism was also for sale from Dinger. Harrison traveled to American Fork, dismantled the frame, and would spend the next 20 years restoring the carousel mechanism (Hopkins, 2006).

The impetus for Harrison's relationship with this carousel began during his tour of duty as a Marine Corps Private in Viet Nam. The specifics of this period in Harrison's life will be described further on in this chapter. Sometime later, while living in San Francisco and working for Amnesty International, Harrison took his children to an Oakland park and saw a carousel. Reflecting back on that encounter he describes the spiritual nature of the animals on the carousel and the thought occurred to him that "now might be the time to begin creating animals." Harrison photographed a rabbit on the carousel that would be his model for an animal carved for the *Carousel of Happiness* after his move to Nederland in 1982 and before he had obtained the *Saltair Carousel* mechanism.

In 1982, Harrison visited a carousel animal exhibit in Oakland California with his family. During this trip, he noticed an old wooden rabbit in one of the exhibits. Although simply carved, the face and particularly the eyes had an enigmatic effect on Harrison. He took several photos and began planning to carve its likeness hoping to capture the essence of this sculpted animal. A few years later, he carved a similar rabbit. It was this animal that inspired the beginning of his carving career.

In addition to these background details, Harrison began working for Amnesty International's Urgent Action Network in 1975. His work focused on building a network through schools and colleges that would advocate for political prisoners held by governments. In Harrison's estimation tens of thousands of people were kept from being tortured over the 32 years he worked for Amnesty International. In Harrison's words, the goal was to "prevent rather than protest." Harrison retired from Amnesty International in 2007.

Once in Nederland, carving carousel animals would follow Harrison's workday with Amnesty International. Believing that one's "professional life doesn't make a man," Harrison conceived of his activities at the time as an equally balanced triad; professional life/family/carousel carving. He recognized that he "needed something else for myself." Unlike his work with Amnesty International, working on the carousel was not deadline driven and was a respite from working on torture cases or meeting family responsibilities.

The second oldest animal on the carousel is the giraffe. Harrison shaped rather than carved it. Later he added a snake after hearing the myth of a snake from Botswana. A journalist friend of Harrison's was in Botswana on a training assignment in 2004. While there he visited a cave complex that included a primitive stone sculpture carved thousands of years ago, of a snake on the back of a giraffe. The legend is that a snake was drowning in a lake and the giraffe with its long neck and legs walked out into the lake, reached down and gently grabbed the snake with its mouth and placed it on his back, thereby saving its life. They became friends and remained together for the rest of their lives. This relationship was somehow important to people then and had a place within the shamanistic culture of Botswana. Harrison also added the snake as a practical design feature to keep people from falling off the back of the giraffe.

Once the *Saltair Carousel* mechanism was obtained, the *Carousel of Happiness* began to take shape. Like the *Saltair Carousel* in its last incarnation, the *Carousel of Happiness* has two rows of animals. Unlike most carousels that have only six to seven carved animals repeated and painted differently, the *Carousel of Happiness* contains entirely unique animals.

All of the wood on the carousel is now new. An original piece of *Saltair Carousel* wood is on display on a wall near the carousel in homage to its predecessor. Harrison has replaced the plywood floor with southern yellow pine originally milled in the 1890s as shelving for whisky barrels. The carousel's scroll decorations are recycled from other carousels. Harrison augmented the Saltair's 1909, 220 ten horsepower motor with a computer to control variable speeds. A General Electric Trolley switch turns the motor on and off. Harrison believes that the squeak that occurs when the motor is first turned on is the carousel's way of offering gratitude by saying "Thank you" or "Hey brother, thanks for the new life."

Art Therapy, Veterans, and Postwar Artistic Work

Harrison and his *Carousel of Happiness* offer an example of a soldier's experience with war and the discovery and pursuit of innate healing imagery. While in Viet Nam, Harrison's sister sent him a music box with *Tristesse* by Chopin. The music had a calming effect on him while serving on his tour of duty. There were moments when Harrison would hold the music box against his head feeling the resonation of the music "off of his skull." This experience inspired "calming visualizations of where I wanted to be . . . in a mountain meadow running a carousel." Harrison explained that when in the war theater people surge adrenalin and therefore need different coping strategies such as "crying, looking at a girlfriend's picture, or music." This early experience with the music box is an example of how the inner psyche can offer up an imaginal remedy that, if followed, can offer therapeutic results (McNiff, 1992). In expressive therapies, locating a primary image within a personal narrative and artistically following its many iterations is why emotional transformation occurs through art. In this case, Chopin's music inspired an image of a particular carousel where "everybody is having a nice peaceful time together." To his credit, Harrison never let go of this initial image and pursued it for decades. The pursuit of these primary images begins to describe the story behind the *Carousel of Happiness*.

The psychological toll on the human psyche from war can be significant. We now have a better understanding of war-based trauma: how it manifests and how to treat it. Since verbal consciousness is interrupted when exposed to traumatic situations such as war, memories can become fragmented and exist without narrative organization. Art used in trauma therapy is a process of re-associating these dissociated memories (Gantt & Tinnin, 2009). Increasingly, art therapy is recognized as an emerging, even necessary treatment option for combat related post traumatic stress disorder (PTSD) (Collie, Backos, Malchiodi, & Spiegel, 2006). These authors discuss the importance of developing a trauma narrative that places stressful memories within declarative memory systems. They suggest that construction of this narrative process, which can be visual, allows for traumatic memories to be reinterpreted and eventually assimilated into a new autobiographical worldview. Furthermore, it seems that art used in therapy offers an oscillating benefit of direct titrated exposure to traumatic material with the opportunity for creating distracting, even self-soothing imagery. The authors of this article synthesize seven "primary therapeutic mechanisms" offered through art therapy, which are (a) reconsolidation of memories, (b) externalization, (c) progressive exposure, (d) reduction of arousal, (e) reactivation of positive emotion, (f) enhancement of emotional self-efficacy, (g) improved self-esteem (Collie et al., 2006, p. 160). Related to these seven categories and from what we learned about Harrison during our interview, it seems feasible to infer the following connections. For example, his early interactions with the music box sent to him in Viet Nam by his sister served as a way to reduce arousal through the self-soothing process of listening to Chopin and imagining his future carousel. His later long-term efforts to carve animals, assemble the carousel mechanism, and build the current site could imply an effective, positive strategy to redirect early convictions and honor long-standing sentiments about peace and justice, thus enhancing emotional self-efficacy.

Due to the bravado culture of the armed forces, many soldiers elect to not seek out psychological treatment until symptoms become unbearable. Still, many soldiers like Harrison make it through their combat service with few symptoms and successfully readjust to their civilian life. Some of these soldiers intuitively seek the benefits of expressive outlets such as music, art, and writing to tell their story and sublimate their bearable anxieties. They innately find their way to self-healing practices, such as art, as a way to consolidate personal convictions, and directly or indirectly, tell some aspect of their personal narrative through aesthetically satisfying work.

There are two primary reasons why image and art, in the context of the *Carousel of Happiness,* resulted in a restorative process for Harrison and perhaps for those who visit the *Carousel of Happiness.* First, it is essential to clarify the contextual meaning of image and imaginal culture in dream and aesthetic work. Basically, imaginal culture is anything that is imagined. According to Hillman (1978), image is not the retinal event of perceiving an object. Seeing a glass of water is not the *image* of a glass of water. Image is the narrative that lives within the object or the memory that is perceived or experienced. It can consist of "mood, context, and scene" that becomes the imaginal territory to explore through art (p. 159). Second is the freedom to imagine, especially when living in restrictive conditions such as war. Berry (1982) refers to the complete democracy available within the image for imaginal exploration. By remaining open and engaged with the simultaneity and multiplicity within the parts of the image, freedom emerges to actively explore this imaginal territory. This process was the primary rationale for Jung's method for actively imagining with an image and wakefully dreaming it onward (Chodorow, 1997; Wallace, 2001). In the example of the *Carousel of Happiness,* the sculpted and painted animals open the door to further access vibrant narratives that can inspire future carvings and evolving insights.

Images call to us to help manifest their existence. In the spirit of true collaboration, a dialogue unfolds between artist, image, and the materials. Harrison, as a self-taught wood-carver, did not try to replicate the old masters of carousel carving believing that it would be "pretentious and a losing proposition." Instead, his style of carving is an amalgamation of disciplined craftsmanship, imaginal fascination with his subject, and the tenacity to follow a dream.

Harrison researches each animal on the carousel prior to shaping and carving. The animals are made from basswood. Harrison describes this wood from the Linden tree as "workable by an amateur, easily carved, and doesn't require being machined." Harrison's animals are inspired by folktales, children's books, and animal sculptures. His goal is to discover the essence of the animal while simultaneously choosing an interesting ride-able pose. Each animal takes three to six months to construct, shape, and carve. On the interior of each animal Harrison places the information that has informed its shaping and carving.

A motivating intention for Harrison is to carve something "peaceful and gentle" for people to experience as well as to embody his animals with their spiritual nature. He is guided by a sincere respect for the animals, which in turn motivates extensive research into the mythology, wisdom traditions, and folk tale stories around each creature. This research method implies an intuitive connection with Jung's active imagination process and Hillman's image work focused on exploring rather than explaining. Harrison actively imagines the personalities of each animal, listens to its message, and follows its communication throughout the carving process. For example, Harrison described his working method for the "big Gorilla" as a process of carving this noble animal while it simultaneously carved him back. For Harrison, it was important that this carving be big, yet also convey gentleness. To this end the Gorilla has a bench next to it that makes it accessible to people with disabilities.

Harrison did not hesitate to have his picture taken with the big Gorilla. Careful examination of this photograph reveals Harrison's genuine affection for this animal (see figure 7.2). Together they hold hands and gaze at each other. This was not a performed or staged pose. Harrison knows these animals from his research and also from his belief that his wood carving brings them to life.

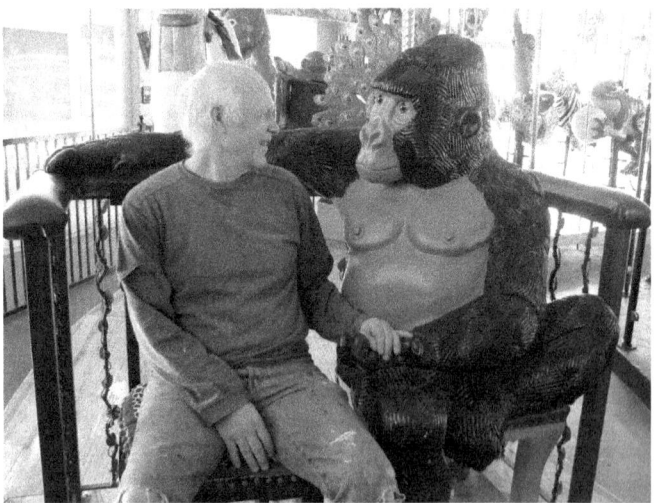

Figure 7.2 *Harrison and Carved Gorilla*. 2011, photograph by Michael Franklin

THE IMPORTANCE OF MATERIALS

Significant to our discussion of the *Carousel of Happiness* is the subject of craftspersonship and materials. Harrison describes his relationship with wood in an almost mystical manner. As mentioned above, the wood that he carves also carves him in return, yielding opportunities for sacred experiences. Harrison remarked that he would leave the radio on for the carvings that remained in the shop after he went to sleep; further evidence of his imaginal relationship to the animals.

Assembling the *Carousel of Happiness* has allowed Harrison to acknowledge that "this project is as spiritual as he has ever gotten" in his life. Part of this spirituality has to do with the nature of wood. The workability of wood initiates an encounter with a living, flexible material. The animals, as well as the wood, pulsate with a living presence that inspires Harrison's work. He begins by laminating pieces of basswood together to rough out the animals general shape. From here he refines the form through subtractive methods of sketching centerlines and stop cuts until he is ready for paint (see figure 7.3).

Upon entering the *Carousel of Happiness,* one is struck by the vibrant colors adorning each animal as well as the overall space. Each figure is meticulously painted, transforming the recognizable form into a living presence. The paint also has to withstand constant surface abrasions as

Figure 7.3 *Harrison and Carousel Animal in Progress.* 2011, photograph by Michael Franklin

visitors mount and dismount each animal. In addition to carving the animals, necessary ongoing repair work is also a part of running the *Carousel of Happiness*.

THE CAROUSEL OF HAPPINESS AS COMMUNITY AND COMMUNITY ART

Each morning Harrison drives into Nederland to visit the *Carousel of Happiness* to be sure that all is as it should be. Located 17 miles southwest of Boulder, Colorado, Nederland, with a population of 1,337, sits in a valley at an elevation of 8,230 feet. The first white settlers came to this valley in the mid nineteenth century. Known by a number of earlier names, the town would be incorporated as Nederland in 1874. As a milling town associated with nearby mining, the population of Nederland has fluctuated over its history along with the demand for local ore. The population waned after World War II increasing again with the arrival of "hippies" in the 1960s (Town of Nederland, 2011b) increasing since that time to its current population (Town of Nederland, 2011).

The center of Nederland is dominated by the Barker Meadow shopping center along with some historic buildings constituting the "downtown." Recent years have seen the addition of a new fire station, library, community center, and the 12-sided steel roofed building housing the *Carousel of Happiness*.

Experiencing the carousel begins with the sound of a gong announcing the start of the mechanism and the animals coming to life. Harrison observes that senior citizens outnumber children. Mindful of the carousel's history, he has made the carousel accessible to people with disabilities through a motorized lift made by the robotics team from a local high school, as well as animals that can accommodate wheel chairs. Harrison's goal is for the *Carousel of Happiness* to be as inclusive as possible; a place where all people feel welcome. When talking to Harrison about the carousel one quickly learns how he believes his carousel is not only contributing to the cultural life of Nederland, but how it also encourages community. For example, Harrison has initiated a "kids docent program" for the purpose of orienting visitors to the history of the carousel. The inclusive community oriented purpose of the carousel also means that visitors will "cry as much as they laugh." Veterans come to the carousel as a site of solace and healing. Harrison likes the fact that the carousel is a "joyous place to remember sorrow." Memorial services are held at the carousel as well as weddings.

The *Carousel of Happiness* exists as a nonprofit organization. The board overseeing the organization employs a director and 10–15 employees. The building housing the carousel was built by volunteers (including children), is almost debt free, and the land is leased to the nonprofit for a dollar a year for 30 years. Harrison donated the carousel to the nonprofit and it has been appraised at $300,000.00.

Harrison's goal from the beginning was that the carousel would be an integral part of Nederland. While Harrison maintains a close connection to the carousel, he believes the carousel's true value is realized through its possession by a community-based nonprofit organization. In this way Harrison believes the carousel liberated itself from Harrison while simultaneously finding people in order to protect itself.

Within Nederland, a community has formed around the *Carousel of Happiness*. There is a group of local volunteers, affectionately referred to as "mechanical monkeys," who meet once a month to assist in the maintenance of the carousel mechanism. The gift shop is run by volunteers and includes the work of local artists. However, the community associated with the carousel is much larger than those who are directly associated with the carousel itself. This community is best perceived through its current and potential interconnections with the people of Nederland as they imagine their future.

Like many rural towns across the United States, the citizens of Nederland are concerned for its future. A March 11, 2011 Mayor's Economic Development Task Force memorandum to the Nederland Board of Trustees details recommendations for sustaining Nederland economically (Town of Nederland, 2011a). The residents of Nederland are also engaged in the *Envision Nederland 2020* project, an effort to bring stakeholders together to imagine the future of their community. The residents of Nederland are considering environmental integrity and sustainability as they plan for the future. The *Carousel of Happiness* holds value in this process as a reminder that along with the environmental, social, and economic factors, the culture of a place must also be viewed as integral to quality of life. In addition, Harrison and the nonprofit that now stewards the carousel, provide Nederland with at least one portal through which children, youth, and adults experience and learn about the history of their community, the people associated with that community along with their stories, as well as the stories of those outside the community who at least for a short time engage with the community of Nederland through the carousel.

The *Carousel of Happiness,* in its current incarnation, epitomizes "community arts." "Community arts" include performing arts (music, theater, dance, etc.), multimedia arts, visual arts, literary arts, culinary arts, clothing and textiles, and the multitudes of other forms that people, individually and collectively, create to make the ordinary extraordinary.

Community arts are first and foremost community based, community focused, and integral to the everyday life of the community. Community art may also focus on a political issue important to a locale. As such, community arts often manifest as a response to the threatened erosion of cohesive, dynamic communities.

In talking with Harrison we know that he views the *Carousel of Happiness* as a place where people learn about where they live and how to live. In this regard, the *Carousel of Happiness* reminds us that learning takes place outside of formal academic settings through informal exchanges like those witnessed by us during our visits to the *Carousel of Happiness* as well as those recounted to us by Harrison. In addition, the political dimensions of community arts are primarily situated within civil society with its emphasis on public discourse, public values, and public language separate from government power. Harrison was deliberate in seeding his carousel to a nonprofit rather than the Nederland government so that the fortunes of the carousel would not be tied to the municipal politics of Nederland. Consider the *Carousel of Happiness* in relationship to other important civic contributions made by quilting circles, hobby associations, and community arts centers. Clearly the Carousel of Happiness functions, in part, as a catalyst for dialogue about individual and group identity as well as local and national concerns.

Conclusion

The lines between persons and things manifest in a variety of ways. In the case of the *Carousel of Happiness,* this line is particularly permeable when one considers its history, the multiple contexts in which it has or does exist, and the people who have shaped its history and contexts—most recently Scott Harrison. We have been able to examine the relationship between the *Carousel of Happiness* and the people associated with it by combining methods associated with art therapy, art education, and material culture studies.

Franklin used an interviewing method recognizing its similarity to how an art therapist would look at artwork and interview a client in a therapy session. However, this method is not restricted to therapeutic encounters. It also has similar qualities to how an art educator might practice art criticism with students. In art therapy and some approaches to art criticism, there is an underlying belief that careful observation of the formal elements will lead to preliminary recognition of content. In essence, rigorous phenomenological observation (Betensky, 2001) of the formal qualities present in the work, and the relational field that begins to surface sparks of meaning. In the case of the *Carousel of Happiness,* the relational field consists of formal qualities within the work and architectural space, verbal exchanges, historical references, and behavioral actions.

Franklin begins an interview with astute silent observations of the relational and imaginal field, which result in empathic resonance (Franklin, 2010). Based on these resonant observations, noninterpretive paraphrased comments are then offered to the interviewee. The process continues with a mutual discussion sparked by these attuned paraphrases. The result is that the interviewee begins to see more of what is familiar and perceive additional uniqueness in well-known imagery. The interviewee is then invited to describe emerging insights as a direct result of seeing "more." These insights surface further dialogue (questions and discussion) as connections are made and revealed information deepens understanding. Most notable is that this cycle of discovery and desire for additional meaning repeats.

An example from the interview occurred when details relating to the roundness of the interior space were paraphrased. This visual summary inspired further comments about other round structures such as mandala inspired shrines, yurts and teepees, and their architectural rarity in our culture. This opened up a discussion on the center pole and the roundness of the building including the "architectural healing" aspects of the *Carousel of Happiness*.

Harrison mused that the center pole of the carousel is the "soul of the enterprise" in that "it has collected the screams and shouts of the people over the decades." With ear to pole one can hear the collective history of the many incarnations of the carousel. Harrison acknowledged that he never thought of the carousel in this way until Franklin's interview. During the interview he continued to independently surface deeper insights into the familiar space and history of the *Carousel of Happiness* as a result of this approach.

The methods Blandy brought to this project were derived from material culture studies and folklore. Bolin and Blandy (2003) define material culture as

> All human-mediated sights, sounds, smells, tastes, objects, forms, and expressions.... When there is purposeful human intervention, based on cultural activity, there is material culture. This being the case, nothing affected by human agency is overlooked as too insignificant for intensive examination, nor viewed as too small for eliciting substantive meaning.
> (p. 250)

The challenge associated with the *Carousel of Happiness* was how to consider the carousel as both material culture as well as the carousel as a manifestation of the way in which people engaged with it and, in turn, the ways in which it affected people. A first step in understanding and appreciating material culture, such as the *Carousel of Happiness,* is to experience it systemically. Becker's (2008) systemic conceptualization of "art worlds" can be helpful in this regard. Art worlds are defined by the people, organizations, institutions, and assorted other entities that as a network facilitate and support the creation, distribution, and appreciation of a work of art. Becker uses the term "art" broadly and it includes, but is not limited to the material created by, fine artists, folk artists, craftspeople, media specialists, as well as the way that we embellish and amplify what we do in our everyday lives.

Fieldwork methods informed by anthropology and folklore are helpful to discovering the larger systems that material culture, like the *Carousel of Happiness,* operate within. Lassiter's (2004) collaborative ethnography is particularly useful in this regard. Lassiter promotes collaborative ethnography as one way to try and achieve a correct interpretation, representation, or description of a cultural group and the material culture it produces. Lassiter's method includes participating in the lives of others, observing behavior, taking field notes, and conducting interviews. For example, Harrison made many references to his studio and carving technique during the interview. It became important to see what he was referring to and learn more about the meaning behind these statements. After seeing his studio as well as carvings in progress, further clarification emerged and our understanding of Harrison's carousel project deepened.

Material collected through collaborative ethnography is in a raw form until it is "interpreted." Lassiter (2004) emphasizes that in representing and interpreting others, a first responsibility is to those who are being represented and interpreted. These individuals should be intimately involved as consultants in all aspects of the program. Self-representation by those studied to the greatest extent possible is desirable.

In the broadest sense, whether working as an art therapist or an art educator, one must always consider the cultural influences on any project. Intrapersonal historical diversity and imaginal ethos is as important to attend to as is diverse interpersonal cultural constructs. Because of this reciprocally embraced perspective, the data gathering methods utilized for this chapter complimented each other. Franklin was observing and listening to the relational field and imaginal culture without an initial interpretive agenda while Blandy was focusing on the systemic relationships necessary to material culture studies. This combined method of trying to understand material culture references with imaginal culture references made this collaborative effort a dynamic process. Although each researcher was attending to the data from slightly different perspectives, the overall information gathered from these points of view mutually reinforced each other. The organic unfolding of candid conversation, initiated by nonjudgmental paraphrased resonant observations, lead to increased insight and further dialogue. When engaged in collaborative data collection, it is important to keep clarifying meaning until all present are certain that they understand each other. Ultimately we came away from our time spent with Harrison and the *Carousel of Happiness* concluding that just as the carousel's center pole is not just an iron pipe, so too the *Carousel of Happiness* is not just a carousel. Like the iron pipe, the *Carousel of Happiness* is absorbing the experiences and stories of all of those who are a part of the smaller and larger communities that surround it.

Postscript

Following is Harrison's recounting, in his own words, of the rabbit carving. We include it here to give readers a sense of Harrison's voice as well as the relationship he has with his carvings.

I glued together wooden boards for the body and head. I then used four by four inch pieces of Douglas fir for the long ears. It was the first time I had tried to carve an animal and amazingly, it began to look like a rabbit. The wood was just scrap lumber from building our house. I had been holding on to a full-size profile drawing of a rabbit that I had created a few years before when we lived in San Francisco. Our family had moved to Nederland, Colorado, and in the new house, for the first time in my life, I had some space to try my hand at carving.

When I was done with the rabbit, I grabbed it up, all one hundred pounds of it, and carried it outside to place it here and there in the nearby woods. It was the middle of winter and I would place it on a box, shove snow up around it to hide the box, and then run back a ways to see if it really did look like a giant hopping rabbit. I think I did a little private dance in the snow, overjoyed with myself that I could create something which, if I went way back and squinted my eyes, looked like an animal. Wow. Good for me.

For the next 25 years, I kept carving wooden animals, all kinds, and I guess I should admit that I did get a little better at it along the way. I soon started using real carving wood, basswood, the preferred wood that carousel horse carvers used a century ago. I got a better set of knives and more expensive carving tools. I watched others carve, and read what I could to teach myself how to be a better carver.

As I continued, the animals got fancier, looked more proportional, and had more details. As people came to visit, I wouldn't show them the rabbit first. Instead, I would show off the cat, then the lion, then the dragon boat, the gorilla, and on and on. A few years later, our house got too crowded with this menagerie and I had to rent space in a local mining equipment warehouse, and the first thing I put in there was the rabbit. Soon, he was joined by others. Eventually I even carved a new rabbit, a bunny really, with a golden mouse in his tail and a paw that tells time.

Many, many years later, the carousel was finished, its house built, and after one year of operating, and close to 100,000 riders, the 60 wooden animals that make up the Carousel of Happiness, are delighting people of all sizes and ages.

For 26 years I have stored Rabbit, first at our old house, then the warehouse and recently in an outer shed next to our new house. There he has been, with grace and patience, lots of patience, sitting on a wooden box again, facing the shed wall, closed up to the sun, the rain, the snow, and the flowers, coming and going, year after year.

A few months ago, George and I took Rabbit out of the storage shed and carried his heavy self into my carving shop. I spent lots of time making it up to him, telling him how much I love him, have always loved him, and have never really meant him any disrespect. It is just that he was the first. A little too big for the carousel frame that I eventually found; kind of plain looking, since I really had no idea what I was doing when I created him.

As I again worked on Rabbit, sanding him, re-carving this and that, just a bit, and giving him a fresh coat of paint, I could feel his wooden forgiveness and understanding, and felt from him just a bit of hope that he was now about to join his friends a half mile away at the carousel. I left the shop radio on at night, not loud, just a whisper of music to keep him company.

Wednesday afternoon, after setting up some scaffolding, during a May snow shower, after being fitted with a nice new steel support cradle, Rabbit came out of his last inside place, and, in the back of a truck, he was brought home—his real home—to the carousel. A local man walked by, under a heavy pack, beginning his westward journey from Nederland, looking for a job and new friends, life on the road under the sky. He laid his pack down and asked if he could help us get this rabbit eight feet up on top of the large sign, looking west, a sign that says Carousel of Happiness. We were busy with our task and didn't notice the bond that this traveler and Rabbit seemed to share. Others came out to help; friends, employees from the nearby grocery store.

The snow comes down wetter, harder. Nobody notices. We have, in one common movement, brought Rabbit up high on his perch. He becomes immediately, The Special One, after all this time. He faces west, toward the highway that brings all those who want to visit the animals at the carousel. But they see him first. He sees them first. It is Rabbit up there presenting the carousel, coaxing the first smiles from those who are looking out their car windows.

This collection of scrap lumber, Rabbit, has taught me patience, respect, and has allowed me his friendship. Look up there at him. Give him a wave and he will return it with an ever so slight (he is made of wood after all) smile.

REFERENCES

Allen, P. B. (1992). Artist in residence: An alternative to "clinification" for art therapists. *Art Therapy: The Journal of the American Art Therapy Association,* 9(1), 22–29.

The American Fork Citizen. (1960). Retrieved from http://www.carousel ofhappiness.org/content/history-img/deseret-news.jpg.

Becker, H. (2008). *Art worlds.* Berkeley: University of California.

Berry, P. (1982). *Echo's subtle body: Contributions to an archetypal psychology.* Dallas, TX: Spring.

Betensky, M. (2001). Phenomenological art therapy. In J. A. Rubin (Ed.), *Approaches to art therapy* (pp. 121–133). Philadelphia, PA: Brunner-Routledge.

Bolin, P. & Blandy, D. (2003). Beyond visual culture: Seven statements of support for material culture studies in art education. *Studies in Art Education,* 44(3), 246–263.

Chodorow, J. (1997). *Jung on active imagination.* Princeton, NJ: Princeton University Press.

Collie, K., Backos, A., Malchiodi, C., & Spiegel, D. (2006). Art therapy for combat-related PTSD: Recommendations for research and practice. *Art Therapy: The Journal of the American Art Therapy Association,* 23(4), 157–164.

Franklin, M. (2010). Affect regulation, mirror neurons and the 3rd hand: Formulating mindful empathic art interventions. *Art Therapy: The Journal of the American Art Therapy Association,* 27(4), 160–167.

Gantt, L. & Tinnin, L., (2009). Support for a neurological view of trauma with implications for art therapy. *The Arts in Psychotherapy,* 36, 148–153.

Hillman, J. (1978). Further notes on images. *Spring,* pp. 152–182.

Hopkins, R. (2006). *Carousel news and trader magazine.* Retrieved from http://www.carouselnews.com/September-2006/Septermber-06/New-Home-for-Saltair-Looff.html.

Lassiter, L. E. (2004). Collaborative ethnography. *Anthronotes,* 25(1), 1–9.

McCormick, J. S. (2011). *Utah history to go.* Retrieved from http://historytogo.utah.gov/utah_chapters/statehood_and_the_progressive_era/saltair.html.

McNiff, S. (1992*). Art as medicine.* Boston, MA: Shambhala.

Perry, L. (1976). Horses run again at state school. *Desert News,* p. 10A.

Saltair Park – Salt Lake City, Utah (2011). Retrieved from http://www.chasingmerrygorounds.com/cohPages/Saltair_Park_Utah.html.

Town of Nederland. (2011a). *Mayor's economic development task force.* Retrieved from http://nederlandco.org/government/town-boards/economic-development-task-force/.

Town of Nederland. (2011b). *Town history.* Retrieved from http://nederlandco.org/about/town-history-2/.

Wallace, E. (2001). Healing through the visual arts. In J. A. Rubin (Ed.), *Approaches to art therapy* (pp. 95–108). Philadelphia, PA: Brunner-Routledge.

CHAPTER 8

Digital Ethnography: Artists Speak from Virtual Ability Island in Second Life

MARY STOKROCKI, ALICE WEXLER, AND
L. S. KRECKER

> *Virtual Ability helps enable people with a wide range of disabilities by providing a supporting environment for them to enter and thrive in online virtual worlds. About half of our group members have one or more kinds of disability (physical, mental, emotional, or sensory) or chronic illness; the other half are temporarily-able-bodied family members, caregivers, professionals, researchers, students, and others interested in disability issues* (from the mission statement on website http://www.virtualability.org). Virtual Ability Inc. runs the Virtual Ability Island on Second Life located at http://slurl.com/secondlife/Virtual%20Abiity/128/126/23.

INTRODUCTION

Second Life (SL) is "a popular multi-user environment where everything is built by avatar-residents, except the basic land" (Robbins & Bell, 2008). Users transform their avatars and creations with SL scripting language and retain copyrights. Although known for its social function, for example, meeting people, virtual parties, and interesting places to visit, these events are also inherently educational and aesthetic. Ondrejka (2008) describes learning in SL as situated, the social interaction providing built-in incentives to apprentice more experienced residents in active, "Vygotsian" collaboration. Over 300 universities worldwide have a home in SL (Michels, 2008). In November 2010, SL claimed to have 21.3 million accounts registered (Second Life, 2011, April). In 2010, approximately 700,000 people used the virtual world for at least an hour a month, the means that Linden Labs uses to measure activity level (Sass, 2010). Because of this unique feature of the platform, SL appeals to artists of all sorts to build and create "in world" (in SL). The result is a rich and varied world, created by its users, for its users.

Deuze (2006) explained its collaborative principles, which included participation, remediation (problem solving), and bricolage (assemblage of tools and emerging findings). Lu (2010) also offered her own principles for designing learning events in SL: "Learning by exploring, being, collaborating, championing, building, and expressing" (Condensed from p. 21). SL has already proven itself as a useful tool for people with limited ability to socialize and connect (Boulos, Hetherington, & Wheeler, 2007). Organizations such as Virtual Ability (http://www.virtualability. org) post lists with resources for people with several disabilities. Diane Carr (2010) investigates the coalescence of disability and technology, particularly in the Deaf community, and how identity is reconstructed in the commingling of real and virtual worlds. She argues "that research regarding online identity, disability and education needs to allow room for self-description . . . recognize the power relations that can lurk within practices of provision or accessibility support" (para 1). Thus, disability studies merge e-learning and accessibility perspectives. For example, the voice feature in SL, which was first introduced in 2007, while beneficial to some disabilities might exclude Deaf residents from both intimate gatherings and large events (Carr, 2010). If one were to follow the social construction theory of disability that Davis (1995) and others propose, then the introduction of the voice feature has changed the social, political, and spatial environment of SL in a way that produces a disability (deafness) where there was none before. In considering such situations that pose the potential for exclusion, even within a site that was designed to support disability, Carr turns to disability and deaf studies that resist representing the Deaf as bereft or passive. Generally, however, many discussions about disability in SL point to the ease with which people with a variety of disabilities might enjoy participating and contributing to events that would not be possible in real life (RL). While there is obviously merit to this perspective, Carr warns that digital ethnography must adopt the kind of scrutiny that disability studies has afforded this conversation; for instance, the inadvertent propagation of an "impairment as problem/technology as solution" dynamic. "Such patterns implicitly define disability as a property of potentially marginalized individuals who are in need of special support" (para 6). Herein lies the difference between the medical model of disability as tragic and in need of support, and the social model, which "attends to the disabling aspects of an environment: as when cultural practices, assumptions, expectations or material phenomena assume a standardized or 'normal' body, and exclude or penalize those who deviate from this pattern" (Davis, 1995).

This cultural shift in the way disabilities are viewed brings to light that the environment determines accessibility (Derby, 2011). Carr suggests that educators in SL might need to find a middle ground between these perspectives, paying attention to the practical aspects of disability, including the support of inclusion and accessibility, as well as the social and political construction of the disabled identity, both real and virtual. The complexity of representing the Deaf community in SL is an example of walking a fine line. The upper case "D" signifies the culture of sign language, but in SL signing is not an option... yet.

Thinking about disability and education in online worlds solely in terms of tools that support participation may be insufficient. It is also necessary to look at the conventions that emerge in the wake of these tools, and the implications for online identity. Investigating these issues also involves thinking about how the disabled or deaf subject is constructed in and through research itself (Carr, 2010, para 12).

METHODOLOGY

Digital ethnography is a systematic study of participants engaged in immersive environments to better understand their ways of life and, in this case, their virtual world (Wesch, 2007). Ethnography implies a case study methodology that investigates situations where interventions have no single set of outcomes (Yin, 2003). Through digital ethnography, we watch online people communicate, build, construct, and transform their avatars, homes, businesses, curricula, and installations, which require patience and attachments for capturing and storing information (Stokrocki, in press).

Historically, Hymes (1974) posited three primary ethnographic assumptions: (a) communication is patterned and can be studied; (b) such patterns are intimately linked with social life; and (c) the nature of communication itself is culture specific, therefore cross-culturally diverse. Carbaugh and Buzzanell (2010) and other authors continued the quest for distinctive communication patterns. Thick ethnographic descriptions uncover a community's communication patterns to include socially constructed symbols, meanings, and rules. We sought to uncover some of these patterns in stages.

Digital ethnography consisted of data collection (DC), content analysis (ConA), and comparative analysis (CompA) stages (Glaser & Strauss, 1967). For DC, we used participant observation note taking, informal interviewing (Kvale, 1996), and photo elicitating (Stokrocki, 1997), in this case, questioning about a specific digital image. ConA entailed searching for repeated themes (art and communication). CompA involved looking for similarities among interviews and the literature on disabilities (Stokrocki, 1997).

CONTEXT

Virtual Ability, Inc. (VAI), runs Virtual Ability Island, where individuals can be oriented to SL. VAI provides people with disabilities tools and support to access and thrive in virtual worlds such as SL. VAI, run by avatar educator Gentle Heron (who Stokrocki and Krecker met in RL when they were attending a major media conference at Arizona State University), assesses each individual and recommends hardware or software to assist them. Furthermore, VAI supports its community through meetings, training, referrals, and socialization. Volunteers and mentors help individuals in manipulating the interface, building, shopping, and integrating into the virtual world. They host coffees, dances, and a virtual art gallery on the island. We conducted most observations and interviews in SL on Virtual Ability Island (http://maps.secondlife.com/secondlife/Virtual%20Ability/136/100/23). Our primary research question was, what meaningful art, learning, and communication patterns emerged from interviews with artists with disabilities on SL?

RESEARCH AND SL PARTICIPANTS

Stokrocki, who had been doing research on SL for three years—empowering different disenfranchised peoples (Stokrocki & Andrews, 2010)—introduced Wexler to SL[1] who introduced SL in her undergraduate course, *Disability Studies in Art Education.* She contacted iSkye Bonde, a mentor in SL who hosts meetings in her cottage where artists with disabilities introduce themselves and their work. Not knowing that Stokrocki and Wexler knew each other in RL, iSkye invited Stokrocki and Krecker to a meeting that she arranged for Wexler's class, which was an example of how SL quickly creates a community of educators with similar research aims. Stokrocki, Krecker, and Wexler were in attendance at iSkye's cottage along with preservice students and VAI artists. Several preservice students had mixed reactions to an unknown virtual territory with artists of unknown identities in RL. But they became more fluent in the program and thus more comfortable as the semester went on. In later semesters, however, undergraduates expressed greater discomfort while graduate students in online courses were more tolerant of the ambiguities of SL and adjusted fairly quickly. This phenomenon invited further questions about the educational effectiveness of SL for students at different levels of maturity.

Stokrocki invited Krecker, her doctoral student with a hearing disability, to join the research team. Krecker was aware of the advantages of using virtual worlds, such as SL, to communicate and learn. She felt distinctly equal in all her interactions in SL. Since thoughts are typically typed on the screen, the running script is visible and understandable. Once a newcomer learns how to control his or her avatar, communicate, and navigate in SL, the dichotomy of disability and normality disappears. Krecker initially set up interviews with three avatar participants. Three students in Wexler's course interviewed two participants, one of whom Krecker interviewed, and Stokrocki and Wexler conducted follow-up interviews. Protocol demanded that we seek participants' permission, and all four avatars allowed their SL names and general RL locations to be used in the study.[2] We sent all transcripts to them and they added or deleted information.

INTERVIEWS WITH AVATARS WITH DISABILITIES

> Sometimes our light goes out but is blown into flame by another human being. Each of us owes deepest thanks to those who have rekindled this light.
>
> (Albert Schweitzer, 1998)

Interview protocols evolved from the many questions that emerged during the initial class meeting with Virtual Ability artists. Stokrocki, Krecker, and Wexler met two artists, Ronin1 Shippe and Carla Broeck, at the meeting arranged by iSkye. Krecker chose to interview these participants because they had hearing impairments, and she found their unique stories compelling. Wexler interviewed Jadyn Firehawk and Levi Ewing. Three students in her class also interviewed Levi and Jadyn in SL, and one student interviewed Carla through e-mail.

RONIN1 SHIPPE

When Krecker met Ronin1 Shippe, he was standing in front of one of the six art galleries where he was showing his work. As they toured the galleries, he talked affably about many of the paintings, describing the stories and his motivations for painting them. One advantage of SL is that artists often show the same artworks in many galleries simultaneously.

A former musician, Ronin sustained a partial hearing loss due to loud music and "other noisy activities." He played the trumpet for more than 40 years, and as a student he was the lead trumpet player at the University of New Mexico's jazz band. He began his university career as a music major, but graduated with a degree in psychology and received a Master's degree in political science. He doesn't describe himself as a professional musician, but he says, "I have played professionally." After graduate school he became a reporter for the *Las Cruces Sun-News* in New Mexico, handling "the crime beat."

Ronin's hearing loss was progressive over several years. He noticed that he couldn't "hear on the phone and I would miss elements of sentences, certain words and sounds getting confused. And it was difficult to hear over background noise." Five years ago he began wearing a hearing aid. He made a quick adaption because "thankfully my hearing loss is not as pronounced as others."

Ronin lives in New Mexico and has been an artist—without formal training—in the real world, working with clay, wood, and metal sculptures. He began his work as an artist in SL about two years prior to our interview. "When I came to VAI I began to think that art might be a way to promote disability awareness and acceptance in SL, as well as promote the cause of VAI." Ronin is a conscientious promoter of his work, always willing to accommodate his viewers. He "paints" on his computer with Windows Paint program because it is a "simple" medium, one in which he can create large format work for no monetary outlay. His self-described work is "a combination of Zen minimalism and impressionism." A Zen painting "captures the essence of a moment in time" in a tradition that is "inexpressible." SL enables him to reach a global audience, and his multiple copies are visible all over the world for display in galleries or in private collections. He has given or sold his artwork to people in France, England, Germany, Australia, Saudi Arabia, the former Soviet Union, Spain, Mexico, Brazil, South Korea, China, and Israel. But Ronin humbly admits that "I'm not a 'technical artist' by any stretch of the imagination, certainly no Vermeer or Da Vinci...so I don't HAVE to be a technical painter. I just have to REACH people."

We started our tour at the Campus d'Arte on Schwanson Schlegel (http://slurl.com/secondlife/Schwanson%20Schlegel/119/160/22). He described this gallery exhibition as a good cross section of his work. As we went inside, we were presented with many large frameless "paintings" displayed tightly across the walls from floor to ceiling. Most noteworthy was *Lesser Wave off Kanagawa,* an image of a massive ocean wave overpowering a small boat. He described the painting as a deliberate "quote" of a famous Japanese woodcut. "I got to thinking that there were probably a lot of waves off Kanagawa."

We then teleported to another venue, called Crossroads Gallery on Lynto Land (http://maps.secondlife.com/secondlife/lynto%20land/50/50/21). We "rezzed" (avatars arrived) in front of the gallery owned by a Frenchwoman and her German partner. Inside we were again presented with images, many recognizable from the first gallery. Ronin lovingly showed us each painting, explaining their meanings. He described a series of three landscapes as a "timeless desert." He explained the inclusion of a delta-winged airplane flying through two panels as "technology sorta comes and goes." Also notable, was a painting of a stucco building with "Josefina's" inscribed above it. He painted it for a friend who "had wanted a painting of the same title that she saw in one of the local restaurants. But sadly, she delayed too long and it was sold . "So, I painted one. But she didn't like it." Ironically, a well-known designer and builder in SL called Sasha, saw the painting "and much to my surprise he said, 'How do YOU know about Josefina's?' You see, Sasha is based in Paris in RL, and it turns out that Josefina's is a rather famous little cantina on the French-Spanish border run by an 80-year-old granny who was active in the Spanish Civil War resistance in her youth." He was astonished, and sent a copy of this painting to be hung in that tavern in RL. "That's the great thing about SL.... A message in a bottle."

Two months after Krecker's interview, Wexler visited Ronin in his home in Cape Able, an affiliate of VAI, filled floor to ceiling with his favorite artists (Da Vinci's *Mona Lisa,* Vermeer's *Girl with a Peal Earring,* and Picasso's *Musicians*), sheet music (Bach's, *Goldberg Variations*), poetry (Ehrman's *Desiderada*), and historical icons (Martin Luther King and Mahatma Gandhi). Ronin's avatar is usually dressed in a suit and bow tie, and in this environment he easily took on the persona of the knowledgeable and well-versed critic. He said with an emoticon smile that the sheet music came with a harpsichord. "I like Bach." Wexler asked "And who else?" "Oh my, you . . . name it . . . Beethoven, John Coltrane, Charlie Parker, George Gershwin."

The rich influences of Ronin's RL displayed in his virtual home, as well as his political science degree, spawned a question about the neutral, primarily aesthetic, and nonpolitical nature of his work. After being asked if he thought about using a political message in his visual artwork, he said, "when so moved, sure," and uploaded *Welcome to Linden Labs,* "suggesting that Linden Labs shoots itself in the foot with their customer relations policies.... Light political humor." Ronin was referring to the recent change of SL policies that phased out their discounts to educational

Figure 8.1 *Welcome to Linden Lab*, Nana and Ronin, photo capture by Alice Wexler

and nonprofit sims. His canvas shows a single foot within the crosshairs of a gun (see figure 8.1).

CARLA BROEK

Carla Broek's story of her disability and her artwork are intertwined. She lives in Belgium, where she worked at an executive level for many years. In 2008, her first sign of illness was tinnitus, a severe and constant ear noise. Troubles began with sleep, work, and contact with the world. About two years before the interview she began experiencing bipolar tendencies, such as instability and uncontrollable impulses. She was treated with medication until a brain tumor situated directly in the emotional processing/regulation center was discovered. Needing surgery and unable to work, Carla created machinima from SL images. Machinima (machine/cinema) are created inside of real-time 3-D graphic-generated environments and shaped into aesthetic cinematography that often uses political or social content (Liao, as cited in Sweeny, 2010). This art form was particularly adaptable to Carla's need to "grasp complete dynamics of images and sounds.... A movie is able to express our human evolving thoughts and feelings. It comes closest to the core of what we are: people in a world moving on." She had no previous experience in art making other than taking "reasonably good pictures" in RL.

Once Carla discovered the people on VAI, they became a support team while she went through medical tests. At the time of our interview, she had been through six months of recovery. She was still, in her estimation, unable to live a "proper life." Although motor skills weren't damaged, unusual fluctuations of blood pressure, temperature, and outbreaks of infection occurred. She described these bodily feelings as invisible to the world, and practically untraceable for doctors. These experiences are also common for traumatic brain injury survivors, who are vulnerable to what is felt as extremes in sensory stimulation, such as in light and sound. She has been recovering, but very slowly over the course of the year. Her motivational and simple task-oriented thinking skills are also still in a state of recovery, and for her, they are the most problematic.

When she came out of surgery her external processes, such as interaction, were damaged by the tumor. She lost her memory of the preceding years, and in an e-mail she explained how memory has changed.

> It took me ages to discover that most of my life was erased. It must have been happening slowly while the tumor grew.... I have learned after a year that memories are difficult to recognize. I had moments that I thought I got my memories back, but without much reference, how could I ever know how much is lost. It comes in sudden shocks, but never is truly complete. I also learned that there is no such thing as one type of memory. I never lost any "experience" or "knowledge," but the context was gone, or incomplete, or changed. Without memory or reference to the past, I feel/felt very incomplete.
> (personal communication, June 28, 2011)

At the end of 2009 her body was giving up because she was losing the will to live. She couldn't sustain the effects that the tumor had on her body, and she went spiraling down,

> because at that time I was literally dying.... I didn't have a "life" outside of my room... I lived inside. My tumor didn't allow me to go further than the supermarket to get food and run back. SL kept me sane, because I could use my abilities that worked: frontal lobes (thinking), and verbal skills.

In addition to Carla's artwork, SL friends supported her before, during, and after surgery, and they "prevented me from doing stupid things. Some people with the same experience helped me convince doctors a surgery was needed regardless of risk, a 50 % chance of survival."

Throughout this ordeal, Carla lost friends, her career, and her personality. The people she met through SL helped her survive. She bought a plane ticket to the United States so that she could give a friend a RL hug. "So that's more or less SL for me."

Carla's machinima are video expressions of her feelings at the moment, recognizing later that each were made during a severe period of illness.

> The ability to express ad hoc feelings, elements of the past or hope for the future, is far more satisfying when making a movie about it ... by expressing myself through movies towards others, no words are needed. The feedback mechanism of others is a major element in keeping or building self-esteem, security, and acceptance.

An SL island called Owl's Bay inspired her first project, *Owls Flight*. With her Owl avatar, she became the actor, filmmaker, and editor. After a few movies, mostly related to music and impressions of the virtual world, she filmed it in one shot with only a mouse and keys. In 2009, she put her avatar in a wheelchair and made *Sorrow and Hope,* intending to portray how "consciousness of poverty matters through a world that deals only with money." A critic saw the machinima on the Internet and asked Carla if she would present it at a film festival in Brazil. She later received an award —a few days before she removed all her work from the Internet.

A second machinima, *Lights On_* (see figure 8.2), showed her hope for a renewed life: "It was made during times of emotional explosions." It depicts images of a vortex of colors with a musical heart beat.

Figure 8.2   Carla Broek, 2009. *Lights On_*. Machinima, photo capture by Carla Broek

Without training, Carla learned by doing. She made *Lights On_* with no preparation, in what she describes as a "linear" method.

> The linear method started with an idea: film, seeking music, seeking film... all put together in a linear way. I had a feeling about the whole picture. But the movies I created in one sequence, from the first to the last second, as if expression gets void while being expressed, moving on to the next piece, the next challenge, the next evolution...
> (personal communication, June 28, 2011)

Sunshine, is a remembrance of a family member.. Afraid that she would not survive surgery, she later called it her "closure movie." She is now unable to make such complex work.. At the time of our interview, Carla was rebuilding her life and continuing to work on other projects in SL.

LEVI EWING

Wexler met Levi Ewing[3] when she was invited to speak about Outsider Art at a Virtual Ability Island gathering in January 2011. He caught her attention during the discussion with provocative but unassuming one-liners such as, "When is art considered to be art?" Until that moment, Levi was writing fragmented and cryptic texts. Only later did she discover that he was from the Netherlands and English was his second language and, as he says, his mind is too fast for his fingers. Another disarming statement was, "autistic people are smart." A complex discussion followed about the autistic artist Jonathan Lehrman, and how he defies assumptions about autism with his highly expressive representations of faces. Representation of facial expressions is unusual for people on the autism spectrum because, for them, faces change mysteriously and are therefore difficult to understand. Objects are much more predictable and they are usually preferred as subjects of art. Levi suggested that "Maybe he just tells us what he sees." And later, "He sees people staring... blabbering at him." The discussion moved on to autistic savants with their hyper talents in one area, typically the arts, and lack of abilities in socialization and communication. Levi bypassed the theoretical discussion of the group and went to the heart of the young man's passionate needs. He insightfully said, "They have no energy left for the rest." Referring to the savant Stephen Wiltshire, who is regularly challenged to draw panoramas of cities within a limited time frame, Levi offered that Stephen "thinks in video."

Only a short time before the interview, Levi discovered that he had Asperger's syndrome (AS), the "higher functioning" end of the autism spectrum. He had a hunch about it and so he was encouraged by Gentle

Heron to be tested. Levi describes the results as "complicated" because he is hyper active without having attention deficit hyperactivity disorder. But typical of AS, he is strong in analysis and below average in interpersonal skills.

Levi is an engaging and divergent thinker and maker. He taught himself with the help of SL tutorials to create Faberge eggs with SL building tools, prims (primitive shapes, such as cubes, cones, and so on) and textures (add-on image files or personally uploaded). Building in SL has indeed given him confidence. Although reluctant to call what he does art (he says he leaves that for others to judge), they are stunning examples of fabrications that he admitted were considered extremely detailed by SL builders.

He enters and, ever so often, wins contests in SL based on themes such as "Bubbles" and "Birds of a Feather Stay Together." In the latter contest, he was only allowed to use elements without textures. In the former he won the competition based on speed,[4] completing the project within 40 minutes (see figure 8.3). But the Faberge eggs are what he calls his own. His intentions and decisions about making such objects as Faberge eggs do not come from the kind of evolution that many consider to be part of the traditional process of art making. When asked "why Faberge eggs?" he stated, "I'm pretty random. To be honest, I thought it would be cool to do." Levi had never seen a Faberge egg except in books, and he has studied them on Wikipedia in which he learned that there are only 50 Imperial Easter eggs in the world and that they were made for Russian Tsars.

Figure 8.3 *Bubbles*, Levi, and Nana, photo capture by Alice Wexler

One could argue that building in SL might be the most ideal setting for an artist with AS. He self-admittedly says that he does not "have to interpret faces in SL." He can be "in the moment, nowhere else . . . no one slowing me down, I can be me. I just look at what I build, 'cam' around it, zoom in and out from all angles, and see if it feels right." Not only can he focus, if needed, for nine hours at a time without the interruption or distraction of real people, but he can also simulate any object in the world that captures his attention. The tools, which are at once phantom-like and highly technological, are a perfect contradiction for a mind that requires that its unique imagination be put to use. Levi, similar to Stephen Wiltshire, with whom he appeared to intuitively engage, also thinks in something akin to video in the visceral way that he perceives time and space In an e-mail he agreed that

> Yes I have videos and pictures in my head which I use to remember things as visual clues. I can wind back "the mental video." I seem to make them with most conversations I have. In that way I can "think back" where I was sitting, the two people that interviewed me, the fact that two other avatars came along and one of them built his own avatar . . . then I remember what is being said. So yes you could argue that a 3D visual environment in SL, with its abstraction levels from real life (with either no or clear facial expressions) helps a visually based memory a lot.
> (personal communication, June 25, 2011)

Levi has a rich inventory varying widely from tiny castles on jewelry to opulent Roman villas with oversized doors, window, atriums, and interior waterfalls. He says that these oversized dimensions "give the rooms air."

> In SL the dimensions need to be about 1.2 to 1.5 times the scale of real life as the camera hovers behind and at a higher height than the avatar's eyes. So you need to build with that factor to compensate for not looking through the eyes, and on the eye-level of the avatar. Although people in SL can use "mouse-look views" hardly anyone uses that. Also, quite a few avatars have heights of 2.20 meters.
> (personal communication, June 25, 2011)

There are grand homes in SL, such as the castle owned and built by Leon Tubrok Beaumont, iSkye's partner. But while Leon's castle is filled with the kind of opulence that one would expect, Levi creates elegance with his judicious choice of materials and the illusion of grandeur through scale.

What was omitted while chatting was kept in notecards sent during the interview. In them was an explanation of how the villa was built sustainably, according to LEED's (Leadership in Energy and Environmental

Design) requirements. An impressive dimension was now brought to the building. Also in these notecards Levi apologizes for his fragmented sentences and explains that he is dyslexic, which was not revealed in the interview.

Levi seems unfazed that these extraordinary models remain unused in his inventory, although he says that SL friends encourage him to be more commercial. He has a shop where he sells work with his brand called *LeviMade,* but "it's in the middle of nowhere." He is satisfied to "build what I feel and how I feel about it." But when pressed about those feelings he circumvents the question, which is easier to do in SL than face-to-face in RL. His comment later in an e-mail was quite articulate.

> For me it is as hard in RL as in SL to specify [the reasons]. It's not that I don't want to talk about it, but it's extremely difficult for me to express exactly what my feelings are mostly because I probably never thought much about them. I probably work far more in direct emotional response levels: that something just feels OK. It starts looking OK without ever defining what OK is. Probably because it's not my strongest point to put my direct emotional responses into a framework of feelings, or the emotional layers which are definitely less present in people with Asperger's than with "normal" people, let alone being able to express those kind of levels. I build often not knowing where I will end. Sometimes a picture starts growing in my head, then I go for it. Sometimes I have an idea, "oh it would be cool to make...this or that...and then I just fiddle along until I have what I want, not having scheduled anything at all."
> (personal communication, June 25, 2011)

In RL, Levi studied industrial design in school, but did not choose building as a career. He says that he has "all these ideas and I could not make good models or draw them." But in SL this is not an obstacle. "People tell me I have a good eye for dimensions, so SL has made me more secure in that aspect." Others tell him that he does "things differently artistically." Currently, he is a publishing editor, but he is evasive about talking about his life, not uncommon for inhabitants of SL, so little else is known about it.

JADYN FIREHAWK

In RL Jadyn was a professor of geography and environmental studies, specializing in parks and reserves. Her first tenure-track position was in a teaching university. Before being granted tenure, however, in 2001 she chose to relocate to a research university. It was shortly after that she was diagnosed with bipolar and post traumatic stress disorder (PTSD).

> I definitely knew I had clinical depression episodically for most of my life. I also had "high" periods that I never recognized as hypomania until later when I was diagnosed. I think I can even rattle off for you the ages that I was when I went through each of the depressive episodes. I didn't have full-blown manias though until I was in my late 30s.

The expectations of the research university, such as book writing, proposing research grants, and so on, exacerbated what she now knows always existed in her life. Stressful life events, she says, or the building of them, is always the manifest cause "that triggers what the psychiatrists call a 'decompensation,' otherwise known as a breakdown." She was soon hospitalized, took a sick leave, and then never went back to the university. She returned to teaching as an adjunct several years later, which she sorely missed, but was fired because of her absences caused by bouts of depression. She is currently on seven medications that fatigue her, and therefore working outside of her home is not possible at the moment. Thus, building and teaching in SL suits her needs.

Between 2001and 2005 Jadyn was "largely just at home, being inactive. In 2005 we found a good combination of medications." She was able to work part time as an adjunct, at first 20 hours a week, and a year later, 30 hours a week. "But by 2009 my condition started to deteriorate and in January 2010 I was fired from my job, and now I'm back on Disability" Her hospitalization as a result of depression was the eighth in ten years.

During the active time in 2006 she bought her first digital camera and became a "self-taught" landscape photographer, at first as a hobby and for her own enjoyment. "Then I started posting my photos on Flickr and that's when I realized that my photos were actually good...It gave me something positive to focus on, and when I started taking photos my therapist was pleased." In those days Jadyn had a wise therapist who tragically committed suicide after the death of her only child. She helped Jadyn to see how making art changed her "inner thinking to outer sensing." Making art neutralized her depression by creating a positive feedback loop through her senses, rather than the cognitive self-effacement caused by bipolarism. "Depression has a strong cognitive component: negative thinking creates and feeds negative moods, depressed moods and anxiety." Jadyn explained that an effective technique, called *grounding* diminishes anxiety with the awareness of one's surroundings: focusing and naming what is seen, felt, and heard.

> Photography is a form of visually sensing the world...so it is in itself a type of grounding exercise. When I focus on seeing, I am thinking less, or

rather; I am thinking about the shot rather than ruminating about negative or fearful things.

During her decline in 2009, Jadyn's activity on Flickr serendipitously led her to SL. VAI was one of the points of entry. Even though she is on Disability once again, she sees a great difference now since finding SL. "This time I'm engaged in the outside world, creating, feeling useful, feeling productive." She quickly learned to upload her photographs and bought a gallery at Las Lagunas, which she fills with her work. She oversees another gallery for artists with disabilities, the well-known Pixel Gallery on Atropolis Island, in a space donated to the Pixel to Pixel Foundation.

Like many artists who work almost exclusively in SL, opportunities arise to exhibit work in RL. In 2010 a curator visited Jadyn's gallery and invited her to exhibit in the Treeline Gallery in Australia, which was simultaneously run in RL and SL. "It vastly encouraged me as an artist ... as well as helped me transform my identity into that of an artist more so now than that of an academic.... I have it in the back of my mind now to submit my photography to RL shows now."

Other than doing errands once a week, she is generally housebound. Unable to take photographs, she turned to building and sculpture in SL. Her interest in building reflects her research and teaching in geography in which she replicates American historical homes, or vernacular architecture, for display or sale. Her sculptures are currently on a building platform next to her replica of a 1910 Craftsman home that she built for the Museum of Architecture. A sculpture called *Cityscape* is a tribute to architecture, *Earth and Mantle* and *Mothership* (the latter was her first sculpture) were submitted to the University of Western Australia design contest. *Surprising Pyramid* is interactive in the sense that an avatar may walk through it and become integrated into the sculpture. By far her floating sculptures are the most innovative, and indeed one was titled *Innovation*. At the end of the interview Jadyn said, "Prims are my new medium! I love 3D more than 2D." Clearly working in 3D would not be an option for her in RL, an example of the fortuitous nature of this virtual world full of possibility.

Conclusions and Implications

Returning to the original research question, what meaningful art and communication patterns might emerge in interviews with artists with disabilities in SL, we found several examples based on our interview questions discussed in the following sections.

Why Do Artists with Disabilities Make Art Here?

Through Virtual Ability Inc. and its mentors, art making helps heal sadness and builds abilities (Stokrocki, 2010). Additionally, some of the building techniques and art forms, such as machinima, are less time intensive and costly in a virtual world than in RL, and can also be widely seen. Carla explains, "Second Life environments can be easily 'modified' to present the concepts of a movie. Also, the ease of moving through the SL world while filming is not achievable without huge investments in RL." Jadyn Firehawk says flatly that she makes art in SL because materials are free (relatively).

Jadyn made a critical observation that her identity was transformed from an academic to an artist. In her interview she stated half jokingly that she kept going to school until there was nowhere left to go. Her knowledge of her field was embedded in research rather than experience. But more importantly, she was saddled with the identity of a bipolar woman who could no longer work in her field. Finding photography was helpful in making the transition from an academic to a woman with a disability, and finally to an artist. It is plausible, however, that she might have remained a woman with a disability if she did not find a sustainable way to make art. SL seems to have served this purpose for artists who are physically frail or with chronic illnesses.

A discussion of identity in SL, however, is far more layered and complex. The addition of the avatar as simulacrum must also be part of this equation. Liao (2010) describes avatars as connecting "body representations with notions of identity in both straightforward and complex ways. Body representation is the visual means of presenting identity online" (p. 183). But it is not solely of the body, she says, but rather in cyberspace an avatar is the location of self-definition and contestation. It is beyond the scope of this chapter to probe the implications of social acceptance via beauty, age, gender, and ethnicity. And indeed, most avatars in VAI appear to be young and beautiful. However, the mission of the community is always apparent to its members and guests: to encourage people with a wide range of disabilities to thrive in a virtual world.

What Art Do They Make?

Interviewees represented a variety of artistic styles: digital painting, film, and building. The interviewees learned how to successfully make art in this arena in different ways. Ronin makes art outside of SL; Levi, and Jadyn make art entirely in SL; and Carla uses SL as the subjects of her art, downloading images for use in her machinima.

While Levi does not want to assume the identity of an artist, he was willing to call what he built "art" for the interview. In addition, his highly professional and sustainable buildings lead the interviewer to believe that Levi is selective about what he will reveal both personally and professionally. Instead, he is self-effacing in interviews. For example, he says, "I just build what's in my head. In RL I don't do art or construction but SL gives me a chance to visualize those ideas." When asked if it was because it was easier, quicker, or more satisfying to build in SL, Levi said, "there are practically no limits in SL, as in gluing, or constructing solidity. You can let stuff float if you like. That's easier than in RL I think."

Jaydyn reformatted her life for her sedentary existence. However, although this transformation was made out of necessity, her excitement about what she is doing is irrepressible. It's not possible to conclude whether or not she is happier as an artist rather than an academic, but she is contributing, as she says, to the world, both in the virtual and the real.

What Communication Patterns Emerged?

While there are some basic generalities that can be inferred in the communication patterns of these artists, their concluding messages are different. Artists have long drawn from their unconscious for inspiration and it is through this unconscious that onlookers get a glimpse of the artist (Naumburg, 1955). Carla, who felt that her friends and experiences in SL saved her life, communicated longings, love and a yearning for "normalcy". She uses color to communicate the fullness of her sensory memory of experience. "Strong warm earth colors represent touch-down contact with reality, fire, hope, power." She didn't consciously choose colors, and she had "no master plan." Ronin used painting to discourse about creativity, reconciling his loss of hearing. Each sought to be heard in various ways through artmaking. As described above, Levi finds that texting in SL through his avatar allows him to talk "face-to-face" without the frustration of interpreting facial expressions. SL is also helpful in facilitating communication and sustaining interaction. Typical of Asperger's syndrome, he says he doesn't have patience for people who live and act from their emotions. He describes his ability to analyze "to the extreme" compensates for his lack of interest or skills in socialization. "Chit chat I find hard to deal with." When at work in SL he says, "I don't have to explain myself as to why...how...or what. I can do what I feel, what I think is right".

What Themes Emerged?

Themes that appeared were expressive and essential, such as collaboration and hope. Collaboration is the key to success by developing social concerns, such as tolerance of different abilities. Art educator Lilly Lu, assistant professor of art education at Northern Illinois University with a background in instructional technology, exemplified collaborative teaching with her students on the SL Art Café site, funded by a National Art Education Association Foundation Grant. Lu (2010) discovered examples, based on Miller's (2004), a pioneer in new media, interactive types. Borrowing her categories, we found evidence of interacting with objects (making digital art, machinima, and architecture), interacting with content information (sending artwork, photographs, and hopeful messages), and communicating with visitors (in class and on tours, text chats, instant messages, avatar gestures, and e-mail). Avatars can also make art together (build and perform). SL transforms users into active collaborators, and Virtual Ability personifies this interactivity through our final themes.

Sharing of resources is also a common thread that emerged. Although we are not aware of the economic status of all the artists, most have disabilities that prevent them from working long hours, such as Jadyn and Carla. Much of Levi's materials are given to him, and gallery spaces are often free, sponsored by their owners, or in exchange for work in VAI.

Implications for Education

SL has proved for these avatars that learning can be personalized in an environment in this context. In their qualitative pilot study, similarly, Andrews, Stokrocki, Jannasch-Pennell, and DiGangi (2010) reported on their curriculum field trials, called *Transitions: A Place for Dreams* within a personal learning environment (PLE) designed by a collaboration of academic researchers and nonprofit volunteers working together in the virtual world of SL. The purpose of the PLE is to provide learners (18 and over) less likely to have access to educational opportunities with a means to create a "new life" in the real world, through a basic web-based curriculum and an advanced SL curriculum.

Similar to our research study, participants engage in introductory and exploratory exercises: orientation, avatar creation, and individualized exploration of the environment, culminating in art an exhibition in a gallery or architectural construction. They learn basic content creation, including simple scripting (program codes—language that gives behavior to *Second Life* primitives, objects, and avatars), uploading artwork or machinima, and building prims. In the part of the program called *Dreaming a future,* avatars designed or rented a home or "hang-out," and planned a simple virtual business, such as a gallery artist, VAI coordinator/mentor, and/or filmmaker. Participants selected the available areas to be mentored, and business ethics and small business practices were learned. Finally, the participants created posters advertising their businesses.

It was also important to give back to the project by mentoring new participants, suggesting improvements for the project, and creating an action plan that would target larger issues, such as stereotypes, loss of political identity, security and seeking funding opportunities. Although SL closed Teen SL for economic reasons, VAI is considering mentoring teen interns at 16 years of age. Some schools are renting and starting their own closed virtual islands.

Therefore, such a PLE can be profitable, emotionally and even financially, for those with diverse abilities and interests. The participatory learning environment with available mentoring is a key ingredient. Such guidelines meet the challenges of artists with disabilities for entry into participatory culture, the new media education for the twenty-first century (Jenkins, Purushotma, Clinton, Weigel, & Robison, 2006).

Final Thoughts

> Computers embody postmodern theory and bring it down to earth.
> (Turkle, 1997, p. 18)

Returning to the medical versus social models of disability introduced at the start of the chapter, Carr (2010) suggests that educators be aware of how research frames the dialogue in unconscious ways. Typically, Carr says, disability is conceptualized as an individual problem, impairment, or deficit, and tools and technology as the solution. Our aim in employing narratives is to override unconscious tendencies to normalize or exclude certain identities and to destabilize the researcher-as-expert model. Narratives explore individual experiences rather than representative samples or generalizations.

In the last few decades disability has become a subject of study comparable in critique and analysis to ethnicity, gender, and sexuality in its lived and constructed realities. Along with these social and political disciplines, disability is now finding its significance in first person, experiential knowing. How do people within the label of disability contribute to this conversation? asks Jim Swan (2002). How do they compare to other silenced groups now finding their own voices? "The answer, I think, is the particular viewpoint that disability studies brings to an understanding of the body—an understanding that writing is not only *about* the body but *of* and *from* the body too" (p. 284, italics in the original). This embodied view of the world, from and of the body, is changing how we think and talk about disability (Wexler, 2011).

Thus, our aim in SL research was to avoid replicating entrenched conceptions about disability that might be carried into virtual worlds. Avatars, as bodily projections of human identities added another layer of the embodiment theory. Meadows (2008), having lived a full second life in the early days of the program, ruminates how deeply woven one's own identity is with the avatar's. Avatars may just be pixels (tiny points that compose an electronic image), but we act as if they are human, bridging the gap between real and virtual. "And oddly, the driver [a real life individual] can also look into himself, as if gazing into his navel, and find a new landscape inside as well.... Somehow my invented self was becoming a part of my real self, as if I'd somehow caused a dream to breathe" (pp. 8, 12).

Meadows also suggests that avatars enable their "drivers" to become more intensely emotional because of a built-in safety feature that at once protects and circumscribes their relationships. But as in RL, the interaction between the researchers' RL identities and the authors' avatars became less artificial as we developed relationships. As discussed briefly, the interviewees' willingness to share their real lives were diverse, but none were limited in their richness, each relationship having its own authentic quality. Each of the authors immersed herself in SL, becoming the student on many occasions by learning from the interviewees how to build, upload images, create power points, and so on. Thus, interaction between researcher and informant was not unidirectional, but mutually beneficial and enriching. Meadows calls this mutual and equalizing experience a *grounding of belief*, which "is all based on the fact that we are sharing a narrative. It is all based on the notion that if I see something and someone else sees the same thing there is a 'grounding of belief'" (p. 51). Avatars, Meadows believes, also build the longed for community, the smaller assembly of people who we care about and who care about us.

NOTES

1. As an undergraduate alumnus from SUNY New Paltz, Stokrocki often visited Wexler. Stokrocki's parents who lived nearby.
2. Linda Krecker saved the original transcripts of the interviews with permissions from the interviewees.

3. Grammar and spelling in Levi's personal communication has been corrected for the sake of understandability, but the content has not been changed.
4. Speed builds are building contests in which avatars interpret the theme.

REFERENCES

Andrews, S. S., Stokrocki, M., Jannasch-Pennell, A., & DiGangi, S. A. (2010). The development of a personal learning environment using *Second Life*. *Journal of Virtual Worlds Research,* 1(3), 36–54.

Boulos, M. N. K., Hetherington, L., & Wheeler, S. (2007). Second Life: An overview of the potential of 3-D virtual worlds in medical and health education. *Health Information & Libraries Journal,* 24, 233–245. Retrieved May 14, 2011 from http://onlinelibrary.wiley.com/doi/10.1111/j.1471-1842.2007.00733.x/full.

Carbaugh, D., & Buzzanell, P. (Eds.). (2010). *Distinctive qualities in communication research.* New York: Routledge.

Carr, D. (2010). *Constructing disability/Deaf in SL.* Retrieved May 12, 2011 from http://learningfromsocialworlds.wordpress.com/social-worlds-and-mmorpg-research/.

Chorost, M. (2005). *Rebuilt: How becoming part computer made me more human.* New York: Houghton Mifflin.

Davis, L. J. (1995). *Enforcing normalcy: Disability, deafness and the body.* London: Verso.

Derby, J. (2011). Disability studies and art education. *Studies in Art Education: A Journal of Issues and Research,* 52(2), 94–111.

Deuze, M. (2006). Participation, remediation, bricolage: Considering principal components of a digital culture. *The Information Society,* 22(2), 63–75.

Dumoulin, H. (2005). *Zen Buddhism: A history,* Vol. 2 Japan (Trans. J. Heisig & P. Knitter). Bloomington, IN: World Wisdom Inc.

Glaser, B. & Strauss, A. (1967). *The discovery of grounded theory.* Chicago, IL: Aldine.

Hymes, D. (1974). *Foundations in sociolinguistics. An ethnographic approach.* Philadelphia, PA: University of Pennsylvania Press.

Jenkins, H., Purushotma, R., Clinton, K., Weigel, M., & Robison, A. (2006). *Confronting the challenges of participatory culture: Media education for the 21st century.* Chicago, IL: The John D. and Catherine T. MacArthur Foundation, Digital Media and Learning Initiative. Retrieved July 1, 2009 from http://www.newmedialiteracies.org.

Kvale, S. (1996). *Interviews: An introduction to qualitative research interviewing.* Thousand Oaks, CA: Sage

Lane, H. (1999). *The mask of benevolence: Disabling the deaf community.* New York: Alfred Knopf.

Liao L. C. (2010). Avatar as pedagogy: Critical strategies for visual culture in the virtual environment. In R. W. Sweeny (Ed.), *Interactions/intersections: Art education in a digital visual culture* (pp. 182–196). Reston, VA: National Art Education Association.

Lu, L. (2010). Demystifying three-dimensional virtual worlds for art education. *International Society for Education Through Art*, 3(3), 279–292.

Meadows, M. S. (2008). *I, avatar: The culture and consequences of having a second life*. Berkeley, CA: New Riders Press.

Michels, P. (2008). Universities use Second Life to teach complex concepts. *Government technology*. Retrieved May 14, 2011 from http://www.govtech.com/education/Universities-Use-Second-Life-to-Teach.html.

Miller, C. H. (2004). *Digital storytelling: A creator's guide to interactive entertainment*. Boston: Elsevier, Focal Press.

Naumburg, M. (1955). Art as symbolic speech. *The Journal of Aesthetics and Art Criticism*, 13(4), 435–450.

Ondrejka, C. (2008). Education unleashed: Participatory culture, education, and innovation in second life. In K. Salen (Ed.), *The ecology of games: Connecting youth, games and learning*. Cambridge, MA: MIT Press.

Robbins, S. & Bell, M. (2008). *Second Life for dummies*. Hoboken, NJ: Wiley Publishers.

Sass, E. (2010, July 29). Second life chugs along. *The Social Graf: Connecting through the Chaos*. Retrieved May 14, 2011 from http://www.mediapost.com/publications/?fa=Articles.showArticle&art_aid=132912.

Schweitzer, A. (1998). *Out of my life and thought*. Baltimore, MD: The Johns Hopkins University Press.

Second Life. (2011, April). Wikipedia. Retrieved May 2, 2011 from http://en.wikipedia.org/wiki/Second_Life.

Stokrocki, M. (1997). Qualitative forms of research methods. In S. D. La Pierre, & E. Zimmerman (Eds.), *Research methods and methodologies for art education* (pp. 33–56). Reston, VA: NAEA.

Stokrocki, M. (2010, May). Art & spirituality on Second Life: A participant observation and digital phenomenological quest. *Journal of Alternative Perspectives in the Social Sciences*, 182–197. Retrieved PDF, June 24, 2010 from http://www.japss.org/japssmay2010.html. Scroll through to find this article with pictures.

Stokrocki, M. (in press). Digital ethnography: Art education qualitative research in virtual worlds. In K. Miraglia & C. Smilan (Eds.), *Inquiry in action: Paradigms, methodologies and perspectives in art education research*. Reston, VA: NAEA

Stokrocki, M. & Andrews, S. (2010). Empowering the disenfranchised through explorations in Second Life. In R. W. Sweeny (Ed.), *Digital visual culture: Intersections and interactions in 21st century art education* (pp. 197–209). Reston, VA: National Art Education Association.

Swan, J. (2002). Disabilities, bodies, voices. In S. L. Synder, B. Brueggemann, & R. Garland-Thomas (Eds.), *Disability studies: Enabling the humanities* (pp. 283–295). New York: The Modern Language Association of America.

Turkle, S. (1997). *Life on the screen: Identity in the age of the Internet.* New York: Touchstone.
Wesch, M. (2007). *Digital ethnography class blog.* Retrieved June 6, 2009 from http://mediatedcultures.net/ksudigg/?p=119.
Wexler, A. (2011). The siege of the cultural city is underway: Children with developmental disabilities make art. *Studies in Art Education*, 53(1), 53–70.
Yin, R. (2003). *Case study research: Design and methods* (3rd ed.). Thousand Oaks, CA: Sage.

CHAPTER 9

Outside the Outside: In the Realms of the *Real* (Hogancamp, Johnston, and Darger)

Jan Jagodzinski

Dilemma of Difference

It is best to start out wondering if there is such a phenomenon as "Outsider Art" in the contemporary *Zeitgeist* where the gallery and museum system immediately tries to capture the new, different, transgressive, and innovative art forms that exist on the "outside," then to be recognized and introduced to a public. Outsider Art suggests exclusion, or a nonrecognition in relation to an inside that is authoritative, hegemonic, and "normative." That is certainly one understanding within an obvious binary that maintains segregation; the social field is territorialized by a fundamental distinction of identity: "one of us" or not "one of us." The institution of art might parade itself as being rather democratic and liberal in this regard in the way it attempts to embrace the "outsider," always letting in what is excluded and thereby broadening the pooled aesthetic. As an institution, it might fulfill the political requirements, which Jacques Rancière (2010) desires: that part which does not belong to the whole is given its equal and just say. In this account, historically the institution of the art gallery has *perverted* the *arbitrariness* of the law,[1] existing outside the official Royal academies, a bourgeois institution that sanctions critique and the new.

This is one way of looking at it.

Another way suggests that such an institution, which sanctions "difference" within the hegemony of the "same," is also vampiric; always in search for fresh blood to display, consume, and sell, like the paradigmatic example of Benetton advertisements. Like capitalism itself, the gallery institution is a vampiric desiring machine, which needs constant critique to feed the blood that it needs; that is, negativity as critique must exist so that it can sustain itself. What draws people into galleries and buyers is controversy, as the performances, installations, and actual objects of art take on a spectatorial aura once "inside," in good Duchampian manner. Its "effects" are brought into the gallery no matter how far physically they may be removed through photographic documentation of earth art, like Smithson's *Spiral Jetty*, or even logged in like Mark Dion's installation, *Neukom Vivarium*, which consists of an actual tree that had fallen in the forest near Seattle. Can the same accusation be made against such galleries as Intuit: The Center for Intuitive and Outsider Art (Chicago), which specializes in what has become a genre? They have their own published magazine, *The Outsider*. Begun in 1992, it has a worldwide circulation of an estimated 8,000.

The dilemma stated above is that of madness itself in the way Reason (the frame of the gallery network) is able to hospice, hospitalize, and host radical difference or alterity. Derrida (2002) coined the term "hostipitality" to point out the ambivalence inherent within hospitality itself as it refers to both guest and enemy. Hospitality is preceded by a necessary hostility and violence of appropriation of space as home. The space is already territorialized so that the "outside" can be welcomed in. There is always a trace of enmity. The fangs can always come out, so to speak. One can say that the gallery system (like Freud) is a "doorman," rather than an outright agent of the law, which does not police the threshold between Reason/madness (inside/outside) as much as it welcomes the "outsider" in; an institution that appears to do justice to madness by being hospitable to it.[2] However, it is this constant territorialization and deterritorialization that keeps it in business.

What is troubling is that "authority," or the law, is continually perverted by the networked gallery system globally. Its hospitality to radical subject positions (for instance, the controversy of Mapplethorpe's photographs back in the 70s as an obvious example) has led to a rather strange situation: a collapse of the inside|outside throughout the globalized capitalist system of the art network where the center and right political agenda have co-opted the moral ground held by the "New Left",[3] the ideas championed by antiracist, feminist, ecological, and gay rights movements to present a conceptual stasis or inertia as to just what *is* a "radical subject"; what *is* an "outsider" in contemporary art, now that there has been a dissipation of social critique throughout the system. As a number of commentators have pointed out, the identity politics of the New Left has become hegemonic, absorbed by right-wing conservatism to further neoliberal agendas (Pitcher, 2009, 2011). Feminism has been harnessed for nationalistic, racialized, and imperialistic agendas in the War on Terror (Riley et al., 2008), as has "homonormative" to make a dividing line between the liberal West and backward Islam (Puar, 2007). Green politics has been absorbed by green consumerism and capitalism, and the antiracist agenda is managed through cultural relativism and forms of multicultural exoticism and identity politics, especially in the arts. The trajectory of 1990s "critical art" has become the norm. So what is "Outsider Art" now?

Foucault, in his groundbreaking book, *The History of Madness* (1973), identified certain "mad" poets, artists, and philosophers, such as Nietzsche, Artaud, Van Gogh, Nerval, and Hölderlin, as transgressors, escapees, outcasts, and drifters. They inhabited a border zone between *epistemes;* they had messianic, visionary aspects to them, heralding a coming episteme, and therefore forming an avant-garde, certainly "outside" the given establishment. This situation has drastically changed, as the clamor of anyone whose voice is not recognized becomes news. Folk art and naïve art (what was pejoratively once called primitive art) have been comfortably accommodated into the gallery system, as has women's art, African American art, and so on. The institution of art has become a "dealer" in social justice, wherein the moral agenda of the New Left has been betrayed by a neoliberalist agenda that has cleverly co-opted what were forms of radical subjectivity into various forms of liberatory transformations based on democratic liberalism within global designer capitalism that is able to manage difference. What was once considered "outside" becomes consumed as quickly as possible in the name of equality and justice, the distribution of power remains unchanged. Walter Ben Michael's (2006) paradigmatic study on the way diversity is politically managed to simply reproduce the current system of inequality in the United States is a case in point.

In many respects I have so far been addressing the juridicial determination of madness with the category called "art" being defined and shaped institutionally by the bourgeois system of the gallery network that established itself in the late nineteenth century. As an institution it did carve out a space where social experimentation as critique could take place—perhaps exemplified by the aesthetic theories of Adorno. My point is that this is no longer the case—critique becomes more empty as the social justice agenda itself becomes hegemonic within the confines of liberalist democracies, confirming perhaps that the moral aspirations of the bourgeoisie have been affirmed. Democratic pluralism is the resultant betrayal of the aspirations of the radical left as managed by the discourses of liberal global capitalism. Foucault's "history of madness," which was objected to by Derrida (1978) on the grounds that there can only be a history of Reason's account of its Other, caused a rift between them for many years. His objection was directed to the institutionalization of madness and had less to do with the "medical" or thought processes of madness. Judicial madness has more to do with justice and the law in relation to identity politics than to the psychic states of madness. It is here, perhaps that we might identify such a politics of representation as the limit of "Outsider Art" as it is defined within the binary oppositions between left and right politics (that is representational politics), which itself is premised on the categorizations that emerge from a difference/same binary that can accommodate the paradoxes arising from the boundary conditions of the inside and outside.

To consider "Outsider Art" that escapes representation is to rethink such art from a nonrepresentational tradition where particular theorizations based on schizoanalysis rather than psychoanalysis are called for. The claim will be made that with such "Outsider" artists, what is required is the radical way that their "schizo" status is able reveal the hegemonically established affective patterns of the social order within what I call designer capitalism (jagodzinski, 2010). While such artists are eventually embraced by the gallery system as well, their perceptions of the social order are never entirely subsumed but remain as "enigmatic signifiers," as theorized by Jean Laplanche (1989). They present the untranslatable excess that continually escapes meaning as such, the hermeneutic question of interpretation. Laplanche in this respect is closer to Deleuze and Guattari's schizoanalysis than Lacanian psychoanalysis in his attention to the signifying aspects of transferencial seduction, the gestures and affective significations that defy the signifier. These constitute the enigma itself where the *materiality of the body is to be found.* "Outsider" artists are like infants (in-fans, without speech) in that they are unable to assimilate the social world, constantly trying to make sense of it by establishing their own imaginary world through art—as an exteriorization of their unconscious *via matter as assembled with their bodies.* In this respect, rather than claiming that "the outside is the inside," as Derrida does in *Of Grammatology* (1976, p. 44), along with his further claim that *"there is nothing outside the text [il n'y a pas de hors-texte]* ... there has never been anything but writing ... that what opens meaning and language is writing as the disappearance of natural presence" (pp. 158, 159). Every opposite is being proposed here: *the inside is the outside with Outsider artists.* This "inside" has everything to do with the body's materiality, cancelling out the preferred stance of psychoanalysis, which posits the "always already" (an absent present) and Freudian logic of *Nachträglichkeit* that privileges the nonsense signifier.

These "artists" are not psychotic as Lacanian psychoanalysis would have it, where the Law of the Father has been barred. Rather, they are schizophrenic, unable to construct an interhuman world.[4] They externalize what they find "alien" on the outside (the chaos of lived popular culture) to make sense of it on their own terms. We are drawn to these schizo "Outsider" artists simply because of their ability to translate and create an Alice-like "wonderland" of their own making. They are "Outsiders" only in the sense that we, as sociologized human beings caught by signification (representation), are not able to operate at this pre-symbolic realm as we once did as infants, when we struggled to make sense of the world through the symbolism that language offers through representation. What is foreign, or uncanny becomes tamed and assimilated into a common sense world to ward off any forms of anxiety. In contrast, Outsider artists are able to continuously try and translate what they themselves are unable to grasp as the primal scenes of their own psychic development through their bodies. They present for us the body's materiality, or the body's "Real," as a Body without Organs (BwO), in Deleuze/Guattarian terms, *without the Real functioning as a negation* as it does in psychoanalysis. "The reality of the unconscious belongs to the realm of physics; the body without organs and its intensities are not metaphors, but matter itself" (Deleuze & Guattari, 1983, p. 27). It is through this continuous translation and failure of translation, the "still not," the "yet-to-come" or "yet to be translated" that their alternative world is constituted as a continuous movement of becoming, generated by an urgency of primal repressions since there are no anchors readily available in the symbolic world they can relate to. In this sense they remain enigmatic, monstrous, and unassimilatable to interpretation. The art gallery precariously celebrates this very notion of creativity as escaping the signifiers of representation.

I hope to illustrate this thesis by turning to three Outsider artists whose schizophrenic unconsciousness is externalized into their own narratological worlds so that they can be externalized and contained within them; so that they might live with their primal traumatizations of their bodies. They confront us with a *singularity* of difference that puts the breaks on the usual assimilation of difference to sameness through the usual nod to Otherness. With Outsider artists, their enigma continues to stare at us with a face of alterity, as "probe heads,[5]" disturbing the usual neoliberalist claims of empathy to what is alien as developed above through consumption, especially in art galleries where such "wild" difference is tamed and readied for tasting as exotic, mad, violent and so on. The three outside artists I have in mind will be presented separately, culled only from the documentary short films that have been made about them. They are presented from the most assimilatable to the least when it comes to their place in the social order.

Marwencol: The Mystery of Time/Memory

I would like to start with the "artist" Mark Hogancamp, creator of the three-dimensional miniature world he calls Marwencol, who has received a great deal of attention through the efforts of photographer David Naugle, and Tod Lippy, the editor-in-chief of *Esopus,* a contemporary New York art publication. Naugle and Lippy enabled Hogancamp to have his first exhibition at White Columns Gallery in Greenwich Village, New York. Touted as a paradigmatic example of "art therapy," there is now a sold out limited edition of a book, *Welcome to Marwencol,* a website with his photo "stories" (www.marwencol.com/gallery/tag/stories), as well as a documentary, *Marwecol,* directed by Jeff Malmberg, which has received many prestigious awards as an insightful documentary. I begin with Mark Hogancamp because the stories he tells with his "dolls" are obviously representational, and his photo-essays appear accessible for easy interpretation and comprehension. Indeed, what is more representational than an entire three-dimensional world (see figure 9.1) constructed to 1/6th scale,

Figure 9.1 Mark Hogancamp. *Marwencol* (2010). Documentary. Directed by Jeff Malmberg (film grab, Jagodzinski)

accurate in every detail, populated by alter egos of his own creation based on people he can vaguely remember, as well as those he continues to work for in the Anchorage restaurant in Kingston, New York? Most everyone reviewing the stories and watching the documentary seem to "get it."

Mark Hogancamp, beaten senseless by five teenage "thugs" in a bar is left in a coma for nine days. He then spends the next 40 days in hospital, left disabled with complete memory loss as to who he is. Hogancamp constructs the fictional world of Marwencol (Mark, Wendy, Colleen), a town in Belgium during World War II, where his alter ego, "Hogie," crash lands his P40 Warhawk and stumbles upon this mysterious town that then becomes his home. Hogancamp repeats, over and over, the primal trauma of his beating (his crash landing). Through picture stories he creates fantasies by positioning his "dolls" in various tableaus and dioramas that are strung together into various narratives of capture and rescue, kidnapping and torture, victory and revenge. The five hooligans are the SS troops that torture and beat him. They invade the town where the locals and the German troops are living peacefully together (friends and enemies get along); the "barbie dolls" (all 27 of them) are there to defend and take care of him. In the town of Marwencol, he "marries" the doll Anna on March 27, while the doll Deja Thoris, his femme fatal, is a Belgian witch who has loved him throughout time. Sounding like déjà vu, she is capable of time travel to rescue him from the SS troops.

The usual explanation of this form of art therapy is that this is Hogancamp's way to sublimate his anger, revenge and fear of being attacked in the actual world. In this fictional world he is safe; it is an enactment of the Real war that is playing inside his head over and over. The repetition of his stories is not to be thought of as some grand narrative, some coherent world of unfolding drama as if it were a movie. Each story that he weaves is singular as such. Marwencol does not exist to represent his trauma; it *is* the trauma of the beating that exists in advance of all the stories he relates, which makes Marwencol's existence possible in the first place. Repetition, in this case, is the universality of the singular. The stories repeat what is unrepeatable. Each is not a second or third repetition, but carries the originality of the trauma to the "nth" power. The trauma remains enigmatic, a source for all of his artistic Xpressions.[6]

It is this aspect of memory loss that I want to examine first utilizing a Deleuzian account to show how the enigma of Marwencol, with its multiple intervening stories that Mark Hogancamp stages, is itself a "crystal-image" of time. Hogancamp's beating in some inexplicable way changed his body chemistry as well as erased his memory. He found out during his recovery that he was an alcoholic, but now the substance has no draw on him. He has become a chain smoker instead. Hence, the bar in Marwencol holds a special place for him. He's like Sam Malone, an ex-alcoholic in the television serial *Cheers,* able to serve others without taking a drink. Yet, he also found out that he had a foot fetish, possessing over 200 women's shoes, and that he liked to cross-dress, especially by wearing high heel shoes. Memory could only be gathered from past photographs, which remained alien to him. But this memory could not be a "recollection-image." Henri Bergson (1990 [1896]) maintained that the recollection-image in relation to the past was always in some sense insufficient. Such an image was virtual by retaining a mark from the past. "Pure recollections" or pure virtuality that are summoned from the depths of memory develop into "recollection-images" that then actualize virtual memory. But in Hogancamp's case there are no recollection-images. When we cannot remember, our sensory-motor extensions remain suspended. The actual image does not link up with a motor image or a recollection-image. It enters into a relation with virtual elements, feelings of déjà vu or past in general dream-images, fantasies, or theatre scenes. Deleuze (1989) sums up what I have been paraphrasing: "[I]t is not the recollection-image or attentive recognition which gives us the proper equivalent of the optical-sound image, it is rather the disturbances of memory and the failures of recognition" (p. 55). Image, thought, and Hogancamp's camera that captures the carefully staged tableaux are united together, falling prey to visual, tactile, sound, and cutaneous sensations. The scenes are dramatic: Hogan's body is mutilated by the SS; he loves passionately; the bar scenes are full of catfights; there are daring rescues—a temporal panorama is presented; yet these images are cut-off from a memory-base and motor recognition.

Marwencol is a crystal image of time displaying Hogancamp's disturbances of memory and his failures of recognition. The crystal is a mutual coexistence of an actual and a virtual image, of the actual and the purely virtual. Marwencol displays the present and a past that *is,* rather than a present and a past that *was.* It is an image of time at the moment of its labyrinthine splitting into a present that passes and a past that is preserved. The crystal is a double-sided image in which neither the virtual nor the actual has yet crystallized. Both dimensions of time are caught up in the process of doing so. This lack of finality of the time image allows for a suspension of the subject in the sensory-motor interval. As long as the past remains purely virtual, the sensory-motor link remains permanently suspended. Although Hogancamp's fine motor skills become refined, there is no habit and attentive recollection that allows for a continuity of the past and present. In the crystal of time, the past is always misrecognized. He proudly displays a "time machine" that he builds for Deja Thoris so that she may magically appear and rescue him.

Hogancamp, by falsifying his past is creating a new memory that is capable of activating a new future. Future time here is empty, it's a potential to be filled, which makes Marwencol a site/sight/cite[7] of therapeutic potentiality. Marwencol becomes a passive synthesis of many different passing presents. His recollected stories ground time so that the past fragments can be explored as a myriad of layers in which they exist as many different past selves. Crystalline time, as a formulation of an eternal return, is a pure form of time. Time is released from its spatial (chronological) progression via habit and recollection. Hogancamp is a split or doubled subject of the time-image, part in the virtual and part in the actual. I call this self-refleXion, the grapheme of the X indicates a formlessness of the labyrinth of time where difference is confronted as Hogancamp's sensory-motor continuum is suspended. He explores the past that *is* and not the past that *was*. What is virtual and actual is impossible to discern. There is no longer a place to ask whether Marwencol is imaginary or real, physical or mental. We don't have to know. Deleuze (1989) calls this phenomenon the "powers of the false" (pp. 126, 155). We can compare Hogancamp's Marwencol to Robbe-Grillet's neorealist description as opposed to the traditional understanding of realism with which many would identify; namely, Marwencol is a miniaturized represented imaginary world where a discernability between the real and the imaginary is possible. Yet, as Deleuze (1989) says of Robbe-Grillet:

> Neo-realist description in the nouveau roman is completely different: since it replaces its own object, on the one hand it erases or destroys its reality which passes into the imaginary, but on the other hand it powerfully brings out all the reality which the imaginary or the mental create through speech and vision.
>
> (p. 7)

In other words the self-assured "discernibility" of realism is not to be had.

While the nonsense signifier Marwencol is the key to Hogancamp's fictional world, psychoanalytically offering up a satisfaction that linguistics, in the Lacanian sense, unlocks the Real (the unconscious is structured like a language), from a schizoanalytic perspective we should look at Hogancamp's bodily desires for the materiality of the flesh that drives his production of desire. Pornography and perverse scenes of seduction are to be found everywhere throughout the delirium that is Marwencol, a lust for the flesh that cannot be consummated. Hogancamp's perverse fantasies are already evident in the drawings he did before the beating and his life as a sailor. His alcoholism prevented any sort of full sexual satisfaction except those of the fantasies that fill his journals that he wrote in an alcoholic stupor. When he read them after his beating, he was shaken by their darkness comparing them to Stephen King novels.

The horror of Marwencol is not the primal trauma of his beating, as much as it is the horror of his sexual disability. It can only manifest itself in the shoe fetish that he has (all 218 pairs) and the cross-dressing that he enjoys.[8] As Tod Lippy comments in the film, there is no irony being staged with his dolls like other artists, such as in the tradition of Hans Bellmer's (1935–1949) plaster dolls and his photographs directed at violent fantasies of the victimization of women by SS that leads indirectly to contemporary artists like Cindy Sherman's doll series of outright misogynistic positions, or to Amber Hawk Swanson's video performances with the PVC Amber Doll who disrupts heteronormative spaces like weddings receptions, tailgating parties and amusement parks. Hogancamp is *in* the work, not using the dolls to represent the seduction, but performs it with them. There is no distance, no subject/object divide as with the artists mentioned. The sexuality is exteriorized like in the film *Lars and the Real Girl* (2007, Craig Gillespie). "Real" here refers to the Lacanian Real but taken to the molecular level that Deleuze and Guattari call for. For Hogancamp, the dolls are materially alive. Silicone at the molecular level forms an assemblage with human flesh in such a way that the fantasy-dream is literalized so that the actual and the virtual are suspended. Chronological time, as developed earlier, is suspended. Time, as *Aion*[9] becomes one long interval of becoming—Bergson's *durée*. Hogancamp can drag his jeep of "losers" along the two-mile stretch to his workplace (The Anchorage restaurant) and back, again and again, waiting for that spark of difference to erupt (as when the photographer David Naugle intervenes, stops him and asks what is he doing). But if it doesn't, it's not unlike weaving string into a ball. The road is an endless walk, back and forth.

The sex dolls in Marwencol satisfy Hogancamp's perverse scopophilic drives under the scrutiny of his eye behind his camera. Not only can he change their outfits, their hairstyles, but they can also be positioned minutely in various poses, making them totally satisfying "living" objects. A comparison with the film mentioned earlier is in order. In *Lars and the Real Girl,* the therapeutic assemblage of Lars and his RealDoll (a sex doll with a posable PVC skeleton and silicone flesh) is composed of an entire community located in a northern Danish town that plays along with Lars's living' fantasy, Bianca. In one sense this is no different from all the characters that are the representative "living" dolls in Marwencol. They too accept Hogancamp's idiosyncrasy hoping that he will get well, and in some sense they are flattered by being represented in his world as doppelgangers. But the similarities stop here. Bianca is completely subordinate and non-phallic. Lars even makes her a paraplegic at the start of their relationship and places her in a wheelchair. She is entirely submissive to him. It is the Scandinavian community who begin to take care of her. They "hold" Lars together as he explores his relationship with Bianca to become psychically well. There is no evidence of this with Hogancamp and his community of co-workers and friends. He remains a recluse. Lars's family (brother Gus and wife Karin, whose pregnancy precipitates Lars's change of behavior) dress Bianca and put her to sleep; the local coiffure changes her hair style and the town folk even take her on therapy and teaching missions. Bianca, on Lars's permission, is allowed to model in a display window.

The difference between the art therapy that takes place in the movie and the fantasy of Marwencol is fairly easy to articulate. Lars is also infantile, impotent and schizo, traumatized by the death of his mother giving him birth, his brother Gus abandoning him, and his disturbed and depressed father who raised him. In many respects Bianca is Lars's "transitional object" as D. W. Winnicott (1971) theorized it. He slowly begins to transfer his love interest from Bianca to Margo, a young woman who is interested in him. His body undergoes molecular changes to the point where he cannot touch Margo's hand without feeling a burning sensation, a sure sign that he is capable of a relationship. A distance begins to develop between him and Bianca (his female doppelganger who is given a similar history as his) as Lars begins to argue with her and (a scene shot from a distance) seems finally to drown her in a lake after he kisses her goodbye; the kiss is indicative of a freeing of his libidinal drives. The violence of the separation and his eventual "killing" is played down in this movie as when transitional objects are simply discarded, tattered and abused from the rough handling as signs of aggression. When Bianca is "dead" and given a proper church burial, the town mourns with Lars, but now he is finally free to begin a "real" (actual) relationship with Margo. Bianca's death can also be equated with the death of his mother, which he is now able to revisit and let go. The actual intervenes into his virtual imaginary and a future is opened. But this is not necessarily the case of Hogancamp: he remains trapped in the time crystal unable to escape as Lars does.

So, in which way is Hogancamp an "outsider?" He did not consider himself an "artist" until being named as one. Only then does he begin to fantasize how an artist should look and behave in what he thought to be the center of "freakdom," Geenwich Village, where he thought he would fit in. Hogancamp is truly conflicted when asked to come to New York and do the exhibit; it demonstrates the suspension he is in between the actual and the virtual, lost, as it were, in the crystal of time as he enjoys the satisfaction of his perverse fantasies. He is truly an "outsider" when in such a suspension, where the "powers of the false" (not in the sense of being opposite of true) play themselves out over and over again; that is, the potential for multiple narratives of actualised time can take place; their power falsifies any singular form of the true. In the time-image of Marwencol, the virtual and the actual are not separate, as they seem to be for the other "doll" artists referred to earlier, but coexist in an interactive relationship: dream and reality are indistinguishable. Time here is actualized along a multiple of divergent paths, each movement falsifying at least one of the pasts that preceded it, creating a difference each and every time. It appears often enough that he is changing his mind as a given narrative undergoes a complete reversal. Hogancamp is a "one-trick pony" who offers up a variation each time he performs. What we cannot see is his *jouissance* in the act, for Marwencol is a *pharmkon:* it both therapeutically cures (remedy) and also entraps and plunges him further into this fantasy world (poison). This then is the enigma of its signification. What it exposes, however, is the other side of fantasy life, that side that we, as neurotics curb or repress so as to make sense of the symbolic order. As a schizo, Hogancamp needs no such protection, for his protection is inside Marwencol. He remains nomadic, outside the symbolic order. In Lacanian terms, he has no need of the Other, unlike Lars who eventually began to pay attention to the demand of the community. There is no identity in the way that it is anchored in the social order; rather Hogancamp brazenly displays the inchoate desires of a fragmented body, referred to by Deleuze and Guattari as a "body without organs" (BwO).

THE DEVIL AND DANIEL JOHNSTON

> Do yourself a favor, become your own savior
> (Daniel Johnston)

The devil, a figure of madness, excess, transgressive acts, and persecution, is evoked prominently throughout the documentary film that bears the same name as this subtitle: *The Devil and Daniel Johnston* directed by Jeff Feuerzeig (2005).[10] The documentary begins with a *mise en abîme* scene of Daniel Johnston as a young man filming himself in 1985 in Austin, Texas, in a mirror. He tells us (the imaginary audience being addressed in the mirror) that he is the ghost of Daniel Johnston, as if Daniel Johnston is already someone else, a question mark, so that the ghost can "tell you about my condition and the other world." It appears as if the cam video he is holding is a gun pointed at his head. It is recording his brain activity as his ghost speaks, but it is also reporting on his death since this recording is but a testament of a past moment in his life. This scene is immediately followed by a statement signed by Daniel Johnston: "I believe in God, and I certainly believe in the Devil. There is certainly a devil, and he knows my name." The documentary ends with Daniel, now in his 40s, dressed as a ghost, Casper the Ghost, the cartoon comic figure. The paradox of Daniel Johnson lies in him being Casper the Ghost: both a *no*-body and *some*-body, flickering in and out of mental institutionalization and star status, someone "pure" of heart but also a devil.

After the statement that stages the conflict of God and the Devil inside of Daniel's head, the documentary immediately projects the audience to 2001 Los Angeles where an older, heavily overweight, frumpily dressed Johnston walks on stage and begins singing. It is shot in black and white. The life led in-between these dates addresses Johnston's "other world." Next, we are introduced to his parents, Mabel and Bill, who reflect on how different Daniel was as the youngest child of five. This interview-like footage appears throughout the documentary as his parents tell stories of Daniel's life. A gifted child, the change in his confidence occurs in junior high, which Mabel identifies as the beginning of his "illness." Another *mise en abîme* scene has Dan (along with his brother) making a humorous movie about not conforming to time: school time and social time, or to the church, which he has never been able to do.

David Thornberry, Dan's best friend in Oak Glen High School, is interviewed next. As the designated artist in high school (he is being interviewed in his studio surrounded by his artwork at the age of ca. 30), Thornberry relates his friendship with Dan throughout high school as two artistic comrades in arms who meet again later in college. What is revealed is that Daniel is a "natural" artist whose introductory trademark was an eyeball, which began to appear on everything. A part-object of fixation, the eyeball was his "inner mind" that has been lost, wandering, detached from his body. The eye connects the body and his soul, which is conflicted by good/evil. It is an ambivalent part-object conflicted between God and the Devil. It is both an evil eye as well as God's gaze on the world when it becomes a "Flying Eye" or an "Eternal Eye." Daniel represents himself as a figure with his brain cut off above his eyes, a zombie body only. Sometimes rays come out of this gaping hole indicating the uncontrollable outpouring of art and music as he processes life, unable to hold anything back. The eye becomes freewheeling, a literal icon he places over everything that he deems evil. It is this gaze, sometimes as the gaze of God, as well as the evil gaze of others **that persecutes** him or whoever the devil has invaded (his hated of **Metallica who had** signed with Elektra records, for example). The symbolism **of Jeremiah the Frog** with two eyes is, again, Daniel in his innocence. But this same figure becomes a many-eyed hydra monster called Vile Corrupt as Satan enters into him and he must struggle with this demon to free himself and once more become "pure of heart." The more eyes the creature has, the more evil it is, embodying the gaze of Lucifer. But the proliferation of eyes can also mean becoming wiser and smarter. Johnston drew an army of ducks to protect him with his battle with Satan. The ducks are phallic symbols, ("a cock and two balls," according to Thornberry). Sometimes the eye turns into a protective Christian fish, the ichthus, the fish symbol for Christ. Johnston was arrested for having "graffitied" these Christian fish-eyes all over the base of the statue of liberty.

Like many "Outsider artists," Thornberry explains that Daniel's artistic process has nothing to do with studying and learning from artists. It is rather a procedure that mimics and explores what he sees, mostly from comic books. Thornberry reveals that Daniel is raised in a very rightwing Christian family, The Church of Christ, which Johnston rejects as a youth, yet at the same time he remains caught by the Great Tribulation. Tape recordings indicate that his mother saw Daniel drawing "satanic cartoons" and "polluting the minds of young people," a "laughing stock," probably possessed by the Devil, doing everything to gain attention. He called himself "an unserviceable prophet" to his mother's "unprofitable servant" of the Lord. When sent to Abeline Christian College, Daniel became disorientated, unable to make the class schedules. He complains of a neuronal disorder, which clears up when he comes home. His parents decide to send him to art school at Kent State University (East Liverpool campus) where he again meets up with Thornberry, as well as the love of his life, Lorrie Allen, a muse that was to remain an unattainable object of desire. A completely passive muse (like Lars's Bianca), she enables a pulsive flow of libidinal pinning that, as an endless production of love songs, speak directly to adolescent angst. University life also ends up in failure and he is sent to live with his brother Dick, in Huston to become productive and integrated into society, which also fails. Only Margie, his sister, seems to befriend him and accept his reclusiveness and his total rejection of social normality.

A series of family video footage of Daniel throughout high school and at home is shown next, edited in random order. Over which is a song composed and sung by Daniel that directly relates to his inability to fit in easily with the expectations of schooling and his parents, calling himself an Outsider artist whose illness makes him misunderstood and unappreciated, like Bobby Dylan or John Lennon. Unlike many Outsider artists, Daniel *does* have the disillusion that he will become famous. The search for recognition from the Other is found by identifying with those artists he thought were also misunderstood—not only Dylan and Lennon but also the musical group *Glass Eye,* led by Kathy McCarthy (Dead Dog Records) whom he meets in Austin, Texas because of an eye that appeared on their poster. His fame came from the embracement of "authenticity" of being "raw and real" that the DIY music culture was into in the early 80s. MTV's *The Cutting Edge* was scouting for upcoming artists and Johnston's songs that spoke of his pain and "schizo" life were eventually embraced. At the 1986 Austin Music Awards, Johnston is awarded best songwriter of the year and best folk artist. Curt Cobain, himself an Outsider artist, spread Johnston's fame by wearing his T-shirt with the image of Jeremiah the Frog from Daniel's debut album, "Hi, How are you." It was contagious. His fame spread quickly as fans who support indie music rallied around him.

Johnston, like other Outside artists, remains infantile, never growing up to fit into the symbolic order. Living in the basement of his parents' home in New Cumberland, West Virginia, he turned the garage and two utility rooms into a "factory like studio." The studio was cluttered with magazines, comics, and paraphernalia, which he later recreates in Waller, Texas, where he again is with his parents, who fear that when they pass on, Daniel will be all alone since he is incapable of taking care of himself.

Johnston has no idea how the music industry operates despite the support of those who genuinely tried to help him, like his long-standing manager Jeff Tartakov. His iconic symbology is pretty much an open book of the struggle between good and evil (God and the Devil) that rages inside his head. Daniel is diagnosed as being manic-depressive and finds himself in and out of mental hospitals, and on and off his meds if he needs to be creative. Otherwise the pills keep him emotionally "dead." The symbolic universe (see figure 9.2) consists of the many headed eyeballed hydra-like creature of evil called Vile Corrupt, the heroic Captain America, based on his father's exploits as a WWII pilot, who defends the American dream, Casper the friendly ghost, his symbol of being "pure of heart," Joe the boxer, which is his "everyman" fighting evil creatures in the ring, and his obsession with numerology, such as 666, the Devil's number. Tarassa Yazdani and Don Goede (2006) try and explain this mythology. The art and songs form a labyrinthian epic of cross references between songs and his art. Like Hogancamp's dolls, the creatures, superheroes and Good Monsters (King Kong, Frankenstein, the Incredible Hulk) that populate his epic myths are "living" beings in that they undergo changes and development in his constantly changing narrative: sometimes they are good, other times they turn to evil.

Figure 9.2 Daniel Johnston. *The Devil and Daniel Johnston* (2005). Documentary. Directed by Jeff Feuerzeig (Film grab, Jagodzinski)

As Johnston admits: "I do believe I lost my soul to the Devil. And I wouldn't be, oh, pursuing my music career if I didn't believe that." Further, "Satan knew my secret heart. I wanted to be famous. You know and he made me famous. And he gonna give me more of that." By all standards, Johnston would be diagnosed as psychotic, hearing voices inside his head, but this is not entirely the case. His uneasy integration into the social order as a musician and artist is maintained through the "holding" ability of his fans as well as a few close friends, like his long-time manager Jeff Tartakov and friend Thornberry, as well as his loving parents, who have much to do with the good/evil narrative that plays out in his head. Johnston's iconic symbology and songs speak directly to what Delauze and Guattari identified as the "body without organs," the body at the molecular level that is dis-organized, a cauldron of productive desire. Each figure in his Bosch-like imaginary universe plays a role in the multiplicity of personalitiess who are all "Johnston" in his schizophrenic state, engaged in an endless eternal and internal dialogue as a battle amongst monsters. He is without a head|brain as his iconic drawing of himself indicates, or rather he has multiple "heads"—the figures are all alter egos that address the materiality of his body. The devil is tamed by the "Polka-dot Underwear guy" who then turns into "Joe the boxer" (Daniel's everyman, who must struggle with his body so as not to lose control in fits of rage), "Jeremiah the Frog" (Daniel as pure innocence), superheroes like Captain America, his army of ducks, and the Good monsters are all there to help him function within the chaos of the world that continually comes at him, which he is unable to entirely screen and organize on a plane of consistency. His iconic symbology is always fragile and in flux, always subject to psychic dissipation—mental breakdown.

Johnston's love of Lorrie, and the pain of his songs are manifested through desublimation; that is, the raw drives are set free to reel as they may, as he pines away. Lorrie is not the sublime object of desire, like Žižek's (1994) account of the knight and the courtly lady; rather she is, in effect, the love object of every adolescent. In an odd way she is desublimated because of her ordinary loveliness, or rather the ordinariness of being a first love who is unobtainable. She is not idealized as a muse would be. Women humiliate Johnston. He fears them, distrusts them and is in awe of them. In his drawings they become objectified things: headless, limbless torsos. They devolve into snakes and lizard bodies. Laurie is Danielss's virtual memory trapped in a crystal of time. She cannot be actualized, although he repetitively tries. Johnston's songwriting is like exposing all one's inner anxieties—Xpressions, rather than expressions; the way he processes information of the outside world. They are the banality of life cast in the ups and downs of God vs. the Devil where the contingencies of fate are always at play. As is the constant desublimation of the "folky" tunes that his fans can relate to, overcast by a religiosity that pervades America's south. Like Casper, who is on the spiritual plane, Daniel is a floating legend that is somehow transparent, and yet the enigma of his body remains forever locked by the constant battle to curb his rage, anger and at times violent outbreaks. Johnston seems to have arrived at a place where his bulky body from overindulgence on Mountain Dew and rich food, begins to mimics Casper's equally shapeless body. Perhaps he has tamed the monsters for now?

IN THE REALMS OF THE UNREAL: HENRY DARGER

I end this thesis with the case of Henry Darger, who is perhaps the paradigmatic "Outsider" artist.[11] Like Hogancamp, who worked at menial tasks at The Anchorage restaurant, and Johnston who was able to hold down a job at McDonalds, Darger worked all his life as a janitor and a dishwasher at a local hospital. The choosing of menial tasks is consistent with the need to be free of the social order as much as possible, where social recognition and responsibility would not take place. Unlike Johnston, whose fame was a source of his bedevilment, and Hogancamp's ambivalence about being elevated to "artistic" status, Darger kept his art and hymn writings songs to himself for all his life. He was "discovered" by his landlords, the Lerners, only after his death, when it was time to clear out his apartment. Like Hogancamp's Marwencol and Johnston's studio space in the basement of his parents' home, Darger's apartment was his sanctuary, his retreat where he worked incessantly to keep the deviled voices at bay. Much like Johnston, Darger was prone to anger and outbursts. Neighbors in adjacent apartments would hear Darger arguing with himself in various voices and tonalities. He slept little, mostly in a chair rather than a bed. Like Johnson's Casper who was the epitome of spirituality and innocence, Darger went to church faithfully two to three times per day. He confined the movement of residential apartments to a small area of Chicago, Lincoln Park.

Unlike Hogancamp and Johnston, who were minimally integrated in their community, Darger was the most reclusive of the three, seeming to be antisocial in nature. He did have a few apartment neighbors who looked out for him, but this came late in life when he was poor and in need of help. The closest he came to having a relationship was with the landlord's pet dog, Ukee. Only three pictures of him exist, another strong indication that he shunned any forms of being seen (represented). Had he been "discovered" during his lifetime, this surely would have unraveled his world. When he was hospitalized and the landlords had discovered his life work of 33 years, he was initially shocked and then told them to "throw it away" (MacGregor, 2002, p. 19). He died a short time later. Effectively his obsession had been "killed." He left behind him an epic narrative that far exceeds Johnston's current artistic and song output, while Marwecol stands pale in comparison. Yet, this 15,000 page narrative epic, *The Story of the Vivian Girls, in What is known as the Realms of the Unreal, of the Glandeco-Angelinian War Storm, Caused by the Child Slave Rebellion* (see figure 9.3), is charged with the same mission: to stave off his demons. It is closest to Johnson's narrative where good and evil are once more at play. It is a never-ending yarn, just like Marwencol's staged dioramas

Figure 9.3 Henry Darger. *In the Realms of the Unreal* (2004). Documentary. Directed by Jessica Yu (Film grab, Jagodzinski)

and Johnson's legendary Biblical dramas. "Yarn" is meant metaphorically, but also literally; "literal" means the collapsing any subject|object distinction. Many Outsider artists, like fiber artist Judith Scott for instance, roll up string or yarn incessantly, as did Darger (see MacGregor, 1999, pp. 92–106). These balls are like condensations of time that act as a form of containment. Darger kept meticulous records of the weather throughout the day *for ten years,* comparing his account to the official weather posts, which were clearly false in comparison. Like the balls of yarn, this is yet another way of distrusting the symbolic order and escaping into the *durée* of time, time as *Aion*. His weather recording essentially mapped his imaginary world that existed apart from the actualized world.

It appears that Darger, like Johnston, was subject to fits of anger and *fear* of losing control over the "self" when the drives (*Triebe*) could not be harnessed without some form of Xpression. It is impossible to know precisely what Darger's traumatizations were as a child that kept him in an infantile state. He had a deprived and tormented childhood. At the age of four, he lost his mother during childbirth and the whereabouts of his sister was lost when she was given up for adoption. He had to live with his lame father (a tailor), and then sent to a school for "feeble minded youth." There is a possible (alleged) killing of a young girl when he escaped the school for "mental retards" at the age of 17. But this is pure speculation. Johnson sinned for want of fame, a direct contradiction of his "condition." Darger also wanted to become pure and a saint to stave off the (possible) traumatic-guilt that he suffered. This required composing the 15,000 page grand-narrative illustrated (some accounts say 23,000 single-spaced typewritten pages, others put it at 30,000 pages) with rolls and rolls of ten foot long butcher paper collage-drawings illustrated on both sides subtitled: *In The Realms of the Unreal* that takes place on a far-away planet where a long and violent history of child slavery erupts into a war between the nation of Angelinia and Glandelina. The obvious conflict here is between his angelic (Angelinian) side and his glandular (Glandelinian) driven aggressive side. Seven Vivian Sister heroines lead the enslaved children against the male Gladelinians who were (in one narrative at least) victorious thanks to the support of the Christian army and the fanciful winged creatures called Blengins. Like Hogancamp and Johnston, Darger incorporated popular imagery he found in magazines and newspapers, the discarded Americana he found in the garbage bins of Chicago's north side including bottle caps and packaging material while walking and talking to himself. He had a profound knowledge of societal events, reading the morning and afternoon newspapers front to back cover. These images found their way into his narrative as well.

Like Hogancamp, Darger's girls were phallic, endowed with penises. Like "Hogie," Darger was their defender, their Angelinian protector. He had scrapbooks filled with traced figures and cutout images. He archived images of pubescent girls such as the Coppertone Girl and Little Orphan Annie; his favorite figure was Little Annie Rooney, the heroine of Darrell McClure's comic strip. Significantly, the collaged work meant that the images were never taken from observed life, but distanced from it. The imaginary epic raged in his virtual world. Adolescent girls, the Seven Vivian Sisters, were perhaps the closest he could cope with his libidinal impotency. Darger in this respect has "n-sexualities." He is neither gay, bisexual, lesbian nor transsexual—categories of the symbolic order; rather sexuality is confused on the "surface" of his body, at the level of the "body without organs." There is no one signifier that buttons down his libidinal investment. The hermaphrodite figures enable the riddle of sex to be suspended in proper ambiguity. Naked children abound in his narrative, both innocent (held captive as slaves) and phallically determined to overpower the male adults (Gladelinians). The tale, in contrast to Marwencol where there is no ambiguity of sexuality, is nevertheless similar, laden with brutality, violence, strangulation, and evisceration of the nude transsexual girls. His fundamental fantasy had nude children and girls in battle with violent adult men, the Glandelinians led by General John Manley. Such are the "powers of the false." Sometimes Manley was defeated, and in the next chapter he would regroup and become victorious. This teeter-totter effect, evident in Johnston's narratives as well, indicates being suspended in the time crystal.

When Darger is still in the asylum-school for feeble boys and girls, he found a photo of a young girl in a newspaper, Elsie Paroubek, aged five, who was found slain in a ditch. Darger made her the child-rebel leader named Annie Aronburg in the flight between Angeline and Glandelian war. Both this picture and the notebook he placed it in went missing in 1915 from his belonging in the school. He demanded that God intervene and have the two items returned to him. God failed to answer Darger's prayers. He began to wage war thinking that God had abandoned him. MacGregor (2002) speculates that just maybe this was the incident that truly threw Darger into a state of repentance. It may well be that Darger had strangled this girl? Annie Aronburg becomes the martyr as the Angelinian forces are swamped by the Glandelinians. Darger commits treason and joins them. Only much later does Darger repent, becoming affected by a comic book where a young man is cast into hell for having committed a terrible crime. Somehow this story turns Darger around and he returns to church.

Darger was never allowed to adopt a child, nor was the suffering of children in the narrative ever ended. Like Johnston, Darger as the heroic protector of children—Captain Henry Darger, head of the secret organization of men called "The Gemeni," was able to instill within himself his own "Law," preventing a fall into a psychosis. Redemption in the form of self-therapy and self-theology at the imaginary psychic register to make BwO "hold" itself within the world where dream and actuality were always decentered in a topsy-turvy state. What is perhaps bizarre is that such a narrative now forms the labyrinthian pathways of a television series like *Lost!*

IN THE REALMS OF THE "REAL": SLAYING MONSTERS

Outside artists make available to us the singularity of their intense and obsessive kernel of their being that is caught in a narrative loop of constant becoming, the *durée* of time that has no closure. They further provide a glimpse of the unconscious Real, Deleuze and Guattari's "plane of immanence," a productive machinic realm beyond the visual and the linguistic, and the Body without Organs (BwO) that lies is adjacent to it.[12] Nevertheless, the imaginary of the visual and the formation of linguistic neologisms enable a way for such schizo-artists to anchor themselves in a world of their creation, and to minimally anchor themselves in the symbolic order through the help of a cadre of friends that can "hold" them in this space, or enable the space (Marwencol, Johnston's basement, Darger's apartment) to exist. In the realm of their symptoms, what Lacan was to call a *sinthome*, there are multiple voices at play, the fragmentation of the self which, like Humpty-Dumpty who fell off the wall, is somehow broken and cannot be put together again in some coherent fashion that could be called a stabilized ego, a consistent core self. The traumas that are lived out by Outside artists require that they slay their monsters (fears and anxieties) through self-refleXive therapies of their own making. The nonsense signifiers that they create attached to bizarre images are ways to stave off madness, the fury of the body acting on its own, out of control. The cauldron of productive creativity is absolutely essential to keep the soul (life as *zoë*) in check as best as possible.

For Outsider artists these monsters are fought on the playing field of the imaginary—incessantly, obsessively, excessively—so that the semblance of a fragile ego can be maintained. Without their "art," they fall into the nightmare of the Real where the Devil awaits in the fury to arouse the uncontrollable drives of the body—aggression, anxiety, fear, anger. What little framing of a world is possible exists only at the level of their imagination. In this "realm of the Real," the molecular level of the body, or "plane of immanence," is an unconscious cauldron of activity that is able to make all kinds of creative connections with materiality. It is a productive plane of open potentialities. This is also the place of Georges Bataille's (1985) "base materialism;" (pp. 140–144) that is, matter that an image cannot absorb. Bataille (along with Jean Dubuffet) identified this as nondialectical materialism—a "desubliminatory heterology"—guided by the constant expenditure in the forms of transgression and excess. Form and matter collapse, which Battaile and Dubuffet characterized as *informe* (formless). Such debris is immediate, uniformed, unstable and unnameable, "by flows in all directions, by free intensities or nomadic singularities, by mad or transitory particles" (Deleuze & Guattari, 1989, p. 40). For these Outsider artists, the symbolic identity, the nelogistic signifiers they make up, become idiosyncratic to them alone, not unlike an ill-formed indistinguishable letter of the alphabet by a child, or a preschematic symbol that holds unique meaning to a particular child alone. Like the chaos of the unconscious, the Outsider artist rummages through the *debris* of his immediate environment, and finds whatever he or she can lay hands on to use so that the narrative that emerges assembles these bits and pieces of found material into the creation of one's own *double*. They enter into a world where subject|object distinction vanishes, where dream|reality twists as in a möbius strip. In Lacan's sense this is a "field of enjoyment" where the repetition to recuperate their fragmentary ego takes place over and over again. This retentive pulse is their libidinal investment, their desire that makes up for their impotency in actual life. The eviscerated bodies that are so characteristic of these Outsider artists are the way they "get off," as moments of heightened *jouissance.* Such enjoyment, their *jouissance* of painful pleasure, sustains them. Their artwork is "scatalogical," formed by the debris of the social order. The Outsider artist does not know that s/he is creating art. In all three cases it is the interested parties that place the work in art galleries for its legitimation.

The fearful world of primal matter, the pre-symbolic realm of formlessness, the unformed (Battaille's *informe*) is the "night of day" that every child must pass through and find framed images and a language to tame it, to become civilized into the symbolic order. The transitional objects such as dolls, blankies, and stuffed animals have to be hugged to weather this "night" when a child's eyes close and monsters appear. There are parents and friends there to "hold" one in this passage. Hieronymus Bosch's *Garden of Earthly Delights* gives us a glimpse of the "realms of the Real" as a desublimated living nightmare, just like Daniel Johnston's symbolic universe, Goya's famous, *The Sleep of Reason Produces Monsters,* gives us a warning that reason alone cannot keep the menacing creatures that swarm the unconscious away while asleep. For Outsider artists, dream and reality are one and the same, suspended in a crystal of time that is just one long endless and perpetual *twilight* they have woven for themselves—what is then deemed "art."

One need not fall into an Oedipal account to explain their schizophrenia as arresting their becoming. They remain infantilized. Lacan states that the fundamental question of existence for obsessional behavior remains "Am I dead or alive?" To keep "alive" Outsider artists illustrate an important characteristic of Battaille's *informe*—entropy, or "expenditure," by which Battaille meant regulation through excess. To the extent that the obsessional Outsider artist can repeat the libidinal pulse of his or her *jouissance,* s/he remains somewhat "grounded" or "horizontal" to call on Bois and Krauss (1997) term, in the way the body remains attached to the imaginary narrative. In short, these obsessional activities (like the rolling of yarn into a ball) provide the expenditure required to maintain the energy necessary to stay minimally (that is) horizontally grounded. The question always remains just when this string, yarn or narrative will snap!: when a psychotic break may take place (like Johnston beating his manager with a lead pipe).

To end what is and will continue to be our fascination with Outsider artists is that they reveal how precarious the creative drive is throughout history. Madness and genius are close allies that are separated by Law that itself is arbitrary. They also reveal the thin line between dream and reality, a border crossing that we make in order to keep our fantasies alive, yet these very fantasies are shaped by ethical and political questions that sustain the symbolic order as it is led. The Outsider artist will always remain "outside" the symbolic order since the signifier is escaped as best as possible. Although the art institution wishes to embrace them, they do so *not* for the purposes of "holding" them in the sense of having them function in the social order; the motives for displaying their work remains questionable and conflicted.

Darger's exposure would probably have meant a psychotic break, whereas in Johnston's case, it is this very exposure as an artist that forms the expenditure of his excesses. Hogancamp's fate is yet in balance. Each, as a singularity, points to each of our own singularity in the way we navigate the symbolic order, living out our fantasies through the art of living itself. In conclusion then, the term, "Outsider" is a misnomer: it should be "insider" that is defined by being "outside the outside," living out the *sinthome* of one's fate where the outside|inside is no longer at issue. What we have in the art of the three singularities presented is simply the *diagrams* of their unconscious—we might call it "Real art."

Notes

1. This is an important point concerning the law made by Derrida (2002) wherein he demonstrates that "the law" is ultimately without legal foundation. *Every* law is premised on a performative act of violence, which then institutes "the law." The law depends only who is before it (prior to it), who produces and founds it and authorizes it.
2. This is a homologous argument that Derrida makes in relation to Freud and psychoanalysis (Derrida, 1978).
3. The New Left in an historical sense of the 1960s and 1970s refers to the pluralistic and social liberal orientation of left activism that expanded beyond the orthodox repertoire of strictly class politics.
4. Schizoanalysis, in contrast to psychoanalysis, does away with Oedipalization, de-sexualization and sublimation. Desire is productive and does not "lack" as formulated by Lacan.
5. The term is developed by Deleuze and Guattari (1988) and used by Deleuze in his book on Bacon (2003) to refer to his paintings. It refers to any device that disrupts faciality, a kind of stammering from within. The three "artists" do this quite powerfully in the way they move into chaos. "Beyond the face lies an altogether different inhumanity: no longer that of the primitive head, but of 'probe-heads'; here, cutting edges of deterritorialization become operative and lines of deterritorialization positive and absolute, forming strange new becomings, new polyvocalities" (Deleze & Guattari, 1988, pp. 190–191).
6. As is customary in my writings, I use the work xpression rather than expression to escape representational thinking (jagodzinski, 2010).

7. The homonym references my other work as a fusion of three psychic registers after Lacan: Real|Imaginary|Symbolic. The "site" of Marwencol is a physical place, but also seeped in unconscious virtuality.
8. A Lacanian reading would maintain that his fetishistic perversion is a response to his discovery that his mother does not have a penis. Such disavowal requires that the mother's maternal phallus be reinstated through a fetish object. According to Freud the shoe is one of the last objects the child sees before seeing that the mother is castrated (Freud [1927] 1991, p. 354). All the Barbie dolls that inhabit Marwencol are armed with guns and knives to compensate for this missing phallus. They are not castrated. Only the mother doll appears in Marwencol. There is no father doll. Hogancamp paints his manicured toenails and even puts a ring on one of them. This crossdressing indicates that he is also castrated but disavows it, substituting his lack with a fetish object (the female shoe) so that his fantasy can be sustained. The women are all powerful and hyper-feminine in Mawencol, big breasts and thin waists. The bar is called "The Ruined Stocking" where catfights take place.
9. Deleuze borrows the term Aion from the Stoics to distinguish this sense of time from time as Chronos (sequential calculated moments of time). Chronos affords the present a privileged ontological status at the expense of both past and future. In relation to Aion the present is nothing but a pure mathematical instant. Aion, in contrast, is immeasurable time. It defies representation. Aion is "constantly [eternally] decomposed into elongated pasts and futures" (Deleuze, 1990, p. 62). This enables Deleuze to consider the "present" in terms of Aion as "always and at the same time something which has happened and something about to happen; never something which is happening" (p. 63). Aion is "always flying in both directions [past and future] at once" (ibid.). In this notion of time, in order for the present to pass on, it must be both past and present at the same time.
10. The documentary film's title alludes to *The Devil and Daniel Webster,* a short story by Stephen Vincent Benét, a Faustian tale of selling one's soul to the devil, which was screen played into a film by William Dieterle in 1941. In this documentary it is Daniel Johnston who sells his soul for fame and fortune to the record industry with disastrous consequences.
11. I have explored Darger in another context in relation to art education (see jagodzinski, 2005).
12. This is an important distinction. The "plane of immanence" is *not* entirely equivalent to the BwO. It is the primordial clamor of becoming that impinges on the BwO as desire. The BwO is the agent of deterritorialization. It is always in a state of becoming—like the endless narratives I have been discussing that try to escape capture to avoid being reterritorialized by bio-power as theorized by Michel Foucault. As Deleuze and Guattari (1983) write, "You never reach the Body without Organs, you can't reach it, you are forever attaining it, it is a limit" (p. 150). "... The BwO is not 'before' the organism; it is adjacent to it and is continually in the process of constructing itself" (p. 164).

References

Bataille, G. (1985). Formless. In *Visions of excess: Selected writings, 1987–1962.* Trans. and Edited Allan Stoekl. Minneapolis: University of Minnesota Press.
Bergson, H. (1990). *Matter and memory* [1896]. Trans. N. M. Paul and W. S. Palmer. New York: Zone Books.
Bois, Y. & Krauss, R. (1997). *Formless: A user's guide.* New York: Zone Books.
Deleuze, G. (1989). *Cinema 2: Time-image.* Trans. Hugh Tomlinson and Robert Galeta. Minneapolis: University of Minnesota Press.
Deleuze, G. (1990). *The logic of sense.* Trans. Mark Lester & Charles Stivale. New York, NY: Columbia University Press.
Deleuze, G. (2003). *Francis Bacon: The logic of sensation.* Trans. Daniel W. Smith. Minneapolis: Minnesota Press.
Deleuze, G. & Guattari, F. (1983). *Anti-Oedipus: Capitalism and schizophrenia.* Trans. Robert Hurley, Mark Seem and Helen R. Lane. Minneapolis: University of Minnesota Press.
Deleuze, G. & Guattari, F. (1988). *A thousand plateaus: Capitalism and schizophrenia.* Trans. Brian Massumi. Minneapolis: University of Minnesota Press.
Derrida, J. (1976). *Of grammatology.* Trans. Gayatri Chakravorty Spivak. Baltimore: John Hopkins University.
Derrida, J. (1978). Cogito and the history of madness. *Writing and difference.* Trans. Alan Bass (pp. 31–78). London: Routledge.
Derrida, J. (2002). *Acts of religion* (Ed.) G. Anijar. Routledge: London.
Foucault, M. (1973). *Madness and civilization: A history of insanity in the age of reason.* Trans. Richard Howard. New York: Random House.
Freud, S. (1991). On fetishism (1927, 1st ed.). In *On sexuality: Three essays on the theory of sexuality and other works* (pp. 345–357). London: Penguin Books.
jagodzinski, j. (2005). In the real of the 'real': Outsider art and its paradoxes for art educators. *The Journal of Social Theory in Art Education, 25,* 225–254.
jagodzinski, j. (2010). *Visual art and education in an era of designer capitalism: Deconstructing the oral eye.* Houndmills, Basingstoke and New York: Palgrave McMillan.
Laplanche, J. (1989). *New foundations for psychoanalysis.* Cambridge, MA: Blackwell Publishers.
MacGregor, J. (1999). *Metamorphosis: The fiber art of Judith Scott: The outsider artist and the experience of Down's syndrome.* Oakland, CA: Creative Growth Art Center.
MacGregor, J. (2002). *Henry Darger: In the realms of the unreal.* New York: Delano Greenidge Editors.
Michaels, W. B. (2006). *The trouble with diversity: How we learned to love identity and ignore inequality.* New York: Metropolitan/Holt Books.
Pitcher, B. (2009). *The politics of multiculturalism: Race and racism in contemporary Britain.* Basingstoke, UK: Palgrave Macmillan.
Pitcher, B. (2011). Radical subjects after hegemony. *Subjectivities,* 4(1), 87–102.
Puar, J. K. (2007). *Terrorist assemblages: Homonationalism in queer times.* Durham, NC: Duke University Press.

Rancière, J. (2010). *Dissensus: On politics and aesthetics.* Trans. Steven Corcoran. London and New York: Continuum.
Riley, R. L., Mohanty, C. T., & Bruce Pratt, M. (2008). *Feminism and war: Confronting US imperialism.* London: Zed Books.
Winnicott, D. W. (1971) Transitional objects and transitional phenomena (1951). In *Playing and reality* (pp. 1–25). New York: Basic Books.
Yazdani, T. & Goede, D. (2006). *Hi, how are you? The life, art, & music of Daniel Johnston.* San Francisco and Colorado Springs: Last Gasp of San Francisco and Smokemuse.
Žižek, S. (1994). *The metastases of enjoyment: Six essays on woman and causality.* New York: Verso.

Author Biographies

Doug Blandy is the associate dean for academic affairs and director of the Arts and Administration Program for the School of Architecture and Allied Arts at the University of Oregon. Blandy's association with schools, community arts centers, and universities and his research and teaching advance art education experiences that meet the needs of all students within a lifelong learning context. His service, research, and teaching also attend to the relationship between art, education, community, and place.

Roger Cardinal is the author of *Outsider Art* (1972) and coauthor of *Marginalia: Perspectives on Outsider Art* (2001). He has written extensively about self-taught artists from Europe and North America, and has cocurated exhibitions of Outsider Art in Britain, France, Germany, Slovakia, Switzerland, and the United States. Cardinal is also an authority on French Surrealism and the early modern avant-garde. He is emeritus professor of literary and visual studies at the University of Kent, Canterbury, England.

Michael Franklin, PhD, ATR-BC, has directed three art therapy programs: the first at the College of St. Teresa, then Bowling Green State University, and his current position at Naropa University in Boulder Colorado. Since 1981, he has practiced and taught art therapy in various academic and clinical settings. He lectures internationally and has published numerous papers in the areas of aesthetics, self-esteem, AIDs iconography, interpretive strategies, the socially engaged artist/therapist, and contemplative and empathic approaches to art therapy. Michael's current work as an artist and researcher focuses on the relationship between art therapy, social engagement, yoga philosophy, and meditation.

David Henley, PhD, is a nationally recognized child art specialist. He has practiced as an educator and art therapist specializing in those on the Autistic and ADHD spectrum, Deaf Culture, as well as typical children in studio settings. He has written numerous articles, chapters, and two texts, the latest being *Clayworks in Art Therapy*. Dr. Henley has taught at The Art Institute of Chicago and Long Island University as a professor of interdisciplinary studies, studio art, art therapy/education, art/social criticism, and performance/poetics. His current research interests explore the biological origins of art, focusing upon proto-creative behaviors of mammals in the context of evolutionary psychology. He currently lives and makes art near Boulder, Colorado.

Jan Jagodzinski is a professor in the Department of Secondary Education, University of Alberta in Edmonton, Alberta, Canada, where he teaches visual art and media education and curricular issues as they relate to postmodern concerns of gender politics, cultural studies, and media (film and television). He is the co-series editor with Mark Bracher of *Pedagogy, Psychoanalysis, Transformation* (Palgrave Macmillan). He is the author of *The Anamorphic I/i* 1996 (Duval House Publishing Inc, 1996); *Postmodern Dilemmas: Outrageous Essays in Art & Art Education* (Lawrence Erlbaum, 1997); *Pun(k) Deconstruction: Experifigural Writings in Art & Art Education* (Lawrence Erlbaum, 1997); editor of *Pedagogical Desire: Transference, Seduction and the Question of Ethics* (Bergin & Garvey, 2002); *Youth Fantasies: The Perverse Landscape of the Media* (Palgrave Macmillan, 2004); *Musical Fantasies: A Lacanian Approach* (Palgrave Macmillan, 2005); *Television and Youth: Televised Paranoia* (Palgrave Macmillan, 2008); *The Deconstruction of the Oral Eye: Art and Its Education in an Era of Designer Capitalism* (Palgrave Macmillan, 2010); *Misreading Postmodern Antigone: Marco Bellocchio's Devil in the Flesh* (*Diavolo in Corpo*) (Intellect Books, 2011).

Phyllis Kornfeld is the author of *Cellblock Visions: Prison Art in America*. She has been conducting visual arts programs with incarcerated men and women—from county jail to death row—for 25 years, in 18 institutions in seven states. She is presently holding weekly classes in five correctional facilities in the New England area. Kornfeld curates exhibitions of the work and lectures on prison art at universities, museums, and conferences. She attended the University of the Arts in Philadelphia, received a BA from the University of Texas, and an MA from the University of Oklahoma.

L. S. Krecker is a graduate student in art education at the Mary Lou Fulton Teachers College of Arizona State University. She is an artist whose focus is printmaking. In her spare time she makes costumes in real life and is learning the ins and outs of building in Second Life.

Tim Rollins was born in central Maine in 1955. He studied at the University of Maine, the School of Visual Arts, and New York University. In 1980 he cofounded the artists collective Group Material, and in 1981founded the Art and Knowledge Workshop and KOS. (Kids of Survival) in the South Bronx. Tim Rollins and KOS have exhibited extensively worldwide and have their works in the permanent collections of over 95 museums and public collections, including the Museum of Modern Art and the Whitney Museum in New York, the Tate Modern in London, and the Museum fur Gegenwartskunst in Basel. Rollins has received numerous grants from the National Endowment for the Arts and was honored with the Joseph Beuys Prize in 1990. A documentary about Rollins's project, *Kids of Survival,* earned an Emmy Award in 1997. Rollins is a professor of fine arts at the School of Visual Arts in New York and has been a visiting professor at the University of California, the University of Virginia, Drexel University, Yale University, and the New Academy of Fine Arts in Milan. Rollins lives and works in the South Bronx and Chelsea neighborhoods in New York City.

Mary Stokrocki is professor of art and area head of art education, Arizona State University. She was former vice president and world counselor of the International Society for Education through Art and webmaster and former president of the United States Society for Education through Art. She received the 2007 College of Arts & Architecture Alumni Award, Pennsylvania State University. She won the following National Art Education Association Awards: 2007 Women's Caucus June King McFee Award; 2005 Lowenfeld Award; and the 1995 Manual Barkan for outstanding research article. She has a Fulbright Award to teach in Taiwan in 2012. Her qualitative research focuses on multicultural teaching/learning in the inner-city Cleveland; Rotterdam, Holland; Ankara, Turkey; Sao Paulo, Brazil; Warsaw, Poland; Barcelona, Spain; Evora, Portugal; and the Yaqui, Pima/Maricopa, Ak-Chin, Apache, and Navajo Reservations in Arizona. She teaches and researches Digital Ethnography on Second Life.

Linda Weintraub is the author of *Avant-Guardians: Texlets in Ecology and Art* (2006–ongoing) and founder of Artnow Publications. She wrote *In the Making: Creative Options for Contemporary Artists* (2003) and *Art on the Edge and Over: Searching for Art's Meaning in Contemporary Society* (1995). From 1982 to 1993, Weintraub served as the first director of the Edith C. Blum Art Institute located on the Bard College campus, where she originated 50 exhibitions and published over 20 catalogues. She is curator and coauthor of *Lo and Behold: Visionary Art in the Post-Modern Era, Process and Product; The Making of Eight Contemporary Masterworks, Landmarks; New Site Proposals by Twenty Pioneers of Environmental Art, Art What Thou Eat; Images of Food in American Art,* and *The Maximal Implications of the Minimal Line.* Since leaving Bard College, Weintraub curated a nationally touring exhibition, *IS IT ART?* She cocurated the internationally touring exhibition *Animal. Anima. Animus* (1999) with Marketta Sepalla. Weintraub is currently a contributor to the international art journal *Tema Celeste.* She lectures frequently on contemporary art and its intersection with ecology.

Alice Wexler is professor and director in the Art Education Program at the State University of New York at New Paltz. She received an EdD in the Department of Arts and Humanities from Columbia University, Teachers College. Her expertise is disability studies in art education and graduate research. In 2007 she was a visiting scholar at the Australian Institute for Aboriginal and Torres Strait Islander Studies, researching art of children from the Stolen Generation. A monograph entitled *Art and Disability: The Social and Political Struggles Facing Education* was published by Palgrave Macmillan in 2009. She has written several articles on the subject of disability for art education journals such as *Studies in Art Education.* The social and political implications of disability and the crossing of boundaries among fields are often the subjects of these articles. The most recent article is entitled "The Siege of the Cultural City Is Underway: Adolescents with Developmental Disabilities Make 'Art.'" She established a community program at SUNY New Paltz called Arts-2-gether for children with developmental disabilities in the New Paltz school district.

Index

ableism, 61
adolescents
　disabilities, 47
　identity, 57
　males, 48
　peer relationships, 56, 57
Aion, 194, 203
alternative reality, 8, 10–11, 15–16, 18–20, 24
Arnheim, Rudolph, 50
　isomorphism, 50
Aroz, Anthony, 102, 103
art criticism, 128
art education, 49, 94, 128
　adaptive, 7, 10–11, 13, 18
　teaching, 64, 65
Art Institute of Chicago, 26
art and knowledge workshop, 37, 38, 44, 45
art therapy, 8, 10, 49, 74, 75, 117, 122, 127, 128, 164, 165, 169
　expressive, 122
　postwar artistic work, 121–3
Asperger's syndrome, 145, 146, 147, 148
attachment and relationships, 14–15, 19–20, 22–3, 29
autism, 1, 6, 7, 13–14, 16, 23, 28, 76–7, 79–80, 145, 150
auto-biographical self, 19, 20–2, 24–8
avatar, 141, 144, 147, 150, 151, 152, 153, 155

Barlow, Dr Barbara, 59, 61, 64
Bataille, Georges, 180, 181
Bergson, Henri, 166
Bethlem Royal Hospital, 17
bipolar disorder, 142, 148, 149, 151
Blake, William, 17
Bluestone, Judith, 79–80
Bosch, Hieronymus, 181
Breton, Andre, 93
Broeck, Carla, 139–41, 151, 152
Byron, Lord, 17

Cardinal, Roger, 8, 17, 49
Carousel of Happiness
　accessibility, 126
　animals, 120–1, 131–3
　center pole, 129, 131
　characteristics, 121
　community builder, 126–8
　contributing to restorative process, 123, 129
　importance to community, 118
　non-profit, 126–8
　number of visitors, 118
　story behind, 122
　visitor experience, 118, 125–6
Carr, Diane, 136, 137, 154
Casper the Friendly Ghost (Johnston), 171, 173, 175, 176
　see also Johnston, Daniel
Catholic Church, 72, 79, 81, 83, 84
Cellblock Visions, 112
censorship, 109
cerebral palsy, 58

Chronos, as time, 183
  see also Aion
cliché, 106, 109
cloud pictures, 105, 106
Cohen, Andrew, 100, 110, 115
collaboration, 107, 110
Collier, Bryan, 49, 62, 64
community, 33, 34, 48, 50, 60
  art, 126–8
  centers, 32, 44
correction officers (COs), 99, 102, 110, 111
craftspersonship, 125
Crawford, Betsy, 59–61
creative impulse, 93
crystal-image, 165, 166, 167, 178, 181

Damasio, Antonio, 9, 18, 24–6, 28
Darger, Henry, 176–9
Davis, Lennard J., 61, 137
deaf community, 136, 137
debris, 180–1
Deleuze, Gilles, 166, 167
Derby, John, 137
Derrida, Jacques, 160–2
designer capitalism, 162
desublimation, 175
developmental growth, 13, 28
devil, 170, 174
Dewey, John, 32, 40
diagnostic labeling, 8
Diez, Braulio, 95
difference, 160, 165
disability studies, 136
Dissanayakake, Ellen, 47, 50
doll, 165, 168
doodling, 93, 101, 102–4, 106
drawing without the brain, 102, 103
drives (*Triebe*), 177
Dubuffet, Jean, 18, 49
  art brut, 49
durée, 168, 177, 179

ego, 97
Eibl-Eibesfeldt, Irehaus, 15

Einstein, Albert, 96
envelope art, 114
epic, 176
ethnography, 136
  digital, 137, 138, 139
ethology, 15–16, 18–20
Ewing, Levi, 139, 145–8, 151, 152
eyeball, as part object, 171, 173

fetish, 166, 168, 188
Firehawk, Jayden, 139, 148–50, 151, 152
Flax, Jane, 10
folklore, 129–30
Foucault, Michel, 160
Freire, Paulo, 88–9

Gallego, George, 34, 35, 36
gallery, 139, 159–61
  Barbara Gladstone, 42
  Crossroads, 141
  Pixel, 150
  Ricco/Maresca, 50, 51, 68
  Ronald Feldman, 41
Golub, Leon, 34, 42
Goodall, Jane, 15, 20
  naturalistic research methodology, 15–16
ground zero (9/11), 31, 32, 35
Group Material, 31, 34, 41

Harlem
  crime, 48
  mortality rate, 59
  poverty, 48
  risks, 49
Harlem Horizon Art Studio (artists of)
  Abraham, 51, 53–4, 67
  Brook, 51, 56–8, 67
  King, 51, 58–61, 67
  Louis, 51, 61–5, 67
  Orville, 67

Harrison, Scott
  Amnesty International, 120
  as craftsperson, 125, 131–2
  life in Nederland, 120
  relationship with carousel animals, 121, 123–5, 132–3
  Viet Nam War, 120, 121
  work on carousel, 120
Hogencamp, Mark, 164–70
hospitality, 160
  see also Derrida, Jacques

iconography, 49, 50
imagery
  appropriation, 8, 13–14, 26
  elaboration, 19, 22, 26
imaginal culture, 123
  image, 123
incarceration, 97, 110, 111, 113, 114
informe, 180, 181
injury prevention program, 64
Intermediate School fifty-two (IS 52), 32, 35, 43, 44

Jeremiah the Frog, 171, 173, 175
  see also Johnston, Daniel
Johnston, Daniel, 170–5
jouissance, 181

Kaprow, Allan, 71, 88, 90
Keigney, Arthur, 96, 111
Knobler, Nathan, 50
Kramer, Edith, 9, 12, 26

Laplanche, Jean, 162
Larson and the Real Girl (film), 168–9
late bloomers, 97, 101, 107
  Creative Drawing Workshops, 94, 102
Learning to Read Through the Arts, 33, 34
Lefens, Tim, 55
  Artistic Realization Technologies (ART), 55
  Flying colors, 55
Lehrman, Jonathan, 145

libidinal investment, 178
Linden Labs, 136, 141, 143
Lippard, Lucy, 35
Liu, Lilly, 136, 153
Lorenz, Konrad, 15, 18
Lovieno, Michael, 112
Lowenfeld, Viktor, 9, 12

MacGregor, John, 17–18
machinima, 142, 144, 151, 153, 154
madness, 161–2
Mahler, Margaret, 22
material culture, 129–30
Matto, Roberto, 5
Meadows, Mark Stephen, 155
Mondrian, Piet, 101
monsters, 179–80
Montano, Linda
  performance art, 71–6, 81–4, 87
Morris, Desmond, 15
Mother Teresa, 74, 75, 76, 87–8
muse, 172, 175

Nadia, 2, 7–8
National Endowment for the Arts, 66
  Beyond Civilization, 66
Naumburg, Margaret, 12, 28
negativity, 100, 101
Neuro-development, 21, 28–9
  aesthetic, 7–8, 18–19, 22–5, 29
  artists, 7, 11–12, 20
  behavioral considerations, 16–17, 22
  child-artist, definition of, 7–9
  exhibiting of, 27–9
  paradigm, 9, 12, 18, 20–3, 29
  pedagogy, 9–13
nonsense signifier, 180
n-sexualities, 178

obsession, 181
occupational therapy (OT), 49
Orwell, George, 40, 41, 43
outpatient, 49, 56

outsider art (artist), 50, 95–7, 103, 104, 145, 159, 160–3, 169, 170, 172–3, 176
art fair, 114

Perseveration (obsession), 8, 13–14, 17, 19–21, 23, 28
Personal learning environment (PLE), 153–4
Persson, Linda, art of
  brush marks, 2, 4, 5
  color, 4, 5, 6
  communication, 2, 4, 5
  ideas about world, 1, 2
  intentionality, 1, 2, 6
  vagueness, 2, 4, 5
phallic girls, 178
pharmacon, 170
physical therapy (PT), 59–61
Picasso, Pablo, 98
  Picassoesque, 48
plane of immanence, 179, 180
  see also Deleuze, Gilles
postmodernism, 9–10, 50
post traumatic stress disorder(PTSD), 122, 148
powers of the false, 167, 170, 178
probe head, 163
projection, 25
psychotic, 174

quadriplegic, 53

Rancière, Jacques, 160
real (Lacan), 165, 168, 179, 180
real life (RL), 136, 138, 141, 148, 151, 152, 155
recollection image, 166
regression, 7–8, 11, 21–3

Richards, Bill, 47, 48, 49, 52, 53, 59–66

Saltair Park, 118–19
  Saltair carousel, 118–19, 121
  Saltair carousel in Utah, 119–20
savant, 145
schizo, 163
scopophilic drive, 168
self
  biography, 20–2, 24–8
  consciousness, 93
  deprecation, 93
  elaboration, 19, 22
  refleXion, 167, 180
Shippe, Ronin, 1, 139–41, 151
singularity, 182
sinthome, 179, 182
Smith, Anna Deavere, 77, 79–80
South Bronx, 32, 34, 35, 37, 40, 41, 42, 45
spina bifida, 58
  cocktail party chatter, 58
Stimpson, Crystal, 111
sublimation, 165
Swan, Jim, 155

time image, 167
transitional object, 169

Virtual Abilty Island (VAI), 136, 138, 140, 141, 145, 150, 151, 153, 154

Weeks, Susan, 48
White, Ronnie, 104
Wiltshire, Stephen, 145, 147

Xpression, 165, 175, 177

zoë, 180

GPSR Compliance

The European Union's (EU) General Product Safety Regulation (GPSR) is a set of rules that requires consumer products to be safe and our obligations to ensure this.

If you have any concerns about our products, you can contact us on

ProductSafety@springernature.com

In case Publisher is established outside the EU, the EU authorized representative is:

Springer Nature Customer Service Center GmbH
Europaplatz 3
69115 Heidelberg, Germany